ABRAHAM LINCOLN'S WORLD

Abraham Lincoln's World
How Riverboats, Railroads, and Republicans Transformed America

Thomas Crump

continuum

Continuum UK, The Tower Building, 11 York Road, London SE1 7NX
Continuum US, 80 Maiden Lane, Suite 704, New York, NY 10038

www.continuumbooks.com

First published 2009

British Library Cataloguing-in-Publication Data
A catalogue record for this book is available from the British Library.

ISBN 978 1 84725 057 5

Typeset by Pindar NZ, Auckland, New Zealand
Printed and bound by MPG Books Ltd, Cornwall, Great Britain

Contents

Illustrations

Plates
Between pages 128 and 129

Text Illustrations

Preface

"A nation may be said to consist of a people, its territories and its laws.
The territory is the only part which is of certain durability."
President Abraham Lincoln, Annual Message to Congress, October 5, 1862.

This book was originally intended to have, as its title, *Land of Lincoln*, borrowed from the Illinois license plates as they were at the time of my first visit to that state in 1953. I then discovered that Andrew Ferguson had got in before me with a book subtitled *Adventures in Abe's America*. These words are sufficient to demonstrate that I have written a quite different book. Nonetheless I found *Land of Lincoln* extremely useful, and the author does a good job in showing that the three states in which he, together with his family, looked for adventure—Kentucky, Indiana and Illinois—mainly disappointed them. The reason is simple. Although Abraham Lincoln spent almost his entire life, before moving into the White House in 1861, in these three states, next to nothing remains of the places he knew. It is difficult to locate, even within five miles, the site of the log cabin in Kentucky where he was born on 1809, and the village of New Salem, where he first lived in Illinois in the years following 1830, has so utterly vanished that there are, once again, doubts about where precisely it was located on a bluff overlooking the Sangamon River.

Lincoln's claim that only the territory of a nation is of a "certain durability" is therefore only half true, as I have discovered repeatedly during my own American travels, which started in the summer of 1941, when I was twelve years old, and continued on into the fall of 2008, when I was not far short of my eightieth birthday. When it comes to Lincoln, and above all the parts of the United States which were important to him, I was from my first day blessed by good fortune. For three years in the middle of World War II—1941, 1942 and 1943—I spent school vacations at Greystone, a wonderful house in Loudoun County, Virginia. It was then, as it still is, home to one branch of the Chamberlin family, first established in the county after the Civil War. Successive members of the family have been my friends now for nearly seventy years.

In the 1940s, however, the events which located Loudoun County in the antebellum years at the vortex of the conflict between north and south, "slave" and "free," were still within living memory. From Minnie Jackson, who cooked for us at Greystone, I heard of her father's childhood years as a slave. Sadly Loudoun County has lost much of its charm, as I knew it in the 1940s: a combination of gentrification, urban sprawl, new industry and Dulles International Airport has produced this result. The charm, also, of Waterford, as a mixed community, has vanished. Where almost every other house during my childhood was home to a negro family, there is now not a single one left. I must also say now that in writing a book whose focus is the nineteenth century—particularly as it was seen by Americans of that time—I use the appropriate language, to talk about "negroes" and "colored people," and not "African Americans"—a designation that would only have confused Abraham Lincoln and his contemporaries.

Loudoun County was also a good starting for getting to know the Atlantic states outside Virginia, and particularly places associated with Abraham Lincoln. In New York state I stayed in Rehoboth House, Chappaqua, home of Horace Greeley, who, as editor of the *New York Tribune* in the mid-nineteenth century, was—together with such men as Thurlow Weed—one of the best known commentators on American politics—and a man whom Lincoln listened to. Rehoboth—incidentally the oldest concrete house in the United States—was in the 1940s the home of Canning Stahl and his family, who were also descended from the Virginia Chamberlins. In Maryland, Mrs. Amelia ("Mimi") H. Walker, whose houseguest I was at her home in Baltimore in the summer of 1942, saw it as her wartime mission to sell the United States to her young guest—who had had the misfortune to be born British. Part of Mimi's program was to conduct us around the battlefield at Gettysburg—a tour which I well remember and have since repeated—and then to bring us, as guests for tea, to the home of a ninety-five-year-old lady in New Oxford, Pennsylvania, who—as a fifteen-year-old—had been in Gettysburg during the battle, and then in November 1863, heard President Lincoln's address commemorating those who had fallen.

There are several estimates of the number of books published about Abraham Lincoln, but they are all well above 10,000. Many new books will undoubtedly be in the bookstores on February 12, 2009, the day of the Lincoln bicentenary, but it could well be that I shall be the only author to have heard a firsthand account of the Gettysburg address. For one thing, most of the others will simply be too young. Even so, I have sometimes worried whether I can offer anything new in such a well-plowed field. Spending a year intensively, and most of a lifetime more leisurely, with Abraham Lincoln and his world, has reassured me that there is still a relatively untouched corner of this field where I can plow my own furrow. I regret not having visited the Abraham Lincoln Bookstore in Chicago, but I certainly saw little in the bookstore of the Abraham Lincoln Presidential Museum in Springfield, Illinois, that covered the same ground as this present book. Nor have my extensive library researches changed my mind.

Although I was hardly out of grade school, three war years in the United States left me fascinated by American politics in a way that I have never lost. In the fall of 1940, when I was at school in Ottawa, Canada, I followed every stage of the presidential election, when FDR fought for an unprecedented third term against the Republican Wendell Willkie. For anyone from Britain—even an eleven-year-old—a Roosevelt victory was essential for continued support in the war against Nazi Germany. I can still remember which nine states—Maine, Vermont, Indiana, North Dakota, South Dakota, Iowa, Nebraska, Kansas, and Colorado—voted for Willkie. I did not conceal the fervor of my support for Roosevelt when, in the summer of 1941, I found myself building sand castles on the north shore of Long Island with none other than his defeated opponent. I must say that Mr. Willkie took my impertinence very well, and when I asked him whether, during his campaign, Roosevelt supporters had thrown rotten vegetables at him, he answered, "Yes, in several places."

"Did they ever hit you?"

"I was hit by a tomato in Pittsburgh."

Pearl Harbor, of course, changed everything, and to one writing about Abraham Lincoln it recalls the Confederate Bombardment of Fort Sumter in April 1861, which started another, earlier war that would transform the United States. To me the parallel goes further when looking at the years before 1861. The ten-odd years from 1850, when Millard Fillmore, as vicepresident, succeeded the suddenly deceased President Zachary Taylor, up to Abraham Lincoln's inauguration, were a time of appeasement—as Lincoln himself always recognized. Seldom has the United States had such inadequate presidents as Millard Fillmore (1850–1853), Franklin Pierce (1853–1857), and James Buchanan (1857–1861)—all three of whom were willfully blind to the fate to which their policies were driving the nation of which they were chief magistrate. Just as in Europe during the 1930s, when leaders such as British Prime Minister Neville Chamberlain—together with the great majority of British citizens—were blind to where the world was being driven by Nazi Germany, so also, during the 1850s, Americans and their presidents refused to face events. This is a constant theme of my book. Lincoln's greatness, like that of Winston Churchill some eighty years later, owes much to the hopeless inadequacy of those who preceded him in office. Basically, Lincoln, like Churchill, got things right: both of them combined judgment with courage in a way seldom equaled in the history of politics.

World War II is now so long a time ago that most of my readers will have no memory of it. Fortunately I was able to return to the United States in 1953—a year that many more will remember—as a research fellow of the University of

Michigan Law School: there I learned how uniquely law and politics combine in the United States. If a "non-political lawyer" is not an oxymoron, it ought to be. Certainly there were few if any in the Ann Arbor Lawyers' Club in 1953–1954, as we followed on television every stage in the downfall of Wisconsin Senator Joe McCarthy. Unquestionably the greatest lawyer-politician was Abraham Lincoln: unfortunately, if one looks at men such as Richard M. Nixon, the combination is not necessarily a happy one.

The year in Michigan left me with many friends, of whom, sadly, few survive. Of these, however, Judge Joseph J. Simeone of the Missouri Supreme Court has proved invaluable when it came to writing this book: his criticism of my text has led me to avoid many pitfalls, his help with documentation has provided a wealth of sources and his introductions to places and professional colleagues, from Nauvoo down to New Orleans, enormously enhanced my experience of Abraham Lincoln's America. My visit to his home in St. Louis, in August 1954, was on the hottest day I can recall in the United States; the coldest, in January 1968, was in Chicago. Significantly both cities were important in the life of Abraham Lincoln, and, if one thing can be said about America as he knew it, it is that extremes of weather and other forces of nature were part and parcel of everyday life—as they still are. (In New Orleans, in November 2007, I saw how the city was recovering from the devastation wrought by Hurricane Katrina.)

The summer of 1954, in which I made three long journeys to and from the Pacific Coast, enabled me to cross Illinois, by three different routes, and then to go on to other states, such as Missouri, Kansas, and Nebraska, that were critical in antebellum politics—as shown by chapters 7 and 11 of this book. In my many American journeys since then I saw comparatively little of this part of the United States, but then I was able to make this good in the fall of 2007, when I saw something of all the states along the Mississippi River, from Iowa and Illinois down to Mississippi and Louisiana, together with Kansas, where many key events of the 1850s took place. In all these states little remains from Lincoln's own time, and what there is—such as the French settlement of Ste. Genevieve, Missouri—is mostly modest in scale. The countryside is seldom spectacular, although often attractive enough, as at those places, such as Quincy, Illinois, and Hannibal, Missouri, where bluffs overlook the great rivers of the Mississippi basin. The road along the east bank of the Mississippi from Hamilton to Nauvoo, with the trees showing their fall colors, was particularly beautiful in the fall of 2007. The rivers themselves are mostly dull, with the same trees lining their banks for hundreds of miles. Of the towns that Lincoln knew, little—except for the odd church or courthouse—remains from his time, although the Lincoln-Herndon law offices and the old statehouse in Springfield are still there (but then special efforts have been made to preserve them). More survives in towns such as Vicksburg, Natchez, and New Orleans on the lower Mississippi, which saw their best days in antebellum times. The rivers themselves have been far from constant: the battlefield of Vicksburg, for instance, overlooked the Mississippi—the river now flows some miles to the west. While the Army Corps of Engineers has over the years made the rivers straighter and largely free of snags, they were certainly more interesting, if more hazardous, in Lincoln's day—you only need to read Mark Twain's *Life on the Mississippi* to confirm this. And as for life at grass roots, Twain's *Huckleberry Finn*, describing life along the great river in the 1840s, is unequaled in evoking a past era. The descriptions of the American scene in Alexis de Tocqueville's *Democracy in America*, published just at the time that Abraham Lincoln was setting up on his own in Illinois, are also worth anyone's time.

The point to be made above all is that all this part of America, in Lincoln's time, was in a state of unparalleled growth, both in population and wealth. This is not what today's traveler sees, some 150 years later. St. Louis is no longer the fourth city of the United States, nor New Orleans the sixth: cities in the east, such as Baltimore, Pittsburgh, and Cincinnati have also moved down several places. The Rust Belt now characteristic of many parts of such key states as Michigan, Ohio, and Pennsylvania, was far from anything conceived of by Lincoln and his contemporaries. My travels in the fall of 2007 revealed to me, over hundreds of miles of modern highway, a countryside that had known better times. The most beautiful places were the well-kept Civil War battlefields, such as Shiloh and Vicksburg, but this is the comparatively recent achievement of the US National Parks Service, and of course the countless monuments—which are much the same at every battlefield—were not there when the battles were fought. Even so, if the man-made elements are disregarded, one still gets a good idea of what the terrain was like in the middle of the Civil War. Lincoln saw a quite different America during his two years in Congress (1847–1849) and his four years in the White House (1861–1865). I describe the Washington scene in chapter 10, but beyond Washington, almost all the eastern cities as Lincoln came to know them had much older roots, going back to colonial times. Most of these cities—Baltimore, Pittsburgh, Cincinnati, Richmond, Philadelphia, New York, Boston—I have visited at one time or another, but apart from some well-preserved historical centers and some first-class museums, there is little to see that Lincoln would have known.

Given my focus on Lincoln's life before the Civil War, my research was largely based on places such as the Lincoln Presidential Museum in Springfield, Illinois, Constitution Hall in Lecompton, Kansas (representing, as shown in chapter 11, the *point of no return* in the events leading up to the Civil War), the Museum of Westward Expansion and the Old Court House in St. Louis, Missouri (the scene of the original trial in the Dred Scott Case), in Mississippi, the University ("Ole Miss," where on October 1, 1962, James Meredith became famous nationwide as the first negro to breach this fortress of white supremacy) at Oxford and the wealthy planters' antebellum mansions at Natchez, and in Louisiana, the Frogmore Plantation (where visitors can pick their own cotton) and the Louisiana State Historical Museum in New Orleans (which as the Spanish Cabildo was where both stages of the Louisiana Purchase took place in December 1803). In the Old Court House I was fortunate to have as my guide Missouri Appeals Court Judge Robert S. Dowd, Jr., who helped me greatly in understanding the legal background to slavery—a matter that was of constant concern to Abraham Lincoln. I am also most grateful to the patient and helpful staff of the other institutions listed above. In addition I would like to recall my visit to the Civil Rights Museum located in Memphis, Tennessee, in the motel where Martin Luther King Jr. was assassinated on April 4, 1968 (an event that can now be seen on YouTube). The presentation of the fight for civil rights goes back to days of slavery, when fighting the cause of abolition before the Civil War was the first stage in a struggle that still continues. I am also most grateful for historical material supplied by the National Cotton Council of America, whose website, http://www.cotton.org, is first-class. Special thanks are due to Nicole Etcheson, professor of American History at Ball State University in Muncie, Indiana, whose criticisms of Chapter 11—largely based on her book *Bleeding Kansas*—greatly improved its contents.

And finally, in New York, I had the pleasure of being shown around the Cooper Union building, the scene, in February 1860, of what is now regarded as Abraham Lincoln's most important speech in the months leading up to the presidential election. For this I am most grateful to my guide, Prof. Greenstein.

As for Civil War sites, my visits were mostly those of a casual tourist, but besides visiting Charleston, South Carolina (where the war started) in 1953, and Appomattox, Virginia (where it ended) in 1999, and Gettysburg (my first battlefield) in 1942, I can recall visits to Antietam, Fredericksburg, Shiloh, Vicksburg, Chattanooga, and the "wilderness" of Orange County, Virginia. If, apart from his memorable visit to Gettysburg, in November 1863, Abraham Lincoln visited very few of these places, he was deeply involved in what happened there. Today's visitor must envisage carnage and horror in quiet and peaceful places, beautifully maintained to commemorate the sacrifice of hundreds and thousands of men, from both north and south, who, when they were there, knew neither peace nor quiet. The ninety-five-year-old lady who recalled for me, in 1942, the battle of Gettysburg, particularly emphasized the chaos and noise that characterized it. As for the events leading up to the Civil War, I have followed the trail of John Brown from Osawatomie, Kansas (his base for organizing the massacre of slave-owning families along the Pottawatomie River), to Harper's Ferry, West Virginia (which I have known since my childhood), where his capture of the Federal Arsenal on October 16, 1859, became emblematic for the abolitionist cause.

Ultimately, however, massive reading from an overwhelming wealth of sources is the only way to get to know Abraham Lincoln and his world. My own sources, as listed in the bibliography, merely scratch the surface. I have, however, reached a point where new sources, in increasing measure, confirm what I already knew—confusing me occasionally with historical contradictions on questions to which, in principle, there should be only one answer. Was, for instance, Democratic Representative Preston Brooks of South Carolina, a nephew or a cousin of Senator Andrew P. Butler of the same state? He could not have been both, but both are reported in the written sources. The question arises as a result of Brooks' notorious attack, with a gutta-percha cane, on the floor of the Senate, on Massachusetts Senator Charles Sumner, who, on May 20, 1856, had called Butler "an aged imbecile . . . lusting for the harlot 'slavery'"? If mistakes, in written sources, came up surprisingly often, this must reflect the difficulty of writing history where every detail counts, whether it relates to a name, a place, a date or whatever. It is, for instance, important to realize that the Lincoln-Douglas debates opened in the fall of 1858 with both sides knowing that the people of Kansas had finally rejected the Lecompton Constitution—a point missed by a number of authors. There are certain to be mistakes in my own book, and for these I accept full responsibility. All I would like to say in conclusion is that I never so much enjoyed writing a book: the company of Abraham Lincoln and his contemporaries has been the source of immeasurable satisfaction.

The American Scene in 1809

THE LIFE OF A FRONTIERSMAN

Although Abraham Lincoln had little to tell of his earliest years beyond the poverty of the household into which he was born on February 12, 1809, his father's livelihood as a small farmer was typically American. In Hardin County, Kentucky, the log cabin in which Thomas Lincoln's two children of his first marriage—of whom Abraham was the younger—were born, was commonly the only sort of dwelling possible for a smallholder on the American frontier. In a restless age Thomas Lincoln was a man of his times: always ready to move in search of a better life, during his lifetime he made six major moves and a trek of several hundred miles. With every move he faced the same problem, which was to set up as an independent smallholder. This meant constructing—with the least possible delay—a dwelling for the family, to be followed by clearing as much ground as would needed for crops. For the most part the natural state of the land in the seventeen states of the Union—as it was in 1809—was forest: this had the advantage of providing wood, though little else, both for building and furnishing houses and making the tools required for farming. It was also an abundant fuel, essential for cooking at all times and heating during the long winter months. The forest was also home to wild animals, notably deer, which could be hunted.

Although wood was the basic natural resource, there were limits to its usefulness. Stone, for some purposes, such as constructing the foundations of a house, or providing it with a hearth and chimney, was a better building material: a quarry was always a valuable local resource. Essential tools, such as axes, scythes, shovels, forks and rakes, hammers and nails, and household implements, such as kettles, pots and pans, required iron or steel—which over time also made for a much more efficient plow.[1] The farmer and his household ate at table with cutlery and crockery, wore clothes of wool and linen—and possibly cotton—and were shod with leather. Oil lamps provided the only lighting. Finally a gun was essential for hunting, as it had earlier been for defense against Native Americans—a lesson Thomas Lincoln had learned as an eight-year-old boy in 1786 when he suffered the trauma of seeing his own father shot dead.[2]

For supplying the variety of chattels listed above, local storekeepers were indispensable, as were blacksmiths—and other craftsmen—for the services they offered. Even so, a frontier family of the early 1800s, such as that of Thomas Lincoln, depended upon household production for all kinds of goods, cloth woven out of linen or wool, leather, tallow for candles, wood for furniture, which a generation later would be bought in stores. In the relations with their farming clients storekeepers all faced the same problem: the typical subsistence economy of the American frontier generated very little cash. The promissory note, whose value turned on the solvency of the individuals who had issued and endorsed it, was the common means of exchange.[3] If the result was chronic indebtedness at every level of the economy, small farmers and tradesmen lived and worked under the constant threat of bankruptcy: here Thomas Lincoln was no exception. The situation was exacerbated by the chaotic state of American banking, which allowed at one and the same time for a massive supply of banknotes, issued by countless local banks—and of such dubious value that as a means of payment they were only accepted at a discount—and a very restricted supply of coin, minted by the US Treasury in Washington.[4]

When Abraham was born in 1809, his Lincoln ancestors had been in America for nearly 200 years. In 1776 they were still to be numbered among the four million Americans who, living within 200 miles of the Atlantic coast, constituted the majority of the citizens of the thirteen British colonies, and whose representatives, meeting together in Philadelphia in that year, signed the Declaration of Independence—which proved to the be the call to revolution. Through six generations the family had been constantly on the move, from the Atlantic coast of Massachusetts to the edge of the Allegheny mountains in Virginia. This migration reflected a consistent and economically rational strategy of "escape and repeat."[5]

In all this the Lincoln family was just one of thousands following the same strategy, and together constituting a vast stream of migration, whose route—from the eighteenth century onwards—followed the Great Philadelphia Wagon Road in southeastern Pennsylvania and the Virginia Road up the Shenandoah Valley. The process transformed the wooded countryside as land was cleared not only for agriculture, but also for small-scale industry: one result of this process was the construction of tens of thousands of water mills—so many, indeed, that the physical geography of the Atlantic states was radically transformed.[6]

Inevitably land scarcity sooner or later impelled families to settle further afield. As with each generation a new family was founded, new land was sought to be cleared for cultivation, with wheat as the dominant crop. Long before the end of the century, geographical constraints, characteristic of a mature system of land usage, required that the process take a new direction. In 1779, while the war against the British was still being fought, the Lincoln family became part of it.

The Shenandoah migration inland led almost immediately into the densely forested Allegheny mountains, part of the great Appalachian chain running hundreds of miles, from upper New York, through central Pennsylvania and western Virginia, to North Carolina and Tennessee. From the earliest days on the American frontier some families had chosen to settle in Appalachia, but it was generally a poor choice, which led to enduring hardship and isolation from the outside world. Even in the twentieth century Appalachia's subsistence agriculture—such as could be found in the seemingly endless hills of West Virginia and the frontier areas of Virginia and Kentucky, North Carolina, and Tennessee—defined a culture of poverty.

The majority of settlers, including those belonging to the Lincoln family, avoided this choice. In the far southwest of Virginia it was possible to turn the corner of the Alleghenies and move west, through the Cumberland Gap, into a land known originally as Kan-tuck-kee, which the colonial government of Virginia had claimed as early as the seventeenth century.[7]

The problem here was that local Indian tribes were strongly opposed to American settlement. This had become a major problem for the colonial government when, in 1763, as a result of the Treaty of Paris at the end of the Seven Year's War, it acquired the vast French territory north of the Ohio River, and east of the Mississippi. In the interests of maintaining peace with the Indians, a Royal Proclamation of the same year forbade all British settlement west of the Appalachians. Whatever its good intentions, this was never going to be enforceable. The local American demand for new land was much too strong. In 1767 the pioneer frontiersman, Daniel Boone, made his first exploratory trip into Kentucky, and with the American Revolution of 1776 there was no turning back the tide of settlement beyond the Alleghenies. Already, in 1775, the Continental Congress—disregarding the proclamation of 1763, and taking a more realistic view of the conflict between Indians and Americans—recognized the Ohio River as the permanent boundary between the two sides. Kentucky, south of the river, was effectively declared open to settlers, while the territory north of the river was reserved to the Indians.

In 1779 Daniel Boone returned to Kentucky, escorting more than a hundred new settlers—including Abraham Lincoln's grandfather, also Abraham, and his father, Thomas—to new land. For the Lincoln family the British concern for Indian unrest proved well-founded. In 1786, Thomas Lincoln saw his own father shot dead while clearing a field for planting.[8] This was no isolated event, but even so there was no turning back new settlers. With the effective

ratification of the Federal Constitution completed in 1790[9] the way was open
to admit Kentucky as the fifteenth state of the union in 1792. (It was also the
first state with universal male suffrage for all free citizens.) Tennessee, until
1781 a territory belonging to North Carolina, followed as the sixteenth state
in 1796, but in this case few of the new settlers, most of whom came from the
southern states, followed the route pioneered by Daniel Boone. By this time
Indian power—mainly in the hands of the powerful Shawnee tribe—was
consolidated north of the Ohio.

The Indians' rights, as recognized by the Continental Congress in 1775, were
soon to be put to the test. In 1787 the new US Congress enacted the Northwest
Ordinance to govern the whole territory, providing at the same time for it to
be divided up into three to five new states to be admitted to the Union when
the time was ripe. (In the event there were to be five new states, Ohio, Indiana,
Illinois, Michigan, and Wisconsin—and even a sixth, Minnesota, of which a
quite substantial part was east of the Mississippi.)

Just as in Kentucky and Tennessee, there was no holding back American
settlement of the Northwest territory. The earliest settlers, who came mainly
from the northern states of New York and Pennsylvania, did not have to
contend with the formidable obstacle presented by the Ohio River. Nor, to
begin with, did they have to confront the Indian tribes, who already in 1795
had agreed to cede the greater part of what, in 1805, became the new state
of Ohio—the seventeenth to be admitted to the Union. As for the actual
countryside, and its potential for agriculture, there was little to choose
between the two sides of the Ohio River. Alexis de Tocqueville, writing in
1835, was plainly influenced by the fact that the Indian name, Ohio, meant
"beautiful river":[10] it flowed "through one of the most magnificent valleys
that has ever been made the abode of man. Undulating lands extend upon
both shores ... whose soil affords inexhaustible treasures to the laborer; on
either bank the air is wholesome and the climate mild." The Ohio's many
navigable tributaries, on both sides of the river, were useful for commerce,
and although too wide to bridge, could be crossed—like the great river
itself—by ferry. The rivers, in turn, were fed by creeks, which could be
bridged and forded, and when in flood navigated by flatboats. Both rivers
and creeks also provided locations suitable for water mills, although—with
the imminent coming of steampower—far fewer were built than in the
Atlantic states. All these factors combined to make a land well suited for
cultivation once the trees had been cleared.

While the land in Ohio state was largely colonized by settlers from the
mid-Atlantic states, the two territories of Indiana and Illinois, both subject to
the Northwest Ordinance of 1787, mainly attracted settlers coming from the
south, across the Ohio River. Although settlement was well under way when

Abraham Lincoln was born in 1809, it was then still somewhat problematic for a number of reasons.

First the river itself was a daunting obstacle: it was far too wide for any bridge to span it, and the strength of the current did not help navigation—particularly for any vessel proceeding upstream. As was true of every river in the Mississippi river system, the Ohio was full of snags, with the level of water varying greatly according to the season. Even so a voyage downstream in a suitable craft had, since before the end of the eighteenth century, provided an alternative route for new settlers from the eastern states. One problem here was to find a suitable point of departure, where the river could be reached overland with no more effort than that demanded by following the well-traveled roads east of the Alleghenies. On the upper river there were two possibilities, Wheeling, in the extreme northwest of Virginia, and Pittsburgh, where the Allegheny and the Monongahela Rivers joined to form the Ohio. Because both cities, although west of the mountains, were reasonably accessible, they were particularly suitable starting points for settlers from western Pennsylvania and the part of upper New York state immediately south of Lakes Ontario and Erie.

Another problem, which became acute downstream, was the presence of Indians in considerable force on the right bank of the river. They were not only an obstacle to settlement, but their experience of navigating the Ohio, combined with their possession of canoes well adapted to the river, spelled danger for Americans choosing it as their way to reach new land for settlement—even when that land was in Kentucky, on the left bank of the river. By the end of the eighteenth century, pacifying the tribes living along the Ohio was a major part of federal government policy, and in principle the process was completed in 1805, when the last piece of land north of the river was ceded by the Indians. Even so, any number of battles were still to be fought in northwest Ohio and the northern part of the Indiana territory. All in all, settlement in Kentucky, south of the river, was still less hazardous than almost anywhere in the Northwest Territories to the north of it. Here in the early nineteenth century, in the land still not ceded to the federal government, one tribe—the Shawnees—dominated the local Indian populations. One reason for this is they were not only the most numerous, but also occupied the most territory. Another, at least as important historically, was that they had a great leader, Tecumseh, who, because of his skill in dealing with Americans, was recognized by them as a formidable and noble adversary. If, however, the Shawnees still counted in 1809, when Lincoln was born, their days as a major factor in the settlement of the land north of the Ohio river were numbered. This is a story told in chapter 3: for the present chapter it is sufficient to recognize that in the successive migrations of Thomas Lincoln in the twenty-odd years after 1809, when his son, Abraham, was growing up, he hardly had to worry about Indians.

The policies pursued by the federal government in response to the demands of settlers on the American frontier, as it steadily moved westward, ensured that Indians consistently abandoned their lands in the face of this advance. In most cases they did so peaceably, if reluctantly, so that—except in the vast territories beyond the Mississippi River—Indians were not part of the American scene.

Even so, the fact that Abraham Lincoln was twice directly involved with Indians must be recorded. The first occasion occurred in 1832, when Black Hawk, who earlier had been an Indian leader in northern Illinois, returned east across the Mississippi River, to reclaim lands in the state ceded by treaty to the federal government. Lincoln, only twenty-two years old, was chosen as captain by the men of a local militia called up by the government to support federal troops in resisting this invasion. He saw little action and his militia was soon disbanded.[11] The second occasion occurred in the fall of 1862, when—during his second year in the White House—Lincoln's main concern was the Confederate General Robert E. Lee's invasion of Maryland. Sioux Indians in southwest Minnesota, who also had been forced to surrender land to American settlement, rose up against local settlers after the local Indian agent had failed to supply the food to which they were entitled by treaty. This was a much more serious insurrection than the Black Hawk War some thirty years beforehand, but news of it only reached Lincoln in mid-October, by which time Union troops had broken its back. His action in the White House consisted of mitigating the harsh sanctions demanded by General Pope, the local Union commander,[12] who wished to execute 303 Indians condemned by a military tribunal. It is a reproach to Lincoln that he was never well informed about Indian affairs; like almost all Americans of his day, he considered American Indians as barbarous and as a barrier to progress.[13]

"FREE" AND "SLAVE" STATES

In the settlement of the land beyond the Alleghenies, one factor, not directly related either to the presence of Native Americans or to the physical geography of the United States, profoundly influenced the ultimate destiny of many settlers. By the time of the American Revolution, the United States had a black population of about 700,000,[14] most of whom were slaves. In 1787, as the time came for the thirteen original states to ratify the new Federal Constitution, the uneven distribution of the slave population among thirteen original states already foreshadowed conflict between them about the status of black Americans. Although at this stage slavery still existed in every state, by 1804— only seventeen years later—eight northern states, led by Vermont, had either abolished it or taken the first steps toward achieving this result.[15] Although this was in part the consequence of an abolitionist campaign, supported both by religious groups, such as the Quakers, and by prominent public figures, such as Benjamin Franklin, expediency was always a key factor. By the time the northern states had joined the Union—a process only completed in 1790—their slave populations had been much reduced as a result of the war of independence, leaving open the way to an economic order in which slave labor would play no part. This was a clear goal of the poorer members of society in the northern states

> among whom could be found neither sympathy for the negro nor understanding of his problems. From its inception, slavery had been detrimental to the working class. On the one hand, the slave system excluded whites from jobs pre-empted by slaves; on the other, it often degraded them socially to the level of the slaves with whom they had to work and compete in earning a livelihood. . . . Whites of the working class hated slavery as an institution, but they also feared the free negro as an economic competitor. They supported emancipation not to raise the negro to a better life but to destroy a system which gave him a fixed place in the economy.[16]

The antipathy toward free negroes also led to some thirty-one states, in the course of time, introducing legislation to restrict voting rights to white males. This process began in Virginia (1762) and Georgia (1777) even before independence. By the beginning of the Civil War in 1861 only four states, Maine, Massachusetts, New Hampshire, and Vermont, were without such legislation.[17] Indeed, except for New England, all new states admitted to the Union after 1790 excluded negroes from voting.

Immediately before the admission of Ohio as a free state in 1805, north and south were evenly balanced when it came to the actual number of states on either side. The "free" north comprised five New England states, together with the important mid-Atlantic states of New Jersey, New York, and Pennsylvania. As to the south, in the six states with an Atlantic coastline which had belonged to the Union from its beginning in 1788, together with Kentucky and Tennessee—the two inland states (carved out of territory ceded by Virginia and North Carolina) which extended to the Mississippi and were admitted to the Union in the 1790s—slavery continued.

Ohio joining the union was the first step in a process—only completed by the admission of Minnesota as a state in 1858—by which time the whole of the Northwest Territory would be incorporated in the Union. This, however, was less than half the story of American expansion in the first half of the nineteenth century.

In 1803 Napoleon, although at the height of his powers as Emperor of France, had lost over 50,000 soldiers in an unsuccessful attempt, after nearly two years of fighting, to suppress a slave revolt on the Caribbean island of Santo

Domingo. This setback—which led to the establishment of the independent negro republic of Haiti in the western half of the island—put an end to Napoleon's dreams of a new empire on the American mainland. Reluctantly he agreed with President Thomas Jefferson to sell the vast territory west of the Mississippi to the United States for $15 million.[18] This was the Louisiana Purchase that, by adding some 847,192 square miles of new territory, more than doubled the size of the country. The extent of the land purchased—which gave America full control of the Mississippi and Missouri Rivers and all their tributaries—far exceeded that of the Northwest Territory. (Until 1820 the Spanish claim to West Florida—which extended to the east bank of the Mississippi—was a minor trial to the United States, but it was eliminated when President Madison—as related in chapter 4—added it to Louisiana.)

Jefferson lost little time in exploring the new land that he had purchased: he commissioned Meriwether Lewis and William P. Clark to lead an expedition which, having crossed the mountains beyond the headwaters of the Missouri, followed the Columbia River to reach the Pacific Ocean on November 17, 1805. Although this was far beyond the limits of the territory purchased from France, it opened up the prospect of a country extending to the Pacific. What this would involve was to become all too clear by mid-century—a story told in chapter 9.

Returning to the seventeen states east of the Mississippi, as they were at the end of the year 1805, the political line-up which they represented in the Ninth US Congress reflects the balance of power. In the Senate, the accession of Ohio tipped the balance—by eighteen members to sixteen—against the slave states. Of the 142 seats in the House of Representatives, the balance was more strongly in favor of the north, with seventy-seven seats as against the south with sixty-five. This balance of power was repeated in the Tenth US Congress, which was just concluding its lame-duck second session when Abraham Lincoln was born in February 1809. In both the Ninth and Tenth Congresses, the Democratic-Republican Party had an overwhelming majority of seats in both the Senate and the House of Representatives. Since almost the entire representation of the minority Federalist Party came from northern states, and particularly New England, it followed that power in the majority Democratic-Republican Party was quite evenly divided between north and south.

Although representation in Congress was based upon a census taken in 1800 (which explains why Ohio only qualified for a single seat in the House of Representatives), throughout the first decade of the nineteenth century, the five states with the largest populations (Massachusetts, New York, and Pennsylvania from the north, and Virginia and North Carolina from the south) dominated the Congress. Representation in Congress—particularly that of Virginia and North Carolina—was skewed by the provision in the Constitution that negroes only qualified for 60 percent of the normal representation in the House of Representatives, and this while they were denied all rights to citizenship, including voting rights. Virginia, with twenty-two seats in the House, was the most powerful state, the more so given that it was the original home of many of the new settlers in Kentucky. In the first forty years (1789–1829) of the United States, all the presidents, except the second, John Adams—a Federalist from Massachusetts—and the sixth, his son John Quincy Adams, were from Virginia. The four presidents from Virginia, George Washington (1789–1797), Thomas Jefferson (1801–1809), James Madison (1809–1817), and James Monroe (1817–1825), were all substantial landowners, who relied on slave labor to work their estates at Mount Vernon, Monticello, Montpelier, and Ash Lawn. Their homes, however, were far from the frontier on the Ohio River, on the other side of the Allegheny mountains. And whatever doubts they had about the ethics of slavery, they were still tied to the rural plantation economy whose prosperity depended upon this institution.

The original plantation crop was tobacco, which, having been introduced in the Jamestown settlement in Virginia in 1612, had become by 1615 a cash crop cultivated for export. In 1619, a Dutch ship transported twenty men from West Africa to serve as bound servants. This was the beginning of slavery in continental North America, although legal recognition, enshrined in the colonial statutes of Virginia, only came in 1661. The formal definition—accepted first in the thirteen British colonies and then, after independence, by the states of the union—is to be found in a South Carolina statute enacted in 1686.

By the eighteenth century the employment of slaves had extended far beyond the tobacco plantations. In South Carolina and Georgia, indigo—used as a dye for textiles—and rice, had become significant plantation crops, dependent upon slave labor. In the last decade of the century, two key events in industrial history gave the institution a new lease of life. In 1790, Samuel Slater, a recent immigrant with knowledge of the new textile machinery of Britain's industrial revolution, opened a cotton mill in Rhode Island. Then, in 1793, Eli Whitney's invention of the cotton gin solved the problem of separating seeds from cotton bolls after harvesting, which is otherwise an extremely laborious manual process. The impact of the invention was immediate: American cotton production increased from 4,000 bales in 1791 to 73,000 in 1800 and this was just the beginning of an incremental process that would continue throughout the first half of the nineteenth century. Overseas the demand came not only from Lancashire's cotton mills in England, but from newly developing textile industries of continental Europe. From its beginnings with Slater's cotton mill in Rhode Island a whole new textile industry developed in New England, a process that culminated in 1822 with the establishment of Lowell in Massachusetts as the first planned textile manufacturing city. Particularly in the northern states this process foreshadowed the growth of an urban working class, recruited from farming families in the surrounding countryside.

In the southern states the consequences of the boom in cotton were drastic. In the lowland areas of Georgia and South Carolina, both soil and climate were ideal for the cultivation of the short-staple cotton required for the mass production of cheap textiles. The process of cultivating cotton, and making the fibers ready for spinning and weaving, is described in chapter 6. The process was labor intensive, and in the social context of the southern states it was inevitably carried out by slaves. This was often the task of women, with the men engaged in other menial tasks on the plantation.

The demand for plantation-grown cotton emerged just at the time when abundant new land, west of Georgia but east of the lower Mississippi, became available for cultivation. Although the so-called Mississippi territory already belonged to the United States at the time of the Louisiana Purchase, the land acquired from France provided it with an unrivaled seaport, New Orleans, whose docks were soon piled high with bales of cotton, waiting to be shipped to destinations both in the northern states and in Europe. Once again the labor force consisted mainly of slaves. Needless to say, plantations were soon established west of the river, so extending the realm of slave labor. Indeed, the French, in their time, had already employed slaves to harvest sugar cane.

A picture of the American South, as it was in the early nineteenth century, based upon a line clearly separating plantation areas from the rest of the countryside, would be an oversimplification. Plantations were themselves far from uniform. Although a large plantation had economies of scale, the fact that the tools used in agriculture were such as could only be used by a single laborer, unassisted by any outside source of power, allowed even the smallest operations to be viable. On the other hand, an abundant supply of slave labor meant that a single proprietor could extend his plantation indefinitely, buying new acres of land with every new slave acquired. It is not surprising then that slave auctions were part and parcel of everyday life. For both land and slaves, it was useful to have access to credit, but both local banking and the extensive use of promissory notes helped solve this problem.[19]

In the lands outside the plantations, which even in the southern states comprised the greater part of their territory, hundreds of smallholders cultivated crops for consumption within their own families or for sale at markets.[20] Other than relative poverty there was no reason why slaves, generally no more than a handful, should not comprise part of the labor force of the individual farmer. A smallholder could own two or three slaves while his neighbors relied on their own families for labor. In either case those toiling in the fields had to be clothed and fed. In economic terms the balance of advantage, one way or the other, was often difficult to determine. Slave labor allowed a certain flexibility: the rule

US Territorial Acquisitions.

that in good times slaves could be bought, and in bad times sold, best applied to the situation of the individual owner as his fortunes changed. In practice the market was much less perfect and most farmers remained content with the number of slaves that they started with. Moreover in times of crisis, such as the Panic of 1837, slave prices could fall by as much as two-thirds, reflecting a corresponding fall in the prices of staple crops—particularly cotton.[21]

Migration, such as that of the Lincoln family in the first half of the nineteenth century, was also a key factor. A smallholder without slaves was probably more mobile but another, who owned slaves, might have an advantage in opening up new land. This, indeed, was a question hotly disputed between the two classes, who for this reason tended to be antagonistic—the more so as time went on in the early nineteenth century. It also provided a reason for the independent smallholder preferring to settle in a state or territory where slavery was outlawed, but in the first decade of the nineteenth century this was problematic. This explains how a frontier state like Kentucky, where the Lincoln family had settled in 1779, remained home to both classes of small farmers. It also explains, at least in part, why this family moved north of the Ohio River—as related in chapter 5.

THE AMERICAN NUMBERS GAME

The political history of the United States cannot be understood without appreciating how important numerical factors were in constituting the rights of the different states. The same was true at state level when it came to the balance of power between different counties and townships. This was something that was taken into account at every stage in the process of writing and ratifying the U.S. Constitution in the late 1780s.

One key question at that time related to the geographical extent of the thirteen original states. The state lines separating the four New England states of Connecticut, Massachusetts, New Hampshire, and Rhode Island from each other, and from New York state, were established in colonial times. The same was true of New York, New Jersey, Delaware, Maryland, and South Carolina, as they related to each other geographically, but these states were also bounded by Pennsylvania, Virginia, North Carolina, and Georgia, four states which claimed territory stretching as far as the Mississippi River. Such extension of the boundaries of these states was never going to be acceptable to the other nine (of the original thirteen), with the result that Pennsylvania, Virginia, North Carolina, and Georgia—as a condition for their admission to the Union—agreed to western boundaries well short of the Mississippi, which are those of these four states as they are today. These boundaries are mainly defined by natural features such as the Ohio and its tributary, the Sandy River, which accounts for most of the western frontier of Virginia, or the Chattahoochee which forms the southern part of Georgia's western frontier, or the long range of forested hills, stretching from New York to Georgia, known as the Appalachians.

Although the British colonial governors' policy was to inhibit settlement beyond the Appalachians, regarding this land as best left to local Indian tribes, the American founding fathers always regarded it as territory for future white settlement. The result was that as early as 1787, the Northwest Territory was created out of the vast expanse of land north and west of the Ohio, and east of the Mississippi River. This was from the beginning a territory subject to federal and not state jurisdiction, where, significantly, the Northwest Ordinance excluded slavery. It was always intended that the territory would be divided into new states, which, in due course, would be admitted to the Union: the actual procedure, which required an affirmative vote by the US Congress, was laid down in the Constitution as it was ratified in 1788, a year later than the Northwest Ordinance.

It is difficult to exaggerate the importance of the Northwest Ordinance as the blueprint for the local government of US territories that had yet to be admitted to the Union. It laid down the procedure for organizing the parts of any territorial "district in which the Indian titles shall have been extinguished,[22] into counties and townships," providing that once there were 5,000 free male inhabitants any such district would obtain the right to elect a representative in the General Assembly of the territory. This provided the essential basis for an administration with its own governor, legislature and judiciary; critically the right to dispose of land was reserved to the US Congress.

The ordinance, having defined the boundaries of the states to be formed out of the territory, went on to provide that:

> whenever any of the said States shall have sixty thousand free inhabitants therein, such State shall be admitted, by its delegates, into the Congress of the United States, on an equal footing with the original States in all respects whatever, and shall be at liberty to form a permanent constitution and State government: Provided, the constitution and government so to be formed, shall be republican, and in conformity to the principles contained in these articles; and, so far as it can be consistent with the general interest of the confederacy, such admission shall be allowed at an earlier period, and when there may be a less number of free inhabitants in the State than sixty thousand.

The Northwest Ordinance was important not only for providing for the eventual admission of six states defined by it to the Union, but also, by extension, for establishing a procedure applicable to other new states—such as notably those included in the Louisiana Purchase (which had not been contemplated by those who drafted the ordinance in 1787). This point was never forgotten by men such as Abraham Lincoln, who were deeply involved in the terms upon which the United States would continue to expand in the nineteenth century.

South of the Ohio River the Kentucky, Southeast,[23] and Mississippi territories were never subject to federal jurisdiction. Instead they were governed, respectively, by Virginia, North Carolina, and Georgia which meant that new states created out of these territories would inherit the legal systems of these states. This had two important consequences for American settlers: first, the institution of slavery would be taken for granted; second, the grant of titles to land would be based on the common-law systems of colonial America—which, being derived from English land tenure, were ill-suited to frontier conditions beyond the Appalachians. Both these factors influenced the advance of settlement, particularly that of the Lincoln family during the first twenty years of Abraham's life.

The territories ceded respectively by Virginia and North Carolina were admitted to the Union as Kentucky (the fifteenth state, in 1792), and Tennessee (the sixteenth state, in 1796). In the north, Vermont in 1791, had already been admitted as the fourteenth state, and was the first state with a constitution that banned slavery. In 1803, Ohio became the seventeenth state, and although its admission as a state was not subject to the limitations of the Northwest Ordinance, the constitution adopted by its citizens none the less banned slavery.

Although there had been no change in the status of the Mississippi territory, the vast increase in cotton production in the early years of the century meant that its economy was developing very rapidly. In 1809, therefore, the thirteen original states had become seventeen, with two new states, Vermont and Ohio, in the north and two, Kentucky and Tennessee, in the south.

Even more significant than the admission of these four states in the course of the first twenty years of the Union, was the acquisition in 1803 of the Louisiana territory from France. Its importance was recognized in 1812 with the state of Louisiana (which comprised only a very small part of the whole territory) being admitted to the Union,[24] an event that substantially enhanced the political and economic importance of the southern states.

From the earliest days of the first US Congress the representation of the American people was based on the rule that while every state should send two senators to the upper house, the number of Representatives in the lower house would be based on population of each separate state, with elections being held every two years—of which the first was held at the end of 1788. The Senate would be in continuous session, with a third of its members being elected every two years to six-year terms, while all the members of the House of Representatives would be reelected every two years. The senators, in turn, would be chosen by the state legislatures—which were at this stage all, like the US Congress, bicameral, with members being chosen on a county basis, according to similar rules. Representatives, on the other hand, would be popularly elected by adult white voters, with, in many states, a minimum property qualification. It was left to the individual states to divide their territory into as many districts as they had representatives, although it was open to elect congressmen at large to represent the entire state.[25]

By the end of the First Congress (1789–1791) there were twenty-six senators, with two from each of the thirteen states, and sixty-five representatives. The latter came overwhelmingly from the larger states, with Virginia in the lead with ten representatives, while Delaware and Rhode Island had to be content with just one each. In its second session (January 4 to August 12, 1790) this Congress provided for the first US census, as it was critical to have reliable figures for their populations in determining the representation of the separate states to the House of Representatives. On this matter the southern states, where the majority of the nation's slaves resided, had forced a concession, incorporated in the US Constitution, allowing for slaves to count on the basis of three-fifths of their actual number—even though they had no voting rights.

The first census, taken on August 2, 1790, counted just under four million residents in the thirteen states of the Union, with only a small balance of 3 percent in favor of the north, whose population was then almost evenly divided between New England and the mid-Atlantic states of New Jersey, New York, and Pennsylvania.[26] By the time of the third census on March 26, 1810 (when Abraham Lincoln was just over a year old) this had nearly doubled to over seven million.[27] While there had been a slight increase in the proportion resident in the mid-Atlantic states, both New England and the south had lost out quite substantially. The new factor revealed by this census was that nearly 4 percent of all Americans resided in the Northwest Territory, mainly in that part of it that had become the state of Ohio in 1803. In the course of Lincoln's life (during which six censuses were held) this part increased very substantially, to the point that in 1860 the population of the six states that had originally comprised the Northwest Territory (Ohio, Indiana, Illinois, Michigan, Wisconsin, and Minnesota) was equal to that of the three mid-Atlantic states, which—with 24 percent of the nation's population—had more or less held their own over this period.[28] In the half century between the censuses of 1810 and 1860 the big losers were New England, whose share of the nation's population dropped from 20 to 10 percent, and even more, the South, whose share dropped from 37 to 17 percent. In this period the population increased fourfold, to more than thirty-one million, which was then greater, for the first time in history, than that of the Great Britain.[29] This was accompanied by a gradual westward movement of the mean center of population: where in 1810 this had been in Loudoun County, Virginia, some forty miles northwest of Washington, by 1860 it had moved to Pike County just north of Cincinnati in Southern Ohio.[30]

In line with the steady secular increase in the American population, the number of members of the House of Representatives also increased—as provided for in the Constitution—but at a much slower rate. In 1809, on the day of Abraham Lincoln's birth, the Tenth[31] US Congress counted 142 members in the House of Representatives, allocated between the seventeen states which then comprised the Union according to the second US census, held in 1800. By the time the Lincoln family moved to Illinois in 1830, the number had increased first to 186 and then 213, following the censuses of 1810 and 1820. In the Twenty-first Congress (1829–1831) the population of Illinois was still only sufficient for the state to be represented by a single congressman in Washington. The fact that Lincoln was elected as one of seven representatives in 1846, to serve in the Thirtieth Congress (1847–1849), indicates how rapidly its population was growing. By this time Ohio, which forty years earlier also had only a single representative, was sending fourteen congressmen to Washington, and Indiana, with ten representatives in Washington, was not far behind. The three states of the old Northwest Territory had thirty-one representatives and given that the total number of members of the House of Representatives was 230, this reflected a disproportionately large share of the American population, attributable almost entirely to economic progress in this part of the nation. The fact that south of the Ohio River, the slave state of Kentucky which, with six representatives in the Tenth Congress (1807–1809), was well ahead at the time of Lincoln's birth, had after twenty years only advanced to ten reflects a significant shift in the balance of power between north and south. On the other side of the Appalachians, Virginia, which for the Tenth Congress had elected twenty-two members to the House of Representatives was entitled to no more than fifteen in the twentieth, a loss that was very keenly felt. As for Abraham Lincoln, he grew up in a climate of growth, with those around him having every reason to be as optimistic as he was about the future.

Until almost the end of the 1820s the balance of power tipped in favor of Democratic-Republicans, among whose number were to be counted the first three nineteenth-century presidents, Thomas Jefferson, James Madison, and James Monroe. All were substantial land and slave owners from Virginia, and each one of them served two terms in the White House. Elected on a restricted franchise, their style of government was patrician rather than popular. The main strength of the Federalists who opposed them was in New England, and as time went on they became steadily weaker, to the point that they only had four senators[32] in the Seventeenth Congress (1821–1823). Then, as so often happens when a party becomes too powerful, the Democratic-Republicans split into three factions in the Eighteenth Congress (1823–1825). One faction was led by William Crawford from Georgia, who was President James Madison's secretary of state, another by Senator Andrew Jackson of Tennessee—renowned for his exploits as a soldier (which included defeating the British at the battle of New Orleans in 1815), and the third by the Speaker of the House of Representatives, Henry Clay, who in the Sixteenth Congress had orchestrated the Missouri Compromise. Crawford was strong in the Senate, Clay in the House, with Jackson—the most radical and ambitious of the three—second in both Houses. All three had their sights set on the presidency of the United States.

In the event these divisions among the Democratic-Republicans led to the 1824 presidential election being decided by the House of Representatives, whose choice, after several rounds of voting fell on John Quincy Adams, a Federalist from Massachusetts and the son of the second president. Adams' election was largely the result of support by Henry Clay, leaving Andrew Jackson firmly resolved to see the whole political house of cards collapse under its own weight. In Congress all the members of both Houses were Democratic-Republicans, and Adams enjoyed nothing beyond a small majority in the House in the Nineteenth Congress (1825–1827), his first. In the Twentieth Congress (1827–1829) Jackson consistently had the wind behind him and his election as president in 1828 was more or less a foregone conclusion. This marked the end of the Federalist Party. While Jackson's congressional opponents became National Republicans, his supporters formed a new populist Democratic Party. A new era had started in American politics, characterized by a wide franchise of all white adult males and a new style of appealing to the public at large and winning its support with patronage and other favors. This extended a practice already well established in places such as New York City, where some ten years earlier the Democrats in Tammany Hall, in an attempt to frustrate the policies of the arrogant state governor, DeWitt Clinton, had launched machine politics onto the American scene.[33] The new politics of the Age of Jackson[34] defined the world which Abraham Lincoln entered when he set up on his own during the 1830s.

What then did the United States add up to? While 80 percent of all Americans still lived in the country in 1860, there had been in the preceding thirty years a disproportionate increase in urban industrial populations. This was particularly true of the states where there had been the greatest proportionate increase in population, from New Jersey in the east to Illinois in the west. This was the period of the American industrial revolution, based on developing natural resources of coal and iron, in which Pennsylvania and Ohio were dominant—as they still are today. The cities that Lincoln would know best, Louisville, Cincinnati, St. Louis, and later Chicago (which did not even exist when he first came to Illinois in 1830), all played an important part in this process. This economic transformation did not, however, extend to the southern states, where, apart from the great harbor city of New Orleans, whose prosperity was closely tied to the cultivation of cotton with slave labor, towns were few and far apart. The plantation economy was content to import manufactured goods, as well as essential skills—such as those required by the railroads—from the northern states.

If the facts related in this section seem as dry as dust, they are still critical for any understanding of American history in the years leading up to the Civil War: one only needs to read the recorded speeches of Abraham Lincoln to realize that he had them at his fingertips. That they constituted material that no serious politician or journalist could ignore is clear from any study of contemporary newspapers and official records. If in all this Lincoln was far from being alone, he was consistently more astute than most of his contemporaries in reading the figures correctly.

THE CAUSE OF ABOLITION

If Abraham Lincoln would himself have chosen to be remembered for having fought and won a long and bitter war to save the Union, it was the abolition of negro slavery, during his administration and on his initiative, that brought about the most radical change in the character of America's society, the development of its economy, and the direction of its politics. The Emancipation

Proclamation of 1863—whose full history is told later—was however the culmination of a process directed to cure what the Frenchman, Alexis de Tocqueville, in 1835, described "as the most formidable of all the ills which threaten the future existence of the Union . . . the presence of a black population upon its territory."[35]

When Massachusetts and New Hampshire, by signing the Articles of Confederation, joined the Union in 1788, slavery was already prohibited in both of these states. The same was true of Vermont when it joined as the fourteenth state in 1791. In the course of the next sixty years the process of abolition would also be completed in New York (1827), Rhode Island (1842), New Jersey (1846), Connecticut (1848), and Pennsylvania (1850). By this time five new states, Ohio (1805), Indiana (1816), Illinois (1818), Michigan (1837), and Wisconsin (1837), which had originally been part of the Northwest Territory, elected to join the Union with constitutions that prohibited slavery; the same was true of Iowa (1846), which had been part of the Louisiana Purchase.

Although the previous paragraph suggests the process of abolition was somewhat protracted, in reality, by 1850 slavery had long disappeared in all northern states. In the case of New York, for instance, legislation passed in 1799 provided for the emancipation of all children of slaves. This not only ensured the steady decline of slavery, but also encouraged slave owners either to move to southern states where slavery was not under threat, or to sell their slaves to new owners in these states. What is more, legislation providing for the end of American participation in the international slave trade, which came into force in 1808, meant that northern harbors, notably New York, had—in contrast to the eighteenth century—little interest in the survival of slavery. In the nineteenth century, therefore, such negroes as lived in the northern states were mostly free. This did not mean, however, that they were citizens whose rights were the same as those of their white compatriots. On the contrary, they had to be content with life in a sort of legal limbo[36] with few opportunities for satisfactory employment. As such they were unwelcome members of society, particularly among working-class white men. As Alexis de Tocqueville noted on the mid-1830s, "the States in which slavery is abolished usually do what they can to render their territory disagreeable to the negroes as a place of residence."[37] They were in any case few in number, so that in 1830, for instance, there were only 120,000 free negroes out of a total northern population not far off seven million. In fact there had been until this time more free negroes in the southern states, but there they were outnumbered by a factor of about twenty to one by the slave population. In the whole antebellum period of the nineteenth century (during which eighteen new states were admitted to the Union) the overwhelming majority of the negro population, which was consistently just under a fifth of the total, consisted—as already noted—of slaves.

Although in principle the abolition of the international slave trade meant that only natural increase could raise the number of slaves, in practice an estimated 250,000 new slaves were imported illegally,[38] over the years, from Africa or the Caribbean. Given that the total number of slaves was counted in millions, and steadily increased in the years up to 1860, the slave community, nonetheless, was essentially one that reproduced itself exponentially.

Rather than being evenly distributed throughout the southern states, as finally defined by the Missouri Compromise of 1821, the slave population was concentrated in areas such as Virginia, the Carolinas, and Georgia, where it was most useful as a source of labor, whereas in Appalachia, few slaves were to be found. However, in such mountainous areas slaves were still employed in transport, small-scale agriculture, metal-working, mining, and forestry.[39] Where slave populations were large, this was because of their employment—often in very large numbers—by plantations. In 1809, while tobacco, particularly around Chesapeake Bay, and rice, in Georgia and the Carolinas,[40] still accounted for large numbers of slaves, the plantation of cotton had already begun to dominate the economy of the southern states. While cotton was first planted in Virginia, Tennessee, Georgia and the Carolinas, from the beginning of the nineteenth century the plantations extended steadily westward across Alabama, Mississippi, and on into Louisiana—to the point that by 1860 they also covered large areas, beyond the Mississippi, in Missouri, Arkansas, and Texas.[41]

The changing economic geography of cotton had critical consequences for the forced migration of slaves. As demand for their labor increased across the cotton belt, their usefulness to the Chesapeake economy declined as farmers, reacting to low tobacco prices caused by increasing overseas competition, switched to corn and cattle. It was then uneconomical to maintain a year-round labor force—however modest its standard of living. This meant a steady sale of slaves in a well-organized market, in which Washington and Baltimore played an important part.[42] The distress that resulted not only led many slaves to attempt escape to free states—much easier from the Chesapeake area than from the deep South—but also fueled the abolitionist cause.

The prospect of slaves escaping to sanctuary in free states was the reason for the US Congress, in 1793, passing the first Fugitive Slave Act, which effectively provided for a slave to be extradited, under Article 4[43] of the Constitution, to the state from which he had fled. With this Act, a slave, who had escaped to a free state, was no longer safe: he need only be apprehended for the law then to ensure his return to his master, if not to trial in the master's home state. Particularly in border areas, such as southern Pennsylvania, professional slave catchers made a good living from the bounties paid for recapturing runaway slaves.

This activity not only gave rise to considerable litigation,[44] but also encouraged northern sympathizers to help fugitive slaves—so much so that their

Underground Railroad finally helped more than 50,000 on the way to freedom in northern states where they could find a safe haven, or even in Canada. This, however, was a comparatively late historical development: in the first ten years of Abraham Lincoln's life the categorical abolition of slavery was a lost cause, adopted only by a handful of religious minorities, notably Quakers. On the other hand, movements directed toward mitigating the consequences of slavery and of the presence of a very substantial negro population were much more successful. One of these was the American Colonization Society, founded in 1816 by Robert Finley, a Presbyterian minister from New Jersey, whose purpose was to send negroes back to Africa. For this purpose the settlement of Liberia was established, and over the years some 13,000 free negroes chose to go there.[45] Needless to say, at a time when slaves were being imported illegally from overseas, there was never any prospect that those born in America would be allowed to emigrate—to Liberia or anywhere else.

That the colonization plan was completely misconceived can be seen from the relatively small number of free negroes who took advantage of it. Instead, during the years 1817–1819, considerable numbers denounced it at well-attended meetings in Philadelphia, which, during the 1820s, led to the emergence of negro anti-slavery associations in major northern cities, together with the publication in 1827 of *Freedom's Journal*, the first black American newspaper.[46] If, in spite of the poverty and low social status of almost all free negroes, there were still a number of successful small businessmen ready to organize in the abolitionist cause, this had little prospect of success without some significant white support. As the record shows, moderate white abolitionists could already claim success as a result of the gradual abolition of slavery in the northern states: then, when the question of admitting Missouri to the Union as a slave state came before Congress in 1820, their influence certainly counted in securing the Missouri Compromise. This, however, did not abolish slavery—indeed it led to its being permitted in the new state of Missouri—but simply restricted its expansion. This was a cause that, over the years, could call upon increasing popular support.

On the other hand outright abolition was not a popular cause, as became clear at the end of the 1820s, when William Lloyd Garrison, its best-known protagonist, entered the arena.[47] This, however, was long after Abraham Lincoln's childhood years, first in Kentucky, and then in Indiana and Illinois. In the latter two states, north of the Ohio River, the future of slavery was seen as a matter for each individual state. It was no problem to the frontiersmen north of the Ohio that slavery continued south of the river: those, such as Thomas Lincoln, who preferred not to live with it in Kentucky, could always cross to the other side, where there was abundant land for new settlement.

2

The American Riverboat

EARLY DAYS ON THE MISSISSIPPI

When I was a boy, there was but one permanent ambition among my
comrades in my village on the west bank of the Mississippi River. That
was to be a steamboatman.

From Mark Twain, *Life on the Mississippi*[1]

The river navigation of the West is the most wonderful on the globe,
and since the application of steam power to the propulsion of vessels,
possesses the essential qualities of open navigation. Speed, distance,
cheapness, magnitude of cargoes, is all there, and without the perils of
the sea from storms and enemies. The steamboat is the ship of the river,
and finds in the Mississippi and its tributaries the simplest theater for
the diffusion and display of its power. Wonderful river! Connected with
seas by the head and mouth, stretching its arms towards the Atlantic
and Pacific, lying in a valley which reaches from the Gulf of Mexico to
Hudson's Bay.

Missouri Senator Thomas H. Benton of St. Louis[2]

In the first half of the nineteenth century steamboats plying the inland waterways transformed the way America traveled and shipped freight. Although
the development of steamboats for traffic in the rivers and along the coasts
of the eastern seaboard was already underway by the end of the eighteenth
century, the center of action in the nineteenth century was far inland, in the
vast area drained by the Mississippi and its tributaries of which ten would give
their names to states admitted to the Union in the sixty-nine years from 1792
to 1861—Kentucky (1792), Tennessee (1796), Ohio (1803), Illinois (1818),
Missouri (1821), Arkansas (1836), Iowa (1846), Wisconsin (1848), Minnesota
(1858), and Kansas (1861). All, in one way or another, would play an important
part in the transformation of the country during the life of Abraham Lincoln.
The key factor, here, was that the Mississippi finally reached the sea in the

Gulf of Mexico, with New Orleans, some hundred miles inland, as the great harbor both for the transshipment of goods brought down the river to seagoing vessels and for welcoming travelers—including countless immigrants—from abroad. Although oceangoing ships, until well into the nineteenth century, were powered by wind and sail, this was out of the question in almost every part of the Mississippi river system—including the great river itself.

There were two reasons for this: first, it was next to impossible to move, under sail, upstream against the current; second, the rivers—led once again by the Mississippi—were constantly changing their course, as on one side they eroded their banks, and on the other created new land by depositing the soil and debris they carried downstream. In what often seemed to be a very wide river, particularly in times of flood, there could be only one relatively narrow navigable channel, and here also the course changed continuously. At every stage there were bends in the river, and also numerous islands. Even so, as a transport artery, the rivers, in the early nineteenth century, had no rival. This meant that the agricultural economies of the states that they drained had to find their markets downstream, with their produce loaded on vessels carried by the river currents.

If, in the subsistence economies of rural America, most production was for local, if not family, consumption, a surplus for sale in more distant markets was essential for ensuring the supply of household goods and farming equipment—such as are listed on page 1. For settlers in the lands drained by the Ohio and its tributaries, the best market was in New Orleans, more than 1,000 miles down the Mississippi. St. Louis, at the confluence of the Mississippi and the Missouri, was even better, but only for farmers close to the tributaries, such as the Illinois, of the upper Mississippi, who could reach the city—which was much closer than New Orleans—by traveling downstream. (At a later stage the tributaries of the Missouri, together with those of the Mississippi west of the river, such as the Iowa, would become important, but they played a minor part in defining the classic Mississippi river scene—such as was later portrayed by Mark Twain's *Life on the Mississippi*.) As settlements were established, in the first quarter of the nineteenth century, in the lands west of the state of Ohio, but north of the river, the advantages of St. Louis over New Orleans encouraged migration across the Wabash River—a tributary of the Ohio—into Illinois and onto that considerable part of the state where the rivers were tributaries of the upper Mississippi. Of these the Illinois River (which gave its name to the state) was much the most important. Rising close to Lake Michigan, it was long and navigable, as were also—in favorable circumstances—rivers such as the Sangamon, that flowed into it. Reaching the Mississippi not far short of St. Louis, it was the first major eastern tributary upstream from the city: this meant that the city was inaccessible to river traffic from almost the whole of that part of the state east of the Illinois drainage basin—a factor with some considerable influence on new settlement. It was also significant that the Illinois River drained a substantial part of the prairie—which predominated in the north of the state—where the future for many, if not the majority of settlers, was to unfold. In this respect the Wabash River, which, defining the boundary between Illinois and Indiana, flowed into the Ohio River, was much less important, as were also tributaries of the upper Mississippi, such as the Kaskaskia, which joined the river below St. Louis.

It was not only the logistics involved in shipping farm produce to market that determined the appeal of the prairie to settlers. The land, if properly cultivated—a skill rapidly acquired by most of them—was far more productive. The great disadvantage was shortage of wood, but in the lands first settled in south-central Illinois, wood grew in sufficient quantities along the creeks and tributaries of the Illinois River catchment area to satisfy the needs of local settlers who took up the challenge of farming the prairie. This made the area acceptable to settlers from Kentucky and southern Indiana, whose farming practice took the availability of wood for granted.

For all these rivers, great and small—whether or not they reached the Mississippi via the Ohio River—the most useful vessel for commerce was the flatboat. This, like many other river craft, was constructed—almost entirely out of wood—for a single voyage, downstream. Its purpose was to bring agricultural produce, such as corn and hogs, to market. Little skill in joinery beyond that needed for constructing a log cabin or a fence was needed. The deck space had to provide for both an economically viable cargo and accommodation for the crew: this generally consisted of young men who had combined in a joint venture. Beyond being easy to build, the main advantage of the flatboat was its shallow draft. That this made steering somewhat problematic meant that too large a boat would be unmanageable. At the same time, a smaller boat could be built further upstream—sometimes even on one of the many creeks that fed the rivers. Most important of all, wood—the essential material needed for construction—was almost always available along the riverbanks.

The journey by flatboat down to New Orleans was made by two successive generations of the Lincoln family. Abraham's father, Thomas, made it several times from his home in Hardin County Kentucky: although it is not recorded who accompanied him, his cargo was home-fed pork. His skill as a joiner, a craft for which he had received some training, no doubt ensured that his flatboats were well made. His journeys were certainly born out of necessity, for he needed cash to liquidate his debts. On both occasions Thomas walked home to Kentucky, a journey that took several weeks, during which time he stopped at farms along the way, paying, with his own labor, for board and lodging—following the standard practice.

Much more is known about Abraham's journeys by flatboat to New Orleans. He made the first of these, in 1828, while still working for his father. Then, in the summer of 1830, he joined his father, together with an extended family which included his cousin, John Hanks, and his stepbrother, John D. Johnston, in setting up a new farm in Macon County, Illinois: this was the end point of Thomas' sixth migration since Abraham's birth in 1809. The time proved to be ill-chosen. At the end of 1830, a blizzard devastated the land, and this was just the first of thirty-one snowfalls in what came to be remembered simply as the "Deep Snow." Remarkably, given the appalling weather, the family still managed to establish a number of outside connections. One of these, made by John Hanks, an experienced flatboatman—who had completed a dozen trips down the Ohio and Mississippi to New Orleans—was with Denton Offutt, a merchant from Springfield, some forty-odd miles west of the new Lincoln farm. When the spring of 1831 came, Offutt planned to float a load of pork, corn, and live hogs (who would certainly consume much of the corn on the journey) down to New Orleans. As the melting snow flooded the countryside, Abraham, with his cousin and stepbrother, bought a large canoe which they paddled down the Sangamon River to Springfield, where, joined by Offutt, they set off in the late spring for New Orleans. There Abraham spent a full month, discovering a whole new aspect of American life, in which the entire economy—both of the city docks and of the local plantations—depended on slave labor. After a month he returned to St. Louis by steamboat: from there he walked the ninety miles back to the farm in Macon County, to discover that the Deep Snow had been too much for his family, who had decided to return to Indiana. They were in fact persuaded by acquaintances to go no further than Coles County, in eastern Illinois, but even so their departure was a decisive rift in the family. Abraham decided that his future was not in the east, but to the west, in Springfield.

THE STEAMBOAT REVOLUTION

The fact that he returned to Illinois by steamboat was the most significant aspect of Abraham Lincoln's journey to New Orleans in 1831: this would have been impossible when his father made the same journey, in the early years of the nineteenth century, from Hardin County, Kentucky, for the steamboat had not then come to the Ohio River.

Even so, the success of steamboat operators along the American east coast and above all on the great rivers flowing into the Atlantic, was certain, sooner or later, to turn their sights to the Mississippi, and more particularly, its great eastern tributary system based on the Ohio—particularly since the whole character of these rivers meant that there was no practical alternative to steam when it came to propelling boats upstream. (Significantly the first time that Lincoln was paid in cash, rather than in goods, for labor, was in 1827, when he earned a half-dollar for helping load tree trunks onto an Ohio river steamboat.[3])

Robert Fulton—a citizen of New York who, in 1807 with the *Clermont*, established a regular steamboat service on the Hudson River—combined with a business partner, Robert Livingstone, to exploit the much greater potential of the Mississippi. They had, however, an immediate setback, because both Ohio and Kentucky refused to follow the precedent established by New York state and grant them a monopoly similar to that which they enjoyed on the Hudson. Undaunted they went ahead and in Pittsburgh built the *New Orleans*, a steamboat on the model of the *Clermont*. Leaving on its maiden voyage in October 1811, it arrived ten weeks later, in January 1812, at New Orleans.

Fulton and Livingstone then decided to use it only on the short run between New Orleans and Natchez, some 200 miles upstream on the east bank of the Mississippi, where it was lost to fire in July 1814. Their decision was purely commercial: upriver from Natchez to Louisville on the Ohio, "a river distance of 1,000 miles, there was only a frontier wilderness with a thinly scattered population of backwoodsmen and no towns of importance to supply traffic and support to steamboats."[4] In any case, with its hull uncomfortably deep for the Mississippi's frequent shallow waters, the design of the *New Orleans* was ill-suited to the upper river. What is more, Louisiana, only admitted as a state in 1812, did grant the monopoly refused by Kentucky and Ohio: Fulton and Livingstone only enjoyed it for three years, for both died in 1815.

By this time an actor much better attuned to the geography west of the Appalachians was already moving center stage. Henry Shreve grew up in Brownesville, Pennsylvania, on the banks of the Monongahela—which, at Pittsburgh, joins with the Allegheny to form the Ohio River. With much better firsthand knowledge of the Mississippi and its tributaries than Robert Fulton, he began to build a boat called the *Enterprise* which took into account their wayward character. In 1810 he took it successfully down the Ohio to the Mississippi at Cairo, Illinois, where he turned upriver intent on loading a cargo from the Indian lead mines on the Galena River—a small eastern tributary which joins the Mississippi in Illinois far to the north of Cairo. The Indians, used to selling to French and English who came down the Mississippi from Lake Superior in pirogues, were at first reluctant to sell to a temperance man who, instead of hard liquor, could only offer household goods such as pots and pans, but in the end they finally traded their entire hoard of some sixty tons of lead to Shreve. This he loaded onto a flatboat specially constructed, under his supervision, in situ, which he towed downriver the whole way to New Orleans.

There he transshipped to a schooner which he sailed to Philadelphia, where he sold the whole cargo at a profit of $11,000.

In spite of his success with his first venture, Shreve realized that his boat was far from ideal when it came to the unpredictable character of the Mississippi river system. In particular it was only because of exceptionally high water that it had been able to navigate the rapids of the Ohio at Louisville. Low water, however, was the great problem, since it occurred in the fall harvest season, when grain traffic was at it heaviest.[5] The success of the flatboat depended on its shallow draft, but this was impossible with the accepted model of the steamboat imported from the east coast. The draft of the conventional Mississippi flatboat was insufficient to accommodate any state-of-the-art steam engine. Shreve, however, constructed a flat-bottomed hull 136 feet long and twenty-eight feet wide, which he decked over, putting the engine and boilers on deck. This he covered with a second deck, and above this he placed the pilothouse, with two high smokestacks just behind it. These were for the two separate, efficient, lightweight, high-pressure engines,[6] each with its own horizontal boiler and piston for powering one of the side-wheels. The *Washington*, a boat built on this design at Wheeling, in the state of Virginia on the upper Ohio, left the city on its maiden voyage on June 4, 1816, with Shreve as its captain. Recovering from a serious accident while still on the Ohio—in which several people lost their lives—Shreve still reached New Orleans in good time, turned the *Washington* around, and steamed back to Louisville in a record twenty-four days. In spite of his earlier success with the *Enterprise*, this achievement removed all doubts and prejudices about the future of steam navigation on the Mississippi and its tributaries, so encouraging the building of shipyards in every convenient locality.[7] The banks both of the main river and its tributaries were transformed, with towns growing up to support the new commerce made possible by steamboats: the economic potential of the vast area drained by the Mississippi was vastly increased. This was the changing world that Lincoln could observe as he made his trip to New Orleans in 1831.

Shreve had designed, built and captained the classic Mississippi paddle-steamer—a model which remained standard for generations. Western steamboats, following his basic design, differed very substantially from the model which Fulton had brought from New York. With little resistance to wear and tear, they were short-lived and extravagant with fuel, but with their high-pressure engines cheap to build: they carried freight as much as passengers who had to accept a safety record quite horrifying by today's standards. Boiler explosions and fires on boats mainly built of wood could destroy both cargoes and the lives of passengers in a matter of minutes. This was a different world from east of the Appalachians, where fast, comfortable, relatively safe and long-lived passenger boats, with low-pressure engines—built at much greater cost—dominated the relatively low volume of traffic. By the 1850s—by which time the voyage upriver took as few as four days—Shreve's steamboats "outweighed in tonnage all the vessels of the Atlantic seaboard and the Great Lakes combined."[8] They were the most notable achievement of the American industrial revolution. By 1840, when the steamboat—which had started thirty years earlier as a haphazard, unskilled, local improvisation[9]—had reached its most perfect form, with engines rated on average at three and a half times the power of those used by industry on land, it accounted for three-fifths of all the steam power used in the United States.[10] In the 1850s New Orleans overtook New York in volume of shipping, with half of all American exports moving through the port. By this time also, the economic development of the Mississippi and the Ohio extended along the whole length of both rivers, with Saint Louis becoming by mid-nineteenth century the fourth largest city in the United States.

It is significant for understanding the United States, as Abraham Lincoln conceived of it, that New Orleans and St. Louis were the first two cities which affected his life—in 1831, when he was twenty-two years old. The success of both cities reflected the remarkable expansion of the Union in the first half of the twentieth century. If this process can be taken to start with the admission of Ohio as the seventeenth state in 1805, the admission of Louisiana, as the eighteenth state in 1812—when Lincoln was just three years old—was historically at least as important.

Following President Jefferson's Louisiana Purchase of 1803, a small stretch of land, comprising the Mississippi delta, in the extreme south of the vast area subject to it, was organized as the Orleans Territory, according to a procedure similar to that established by the Northwest Ordinance of 1787.[11] This new territory was then admitted to the Union as the state of Louisiana in 1812. Its great harbor city of New Orleans was the gateway to the whole drainage basin of the Mississippi, including lands belonging the Union before 1803—which in that year meant the states of Kentucky and Tennessee, together with the Northwest and the Mississippi Territories. Much the greater part of the land purchased in 1803 was drained by rivers that flowed into the Missouri before it joined the Mississippi at St. Louis, but in contrast to the great eastern tributaries of the Ohio—such as the Cumberland, the Tennessee, and the Wabash—these western rivers often carried very little water: there was simply too little rainfall in the prairies through which they flowed.[12] Notwithstanding the substantial differences between the eastern and western river systems, in the first half of the nineteenth century their economic potential could never have been realized without the transport infrastructure defined by the countless steamboats which served them. New Orleans, which could be reached downstream from every part of the whole vast system—while at the same time being accessible to ocean shipping—was the gateway to the outside world.

The great economic advantages of the harbor of New Orleans inevitably encouraged the location of plantations in places where both the lower Mississippi and its most important tributaries were easily accessible. This was above all the case with crops grown for export: in the American South, in the first half of the nineteenth century, this meant cotton above all—and as chapter 6 demonstrates, cotton meant the large-scale employment of slave labor. (The same was equally true of other crops, such as sugar, grown in areas easily accessible to the Mississippi.) The secular shift in cotton production is well documented. Whereas in 1800 the areas planted in cotton were to be found mainly in southeastern Virginia, the central parts of North and South Carolina, and northwestern Georgia—all founding states of the Union—by 1850, production had extended right across Georgia into Alabama and Mississippi, and beyond into Louisiana, Texas, and Arkansas. Large cotton plantations were characteristic of both banks of the lower Mississippi, and towns such as Vicksburg and Natchez became famous for their patrician lifestyle, in which service rendered by slaves was an essential component. This was equally true of the docks of New Orleans, where bales of cotton were piled high, waiting shipment overseas—whether to New England's textile mills, or to the same industry in old England's county of Lancashire. As the south's commercial center, New Orleans was inevitably a center for buying and selling slaves. All this would have been apparent to Abraham Lincoln in 1831 in the course of his journey from St. Louis to New Orleans and back. At this time the development of cotton planting and of the infrastructure it supported would still continue for another generation—although by the 1850s riverboats would be competing with railroads. In a real sense, Lincoln saw only the half of it: where in 1831 there was little cotton north of Louisiana—except in Tennessee—thirty years later it had extended as far north as the banks of the Missouri River.

What then did the Mississippi system add up to in its heyday? One of the great pioneers of western expansion, Senator Thomas Hart Benton (1782–1858) of Missouri—which in 1821 had been admitted as the first state wholly west of the Mississippi—reckoned that some 50,000 miles of water in the Mississippi system were navigable by some kind of boat: in any case some 16,000 miles of steamboat routes are recorded—although many of them had not yet come into operation in the early 1830s.[13]

These routes differed considerably both in the character of their waterways and in that of the traffic they carried. The geography of the system defines four main sections. The first of these, traveling downstream, comprises the stretch of the Mississippi from Minneapolis—the highest point of the navigable river—to St. Louis, Missouri, where the Missouri River flows in from the west. In 1823 the *Virginia* became the first steamboat to complete the journey upstream from St. Louis to Fort Snelling—as Minneapolis was then known. Although this northern section would later become important, it was not until the 1840s that the states comprised in the territory north of Illinois and Missouri were admitted to the Union—which gives some indication of their modest economic development before this time.

The course of the river from St. Louis down to the Gulf of Mexico, some hundred miles downstream, defines the classic southern section, discovered by Lincoln on his journey to New Orleans in 1831—and made famous, later in the nineteenth century, by Mark Twain. Equally important in 1831 was the eastern section, defined by the Ohio River and its main tributaries, which Lincoln would have discovered as a boy as his family constantly moved home from Kentucky, through Indiana and on into Illinois. With the admission of Kentucky as a state in 1792, the Union reached both these sections of the Mississippi river system, and after Arkansas became a state in 1838, they were contained entirely within it: by this time their economies had long been dependent upon constant steamboat traffic on their navigable waterways. The fact that along the 1,200-mile-long southern section there were 1,327 landings at which boats might stop[14] gives some idea of what this all involved. Significantly there were more than a thousand along the 135 miles of river in Louisiana between Baton Rouge and New Orleans. For shipping cotton and sugar the steamboat was plainly indispensable. No wonder, then, that in the early days of the river steamboat Fulton and Livingstone confined the service they offered to the busy stretch of river between New Orleans and Natchez.

Although there were far fewer landings, the eastern section of the Mississippi river system was also extremely busy. For one thing this was where the majority of steamboats were constructed. Since, however, distances downstream were much longer—particularly for loads originating along the Ohio—there was everything to be said for allowing the current to carry cargoes downstream on flatboats: the strategy adopted by Abraham Lincoln and his three associates in the early summer of 1831 was common practice—for sound economic reasons. For them, and many others, the usefulness of the steamboat was in bringing them back home.

The western section of the whole river system, although mainly defined by the Missouri and its tributaries, may be taken to include the western tributaries of the lower Mississippi, which had much the same character. In its natural state the country drained by these rivers was grassland, rather than forest; such trees as there were to be found were mainly along the creeks and rivers—which by the end of the summer often ran dry. On the other hand when water did come, the rivers were often in flood, with the power of the water eroding their banks. The results could be dramatic, as could be seen along 150-odd miles of the Red River below the point where—after forming the whole long frontier between Texas and the Oklahoma territory[15]—it entered Louisiana. Trees along the riverbanks were constantly undermined, and inevitably after falling into the waters created a succession of logjams. As the logs piled up, often over a distance of several miles, they formed the Great Red River Raft, a unique obstacle to shipping with nothing like it east of the Mississippi. Given that the Red River was the first major tributary encountered when moving upstream from New Orleans, there was a considerable incentive to clear the Raft.

This was an epic task, begun in the 1830s by Henry Shreve, whose *Heliopolis*, a double-hulled snag boat, was purpose built for clearing the channels of the Mississippi—which were continually blocked by debris. This he used to clear the logs at the bottom of the Raft, allowing them to be carried downstream by the current. This accelerated the natural process by which these logs were dislodged, so that it occurred more rapidly than that of new logs accumulating at the top of the Raft. Shreve's successes with the *Heliopolis*—although often spectacular—were never more than partial, and it was not until the mid-1870s that the Raft was finally cleared—and by this time the river traffic was already declining in the face of competition from railroads.

The Red River Raft was an object lesson in the hazards involved in mastering the western rivers. Progressively, as the Raft was cleared, the river flowed faster in times of flood, deepened its channels, and increased the rate at which its banks eroded. Valuable alluvial soil was carried downstream, to be deposited as shoals lower down the river: the hazard created in this way, while already only too familiar on the Mississippi, was still waiting to be discovered along countless stretches of the Missouri and its tributaries. Even so, steamboat operators persisted in moving further west: the political consequences were critical, since the opening up of the west was certain to lead to the admission of new states, carved out of the Louisiana Purchase. Here Missouri, admitted to the Union in 1821, was inevitably in the vanguard: St. Louis, the gateway to the west, and—next to New Orleans—the most important city on the Mississippi, was first reached by a steamboat in 1817. The *Zebulon M. Pike*, after setting out downriver along the Ohio from Louisville, Kentucky, took six weeks—traveling only by day—to reach its destination. Two years later, in 1819—and four years ahead of the *Virginia*'s journey up the Mississippi to Fort Snelling—the *Independence* became the first steamboat to navigate the Missouri River—which joined the Mississippi just above the city—and in 1831 a steamboat reached its headwaters, more than a thousand miles to the west.

The main long-term impact of the Mississippi steamboat on the future of the United States was demographic: from the 1820s onward, steamboats carried thousands of new settlers to the territory west of the Mississippi. In the United States, as it was then, the question that concerned almost all of them was whether they owed their allegiance to the north—where by this time every state was at least on its way to abolishing slavery[16]—or to the south, where every state retained it. Geography made certain that the state of Missouri—which from 1821 until 1838 would be the only state entirely west of the Mississippi River—would be the vortex of the new tide of immigration. As the *Missouri Republican* reported in 1835:[17] "Every Steamboat that arrives at our wharves is crowded with passengers. Some of the Louisville boats bringing three hundred at a time . . . many of these remain with us."

The fact that steamboat traffic was only just beginning to develop in the early 1820s meant that almost all of those who had already settled on the west bank of the river had come overland from the eastern states, and of these many had come from the south bringing slaves with them—mostly in very small numbers. One way or another all the settlers would have had to cross the Mississippi, but particularly for those from the south this could have meant no more than a short journey by ferry—for, given the direction of its flow, access by the river itself was much more useful to those coming from the north.

Geography also meant that Missouri—except for the advantage provided by the communications infrastructure of its two great rivers—was not well suited for plantation agriculture. Even so, cotton was planted in the southeastern corner of the state (known as the "boot-heel") and on the bottom lands of the Missouri River. Quite simply the state, with its northern frontier almost on the same latitude as New York City, belonged as much to the north as to the south—certainly that was the way many saw it in the northern states. Missouri was admitted as a slave state in 1821 as a result of the Missouri Compromise of 1820. The crucial importance of this event to American history is the subject matter of chapter 7: this chapter is only concerned with how subsequent events, in the short term, were influenced by the development of steamboat traffic in the Mississippi river system. Here two separate historical processes occurred over much the same timespan.

The first of these was the arrival, by sea, of new European immigrants at New Orleans, who, while having every prospect of settling new lands up-river, had none whatever in the plantation economies of the southern states. Starting as a trickle in the 1820s, new settlers, mainly from Ireland, Germany, and Scandinavia, arrived in increasing numbers to seek their fortunes in the territories drained by the upper Mississippi and the Missouri. Single men among them were often recruited immediately as roustabouts, "the proletariat of the river population."[18] Working twenty-four hours a day, with little respite, they loaded and unloaded cargo with little mechanical help, and just as important stored it in such a way that the boat remained stable. When the steamboat grounded on a shoal, their task was to transship the cargo onto flatboats to lighten the steamer. On top of all this the roustabouts had, twice a day, to carry four-foot logs on board as fuel for the engines.

Other immigrants traveled as lower-deck passengers, who, charged next to nothing for their journey, were little better off than the roustabouts. Both groups—with much the same European background—were intent on making their homes far upriver. Particularly on the lower river, even their lives counted for little: on one occasion reported by the Memphis *Daily Eagle*, a hundred German immigrants were put ashore, in freezing weather, on an island, to lighten the boat so that it could cross a bar—an operation in which roustabouts played an essential role. The boat then sailed on, leaving the immigrants to their fate.[19]

Conditions were much the same on the Ohio and the Missouri. If they were somewhat easier it was because lower-deck passengers and roustabouts were mainly Americans from the eastern states, rather than European immigrants. From the early 1840s onward, steamboats on the Missouri, after leaving St. Louis, brought countless settlers to Independence, on the other side of the state, the starting point of the Santa Fe and the Oregon Trails, whence they continued their westward journey in the covered wagons familiar from many a Hollywood epic. During the 1850s, as related in chapter 11, the eastern counties of the Kansas territory were often the destination of Missouri River passengers intent on taking one side or another in the fight for and against slavery—whose outcome would be critical once the territory was admitted as a state of the Union. The contest was often fought out on the actual riverboats as they went upstream, with passengers attacking each other even at the breakfast table.[20]

In the 1830s the lower Mississippi witnessed the transport, under the hardest possible conditions, of the saddest of all the steamboat passengers—Indians from the eastern states transported under the federal Indian Removal Act of 1830, which required all belonging to this category to be moved west of the Mississippi. In 1831 the law was brutally enforced by President Andrew Jackson, with Indians belonging to the eastern tribes brought down to the lower Mississippi and then transported by steamboat up its western tributaries, such as the Arkansas, which was navigable for several hundred miles: their destination was a vast area comprising the whole of the present state of Oklahoma, and parts of Kansas and Nebraska, formally set aside in 1834 as Indian territory.[21] The transport of Indians in the 1830s was, however, exceptional: in these early days the steamboat services on the western tributaries of the Mississippi, including the Missouri, were developed mainly for transporting soldiers and supplies to the forts established by the US Army in the process of opening up the west to settlers.

By the end of the 1830s, boats could hardly be built fast enough to deal with the flood of immigrants, and by the end of the 1840s, when their numbers multiplied as a result of settlers moving overland to California—to seek their fortunes in the gold rush described in chapter 9—there were a hundred steamboats on the lower Mississippi, seventy-five on the upper river, fifty-eight on the Missouri, twenty-eight on the Illinois, fifteen on the Tennessee and a staggering 150 on the Ohio.[22]

These figures tell their own tale. Two points stand out. First, with the Tennessee—although a tributary of the Ohio—as the only southern river that counted, relatively few immigrants from the south came by steamboat. As already noted, there were alternative routes overland, but even so the low level of river traffic on the Tennessee suggests also that immigrants from the south were hard put to match the numbers coming from the north. After all, settlers from Illinois could also travel overland, yet the twenty-eight steamboats on the Illinois River outnumbered those on the Tennessee almost two to one.

Even more significant are the 150 steamboats on the Ohio, above all in relation to the hundred on the lower Mississippi. Some taking the boat down the Ohio were no doubt southerners—often with their own slaves—who came on board from the Kentucky shore. (Louisville, the state's largest city, was one of the places where the young Abraham Lincoln observed the commerce in slaves.) Another factor, however, was much more decisive: starting with the opening of the Erie Canal in 1825—providing a continuous waterway linking the Hudson River just above Albany to Lake Erie close to Buffalo—settlers from the north had a new route not only to the lands of the old Northwest Territory, but also to those of the Louisiana Purchase beyond the Mississippi. Seven years later, in 1832, the Erie and Ohio Canal linked the Cuyahoga River, which flowed into the lake at Cleveland, with Portsmouth on the Ohio River. Other canals followed, culminating in the Illinois and Michigan Canal, opened in 1848, which linked the river with the lake at Chicago, which by this time had grown to be a city with more than 20,000 inhabitants. Although steamboats were slow in replacing horse-drawn barges, transport by canals was—until the coming of the railroads in the 1840s—superior to any alternative transport overland. The same was true the Great Lakes, even before steam had taken over from sail.

As chapter 8 will show, the coming of the railroads transformed the American transport infrastructure, including that part of it defined by steamboat traffic on the Mississippi river system. After the mid-nineteenth-century, river and rail traffic both complemented and competed with each other, with the terms on which they did so defined mainly by economic factors. As a general geographical statement, the bias of the Mississippi river system was north-south while that of the railroads was east-west. In the days before the American Civil War (1861–1865)—during which time Lincoln lived and worked mainly in Illinois—river traffic dominated: steamboats had had, after all a quarter-century start on railroads. It was only in 1852 that the first line built west of the Mississippi—that of the Missouri Pacific Railroad linking St. Louis with the west of the state of Missouri—was opened, with much of its early traffic consisting of passengers brought to the start of the western wagon trails. It was another five years before the first railroad link from the east was completed by the Baltimore & Ohio Railroad, reaching the Mississippi at East Saint Louis, Illinois, in 1857. In the same year the Chicago, Rock Island & Pacific Railroad, based on Chicago, was the first to actually bridge the river—from Rock Island, Illinois, to Davenport, Iowa.

Although—until a very late stage—the rivers constituted the main traffic arteries for immigrants, upstream from Memphis, Tennessee, neither the lower Mississippi nor the Ohio had much to offer to the southern states. The railroad network in these states, disjointed in comparison to that of the north, hardly made up the deficiency. What is more, as southerners in the end realized only too well, the number of those willing to play a part in establishing slave-based economies beyond the Mississippi was limited. Once in the new lands they were unlikely to make converts either among settlers from the existing northern states (many of whom would be of recent immigrant stock) or among immigrants coming directly from Europe.

This was a numbers game with only one possible winner, and Abraham Lincoln, after he set up in central Illinois, on the Sangamon River, would have been a close and percipient observer. What he saw—together with many others—was a demographic tide that could only run in one direction. Without the river steamboats the tide would have flowed much more slowly: it flowed even faster when the flood of immigrants could also be carried by train.

3

The British Connection

THE COLONIAL HERITAGE

Few young nations have been more lavishly blessed, if that is the
right word, by the existence of an enemy than the United States in the
early years of independence; few have made more effective use of the
techniques of comparison in the search of an identity. Whether this
enemy was Europe as a whole, as it was symbolically in much writing
and orating of the time, or that special corner of Europe called Britain
or England, it was literally in 1812 and prospectively in 1845, its
mere presence in the world [that] helped speed up the course of self-
identification of the United States.[1]

The United States, in the first half of the nineteenth century, was far more
British than it ever was after the end of the Civil War in 1865. Indeed, until the
inauguration of John Tyler in 1841, every president[2] had been born a British
subject. Although with some, such as notably Andrew Jackson, this was the cause
of implacable hatred of almost everything British, it was impossible to deny the
stamp of British institutions upon life in the United States. Leaving the Native
American population out of account—according to the common practice of the
day—English was the mother tongue of the great majority of the population,
including more than half a million slaves of African descent. Those belonging to
the population of European descent, if not themselves immigrants, were mainly
descendants of British settlers in colonial times. There were local communities
of German descent, mainly in Pennsylvania, of Dutch descent in New York
state—which until 1664 had been a colony of the Netherlands—and following
the Louisiana Purchase in 1803, of French descent. After the 1840s, Texas and
California, and the other territories acquired from Mexico, added a Spanish-
speaking element, but this was very small in relation to the millions of Latinos
now resident, legally or illegally, in the United States. By the 1840s immigrants
were also beginning to arrive from Scandinavia and southern Europe, while the
California gold rush was beginning to attract immigrants from China. It was

only in the 1850s, however, that the new immigrant communities, which were beginning to take shape, began to be a major factor in American politics[3]—with significant consequences, described in chapters 7 (relating to Missouri) and 9 (relating to California) on the way the balance of power shifted in the years leading up to the Civil War. Even so, of the members of the Thirty-sixth Congress—elected at the end of 1858[4] and the last to serve a full term before the secession of southern states in 1860 and 1861—all sixty-eight senators and all but four of 194 representatives—had English names. One name that stands out is Spanish, that of Miguel A. Otero, not a representative with voting rights but a delegate from the New Mexico Territory only ceded to the United States in 1848—in circumstances related in chapter 9.

The ancestors of these members of the thirty-sixth Congress—who had left Britain for North America at various times in the seventeenth and eighteenth centuries, and one or two even in the nineteenth—were hardly a cross-section of the British population. Quite disproportionately they were Puritans, coming from those parts of England—notably East Anglia—where religious dissent was strong, and, as such, subject to discrimination, particularly when it came to election or appointment to public office. From the earliest days, settlers in the new North American colonies claimed—in a process that the colonial authorities were powerless to restrain—political rights and religious freedoms, beyond anything that was possible in Britain. This was true of Congregationalists in Massachusetts, Quakers in Pennsylvania, and Catholics in Maryland. Even so the settlers readily gave the names of the towns they had left behind to their new homes across the Atlantic: where else could the name of Plymouth, chosen by the Pilgrim Fathers for the community they founded in 1620, have come from?

The same was true of the thirteen new colonies, of which only Connecticut and Massachusetts have native American names. In the southern states, the English connection was even more pronounced, with Maryland, Virginia, Carolina, and Georgia all reflecting ties to the British monarchy, as did also many of their counties and townships. With such counties as King William, Prince Edward, Prince George, Caroline, and Orange—to say nothing of King and Queen—place names in Virginia undoubtedly lead the field when it come to the British royal connection. There, as in much of the rest of the south, the British settlers were not so much religious dissenters but fortune hunters, seeking to turn lands granted by their British governors into profitable plantations—an enterprise in which only relatively few succeeded. It is not for nothing that the Anglican Church, established by law in England, dominated religious life in the American south—particularly in Virginia.

Geography was never going to allow the patrician lifestyle of the plantations to extend far inland. This was characteristic of the tidewater Virginia, with rivers, such as the James and the Rappahannock, which were accessible to seagoing ships. The abundant land beyond the Blue Ridge, and along the Allegheny mountains, attracted smallholders—who as likely as not were religious dissenters from the northern states. This, as already related in chapter 1, was the route followed by the family of Abraham Lincoln.

It was not just language, and the names which are part of language, nor their characteristic forms of religious dissent, that the British brought with them to North America. At a time when there was no international standard for weights and measures, the American colonies measured distances in miles, areas in acres, weights in pounds, fluids in gallons—all units taken from Britain. The one complete break was the American dollar with a hundred cents: the new republic, founded at the end of the eighteenth century, had nothing to do with pounds, shillings and pence.

Most important of all, when it came to British institutions established in the American colonies, was the common law, quite different both in principle and practice to the civil law of continental Europe. This became the foundation of American law—particularly at the grassroots level. Trial by jury, the examination of witnesses in open court, advocates who saw each other as adversaries, and the reliance on precedent established by cases already defined an institution which was at the heart of township government in the new American colonies—to survive, almost unchanged, in the new republic. The courthouse, whatever its English background, became a defining American institution, and the stage upon which political battles were fought out. If the politics were native American, the best guide to the law to be applied by the court was William Blackstone's *Commentaries on the Laws of England*—published in London in the mid-eighteenth century without any regard to its possible impact in the North American colonies. If it was indispensable on the other side of the Atlantic, this was because there was no alternative to it. Abraham Lincoln, during his first months—in 1835—devoted to the study of law, read Blackstone twice.[5]

It is natural to ask why, if British institutions were so well established in North America, the men and women whose lives they governed ever chose to revolt against them. Since this is not a book about the American Revolution, the question does not have to be answered. It is better to ask what the British connection meant to Americans after the War of Independence had been won. The simple, but essential answer, is that King George and his parliament in London no longer had any voice in the way that North America, outside of Canada, was governed. The United States was free to develop its own institutions—particularly in law and politics—in a process which began with the Constitution as it was finally agreed upon in the period 1787–1790. Even so, as Thomas Jefferson wrote in a letter to his friend William Duane, "Our laws, language, religion, politics & manners are so deeply laid in English foundations, that we shall never cease to consider their history as part of ours, and to study ours in that as its origin."[6]

Canada, however, was problematic, at least for many Americans anxious to defend and retain their new-won freedom. Britain still maintained a military presence in Canada, and it was not there just for show. In addition, some tens of thousands of Americans who preferred to remain loyal to the British crown set up new homes in Canada. Although, in the early nineteenth century, this meant that Upper Canada (the present province of Ontario), the promise of new land in the west—following on President Jefferson's purchase of the Louisiana Territory in 1803 and the successful Lewis and Clark expedition in 1805–1806—was certain to require the frontier between the United States and Canada, west of the Great Lakes, to be settled one way or another.

Another significant factor was the way that the British presence in North America had been enormously strengthened by the peace terms agreed with France at the end of the Seven Year War in 1763. Effectively these left the whole continent divided between Britain and Spain, an outcome of great strategic advantage to Britain at a time when Spanish imperialism was becoming steadily weaker. What is more, the British, as rulers of all the land (except for Florida) east of the Mississippi—including the thirteen Atlantic colonies—were effective owners of all that counted economically in North America. It is no accident that the colonists, after 1763, only waited for thirteen years—that is until, 1776—before rising in revolt. The new North America was clearly a prize worth fighting for, and with the acquisition of the Louisiana Territory in 1803 it became even more valuable. But the British, in the opinion of many American citizens, were still breathing down their neck.

THE WAR OF 1812

In the early years of the nineteenth century—following the short peace of Amiens from 1801 to 1803—United States foreign policy had to come to terms with the fact that France, under its emperor, Napoleon, was fighting a war in which it sought to dominate the entire European continent, from Lisbon to Moscow, with key battles on land fought in Portugal, Spain, Italy, Austria, Prussia, the Netherlands and Russia, and at sea, off the coasts of Egypt, Spain, and Denmark. Before 1801, American merchant ships were able to make vast profits from trading between the French islands in the Caribbean Sea and the mainland of Europe—so long as they called in at a port in the United States.[7] This was a result of the Jay Treaty of 1794, by which Britain and the United States agreed to regulations that would govern the maritime trade of the two nations in time of war. These were so favorable to the United States that they allowed exports to increase threefold in the period 1794 and 1801. French maritime trade, successfully blockaded by the British navy, paid the price: France retaliated by giving its frigates, together with much more numerous French privateers, a free hand in capturing American merchantmen. By 1798, by which time the privateers had seized some $20 million worth of American cargo, this had become so intolerable that American ships of war were let loose on the French in the Caribbean, capturing over a hundred privateers and recovering seventy American merchantmen. This so-called "Quasi-War" ended with the convention of 1800, by which France agreed to the suspension of all the treaties made with the United States since the revolution. To many Americans this was a hard blow, because the French, in their revolution which started with the fall of Paris' Bastille prison in 1789, were seen as fighting for the same cause. To others, however, Napoleon's wars and imperial designs meant that France forfeited all the goodwill earned for putting an end to its monarchy.

This polarization was reflected in the American political lineup: the Jay Treaty, agreed with Britain when George Washington was still president, was essentially the work of the Federalist Party, which was only too ready to be reconciled with Britain—the community of interests counted for more than the fact that the two sides had fought a bitter war. After 1801, and the election of Thomas Jefferson to his first term of office as president, power shifted to the Democratic-Republicans, who favored a policy of disengagement and disarmament, but when, following the Peace of Amiens in 1801, the French were able to restore their own maritime trade, the losers were the Americans.

When war came once more to Europe in 1803, Americans could make good their losses, for the British naval blockade once more effectively excluded France from the Atlantic trade. American commerce boomed, as it had in the years before 1801—so much so that James Monroe, the American minister in London, could report: "The truth is that our commerce never enjoyed in any war, as much freedom, and indeed favor from this govt. as it now does."[8] Monroe spoke too soon. A year later he detected a British plan "to subject our commerce at present and hereafter to every restraint in their power." The terms declared by the Polly decision were enforced much more stringently, with the Royal Navy seizing any number of American merchantmen which allegedly failed to satisfy them. Although most were released by the British courts, Americans were up in arms. Enmity between the two sides was exacerbated by another practice of the Royal Navy, the use of press-gangs to round up men—mostly from the streets of the big cities—to serve as sailors.[9] In the war with France this was essential if crews were to be kept up to strength. American merchantmen, equally short of crews, readily engaged press-ganged British sailors who had deserted from the Royal Navy. The result was that British warships boarded American ships to reclaim British subjects—a process that led to several thousand US citizens being taken as well. To some extent Americans, who were not particular about issuing certificates of citizenship, were themselves to blame.

There were also disputes about the way the Royal Navy seized contraband destined for France from American ships, and all this was happening under a president, Thomas Jefferson, who almost from his first day in office had an aversion to treaties, calling, in particular, the Jay Treaty a "millstone round our necks."[10] What is more, Jefferson, had spent the five years preceding the fall of the Bastille in 1789 in France, first as a special delegate of the US Congress for negotiating treaties, and then—as successor to Benjamin Franklin—as US minister in Paris. He returned to America too early to witness the terror of the 1790s, or the rise of Napoleon at the end of the decade, but the time spent in France led him, after his return home, to support French rather than British interests—while the Jay Treaty, as he saw it, leaned in the other direction.

The status of Indians in federal territories provided another reason for Americans to distrust the British. Indian opposition to American settlement beyond the Appalachians, and particularly north of the Ohio River, has already been noted in chapter 1. If, in principle, the federal government was committed to protect Indian rights to land, it was powerless to prevent trespass by American frontiersmen intent on establishing homesteads—even where this meant murdering Indians. The Indian reaction was to be found in religious fanaticism among the Shawnees in the north and the Creeks in the south. In the north the hand of the charismatic Shawnee leader Tecumseh, strengthened by the Treaty of Fort Wayne in 1809, was turned to establishing an Indian confederacy in Ohio[11]—admitted as a state in 1805—and the Indiana territory.[12] Here Americans on the frontier believed, with little justification, that he was supported by the British,[13] who on the northern *Canadian* side of the Great Lakes—notably Ontario and Erie—were at least as well entrenched as Americans were on the southern side. The most that could be said is that Tecumseh enjoyed some moral support: after all, the British still had reason to be grateful for the support of Indians west of the Appalachians during the Seven Years' War (1756–1763)—which not for nothing is known to Americans as the French and Indian War. On the other hand the British had neither the will nor the means to block American settlement south of the Great Lakes. The threat of British intervention was however a factor in deciding American policy at a time when new settlers, such as Thomas Lincoln and his family, were moving north of the Ohio River in steadily increasing numbers. One can be certain, however, that none of them ever encountered any significant British presence on the new land they opened up.

To many Americans the various events recounted above meant that there was still a final account to be settled with the British, in spite of the fact that Britain had kept to the terms of the Treaty of Paris—that formally ended the

Revolutionary War in 1788—and had also honored its obligation under the Jay Treaty to withdraw its troops from the Northwest Territory, so in effect leaving it up to the Americans as to how they dealt with Indians, such as notably the Shawnee under Tecumseh. For Britain, the heart of the problem at least since 1803 when the country was once more at war with Napoleonic France, was to prevent help from America from reaching France in any form. It mattered little that France had a similar problem when it came to British imports from America. Critically, the Royal Navy, much more than any French naval forces, was far better able to engage in counteraction directed at North America, and did so in a heavy-handed way. After all, Britain had defeated the French in a number of significant battles at sea—of which Trafalgar, fought off the coast of Spain in 1805, is the best known. There is no doubt, however, that Americans—particularly those engaged in overseas commerce—were only too ready to fish in troubled waters. This was particularly true of a city such as Baltimore—after New York the United States' leading seaport. At the same time, in this city—home to many Irish, German, and French traders—there was a strong popular demand for war against Britain, and this was widely shared elsewhere in the country. Politically those in favor of war belonged to the Democratic-Republican Party, to which the first three nineteenth-century presidents—Jefferson, Madison, and Monroe—belonged.

For so long as he was president Thomas Jefferson (1801–1809) was able to maintain peace with Britain and France, but his friend and successor, James Madison (1809–1817), finally succumbed to the pressure exerted upon him by the war party. He was a weaker man than Jefferson at a time when American losses at sea were steadily increasing as the scale of the war in Europe was stepped up. Finally, on June 1, 1812, Madison asked Congress for a declaration of war,[14] which came on June 17, to be signed by him the next day;[15] American honor was at stake.

For both sides the war of 1812 was futile from the very start of hostilities. On land, the fact that Lake Erie and Lake Ontario separated the two countries at war, meant that vast distances separated the actual battlefields. While communications were slow and troop movements problematic, neither side had much to gain from any local victory—as soon proved to be the case. If "Win some, lose some" was for both sides the order of the day, in September 1813, a key American victory just inside Canada was decisive for the outcome of the war.

Although at almost every stage the United States could mobilize more troops, Britain made good the deficit in the number of its own soldiers by enlisting the help of its Indian allies, whose support was indispensable on many occasions. Alliance with Britain was particularly appealing to the Shawnees, for any American defeat would enhance their power south of the Great Lakes. The

British alliance, however, proved fatal to the Indian cause. In September 1813, a well-trained mounted force, recruited mainly in Kentucky and commanded by one of the state's congressmen, Richard M. Johnson, crossed over into Canada from Detroit, seeking battle with a British army, commanded by General Henry Procter, which was retreating up the Thames River.[16] Battle was joined at Moraviantown, some thirty miles upriver, and the poorly commanded British and Canadians were defeated. On their side only the Indians put up a good fight, but this ended when they heard the news that Tecumseh had been killed—for which Johnson immediately claimed the credit.[17]

Finally, in the summer of 1814, in a campaign fought mainly along the Canadian side of the Niagara River—separating, together with the famous falls, Lake Erie from Lake Ontario—American regular soldiers under General Winfield Scott won two decisive victories, at Fort Erie on July 3 and Chippawa River on July 5:[18] this was not enough, however, to secure an American foothold in Canada.

By this time Napoleon, who had abdicated on April 4, was in exile on the Italian island of Elba, so that Britain was free to concentrate on fighting the war in North America which until then, as seen from Europe, was little more than a sideshow. Admiral Cochrane crossed the Atlantic with a powerful fleet and 3,000 veterans from the war against France: its first targets were along the coast of New England, where Federalists cheering every British victory made manifest the division of loyalty within the United States. Worse was to come in August 1814, when Cochrane moved his fleet south to sail into Chesapeake Bay, and after routing a small, hastily improvised defense force at Bladenburg on August 24,[19] went on to sack Washington—burning down both the Capitol and the White House[20] (where President Madison's high-spirited wife, Dolley, achieved fame for rescuing the full-length portrait of George Washington).

From Washington, Cochrane moved on to Baltimore: there 15,000 American soldiers, ably led by General Samuel Smith, repulsed the British after a sharpshooter had killed their commander, General Ross.[21] Cochrane did not give up: attempting once more to take Baltimore, he decided first to have his rocket vessel, HMS *Erebus*, bombard the American Fort McHenry, which guarded the sea approach to the city. The bombardment started at dawn on September 13, and although it continued throughout the day and the whole night that followed, the Stars and Stripes still flew over the fort on the morning of September 14—an event that inspired Francis Scott Keyes, who witnessed it, to write the words of "The Star-spangled Banner."[22] Failing to reduce Fort McHenry, Cochrane gave up the attempt to take Baltimore—so ending the fighting in that part of the United States. Three days earlier, on September 11, another British force, which had moved down from Canada, was finally defeated in an attempt to capture Plattsburg, the key to the defense of Lake

Champlain—a normally peaceful stretch of water shared by New York and Vermont, and close to the Canadian frontier.[23]

In principle Lake Champlain should have been the last battle of the war, since by this time both sides had had enough: from August 8 to December 24, 1814, delegates from both the United States and Britain met at Ghent—then a city in the Austrian Netherlands—to agree the terms of peace. The reason why negotiations lasted so long was that the British delegates started off with demands which the Americans were never likely to accept: the main British concern was for the security of Canada, for as claimed by one British delegate, it was "notorious to the whole world that the conquest of Canada and its permanent annexation to the United States was the declared object of the American Government."[24] What is more, Sir George Prevost—whose final command was that of the British forces at Lake Champlain—had assured a group of western Indians earlier in the year that "Our Great Father considers you as his children and will not forget you or your interests at a peace."[25] The British commitment to making good their promises to the Indians was bound to be a major stumbling block in Ghent. The first proposal—to create a permanent Indian reservation in the Northwest Territory—was never going to be acceptable to Americans. It was not only a massive denial of American sovereignty, but also a flagrant disregard of a process of settlement—such as that of which the family of Thomas Lincoln was a part—that was already well underway. Although the treaty did commit both sides "to restore to such [Indian] tribes ... all the possessions, rights and privileges, which they may have enjoyed or been entitled to, in one thousand eight hundred and eleven, previous to [the] hostilities" there was no way in which the Indian cause would be protected by law. On the contrary, the death of Tecumseh sounded its death knell in the Northwest Territory, and although battles with the Indians were still fought after the end of the War of 1812, they were fighting a lost cause, with one new treaty after another providing for tribes to migrate westward, after having ceded their traditional homelands to American settlers. This was a process in which Abraham Lincoln, as related in chapter 1, played a minor role in the mid-1830s.

The Treaty of Ghent also provided for both sides to "use their best endeavors to stamp out the slave trade,"[26] but this was little threat to slavery itself as it was established in the United States. When it came to the territory in North America of both the United States and Britain, the treaty simply restored the position that existed before the war. Maritime issues, although part of the negotiations leading up to the treaty, were not resolved—in spite of the fact that these provided the original grounds for the American declaration of war in 1812. By the end of 1814, however, war against France was over—at least at sea[27]—and American merchantmen in the Atlantic had little reason to fear the

Royal Navy. (Although sailors would continue to be recruited by press-gangs, crew members of American ships, even if British, would no longer be at risk.)

The war had a memorable historical aftermath at the Battle of New Orleans, fought in January 1815. Although this occurred two weeks after the treaty to end the war had been signed in Ghent, the news had yet to reach either side in the southern theater of war. This meant that the commander of a British naval force chose to confront American land forces on high ground just outside the city of New Orleans: although the British were equal in numbers, the Americans, much better led under the command of General Andrew Jackson, won a decisive victory.[28] Because the news reached the east coast before the arrival of the ship carrying the terms of the Treaty of Ghent in New York—on February 11, 1815—Andrew Jackson's victory, combined with the news of the treaty, led to great popular exultation, so that when President Madison announced the end of the war to Congress, he congratulated the American people "upon an event which is highly honorable to the nation, and terminates, with peculiar felicity, a campaign signalized by the most brilliant successes."[29]

Orators and newspapers supporting the Democratic-Republican Party took up this theme, with, for example, the New York *National Advocate* boasting how "this second war of independence has been illustrated by more splendid achievements than the war of revolution."[30] Although this was the last time that Britain and the United States were ever at war, the Peace of Ghent did not put an end to disputes over territory—as will be shown later in this chapter.

FROM JAMES MADISON TO JAMES POLK

In the generation after the Treaty of Ghent, however, the economies of Britain and the United States were linked in ways profitable to both sides, and few who counted in either country denied that this was so. The reasons were quite straightforward. Britain, throughout the lifetime of Abraham Lincoln, was the world's leading industrial power, and already by 1800 two-thirds of the goods produced by the new factories born out of the industrial revolution went to America. These included steam engines designed by James Watt, imported not only for use on land but also on water for powering the new steamboats pioneered by Robert Fulton and others in the Atlantic states. In the early nineteenth century the problem facing Americans, particularly in the northern states, was that they had little to offer in exchange. The answer was to be found in trade with the British Caribbean islands which, with economies based on the monoculture of sugar, were a ready market for fish caught by American fishermen off the Grand Banks, wood from New England, and agricultural produce from the middle-Atlantic colonies.[31]

The case of the southern states was quite different, and that for one reason only. Following the final defeat of Napoleon in 1815 the steady, unchecked development of Britain's textile industry meant that by the middle of the 1830s cotton products comprised some 50 percent of all exports, measured according to their value, while some 20 percent of net imports[32] consisted of raw cotton imported from the American south. Already—by the beginning of the nineteenth century—cotton sold to Britain was overtaking tobacco as the most important export crop of the southern states. As the frontiers of the plantation economy moved west across the new states of Alabama (1819) and Mississippi (1816), to extend far into the land on the other side of the great river acquired as a result of the Louisiana Purchase, Lancashire's capacity to absorb cotton imports steadily increased, adding enormously to the prosperity of the American south—particularly after the British parliament abolished the import tax on raw cotton in 1845.[33] Significantly, every increase in this trade also helped entrench the institution of slavery as the basis of plantation labor.[34] The increase in scale can be measured both according to the rise in production of American raw cotton—which in the fifty years up to 1860 increased by a factor of twenty-five—or by the relocation of the slave population, which in the same period meant that more than a half a million negroes were constrained to move from the Atlantic states to cotton plantations in Alabama, Mississippi, Louisiana, and Texas. And all this was to satisfy the demands of an industry that was located mainly in England: although in both cases only one part of the country was directly involved, the economic symbiosis linking the plantation agriculture of the American south to the industry of Lancashire provided both the United States and Britain with a compelling reason for steering clear of any form of conflict. If, with the steady growth of American manufacturing—mainly for the home market—and the development of steam transport, first by river and then by rail, plantation-based exports from the southern states became steadily less important to the national economy, their contribution was still not only very substantial but also critical for the continuing prosperity of the south.

Turning away from the south, the possibility of conflict between the United States and Britain is shown by a number of disputes between the two countries which at the beginning of the 1840s were still unresolved. Significantly it was toward the end of this period that Abraham Lincoln, from 1847 to 1849, represented the Illinois Seventh District in the US Congress as a Whig: this was also the party of John Tyler, who, as president from 1841 to 1845,[35] worked hard to improve relations between Washington and London—which during the administration of President Martin Van Buren (1837–1841) had reached a low ebb. For Secretary of State Tyler chose Daniel Webster, whose guiding principle, while at the State Department, was peace with Britain.[36] At much the same time the government of Sir Robert Peel—who had become the British prime minister (for the second time) in 1841—was represented in Washington by Lord Ashburton, a personal friend of Webster. Webster and Ashburton were able to agree to a compromise on two boundary disputes, one relating to the frontier between Canada and the American states of Maine and New Hampshire, and the other to that between Canada and Minnesota: the Webster-Ashburton Treaty, once ratified by the Senate by a vote of thirty-nine to nine, established the boundaries in both cases as they still are today.

This left unresolved a third and much more critical boundary dispute, which was the result of the opening up of the American west from the 1830s onward. As American pioneers, in their tens of thousands, followed the great trails across the prairies to the land beyond the western mountain ranges, they entered into territory to which any American claim had little solid basis in international law. While victory in the Mexican War, and the terms of the Treaty of Guadalupe Hidalgo—as related in chapter 4—resolved the matter definitively in favor of those who took the southern Santa Fé Trail, the question remained open for the many who took the northern Oregon Trail, which ended in territory bounded only by the Pacific coastline, beyond the limits of that comprised in the Louisiana Purchase.

Although those who chose to follow the Oregon Trail had little doubt about their right to settle in what, in their view, was indisputably American territory, this was a view which London could rightly question. Not only had the American west coast north of California been explored from the sea by James Cook in 1779, but Britons and Canadians—generally connected to the British Hudson's Bay Company—had come there overland and settled in some numbers, without confronting any Americans. The notable success of the Lewis and Clark expedition blinded almost all Americans to the fact that Alexander Mackenzie, who was British, had reached the Pacific coast more than ten years earlier. What is more, the Columbia River, which provided the route taken by Lewis and Clark in the final stage of their journey, rises in Canada, and long before the 1840s Canadian trappers and traders associated with the Hudson's Bay Company had used it for their commerce, with their own outpost, Fort Vancouver, about a hundred miles from where it reaches the sea. The fact is that a vast area of land, with a long Pacific coastline, was up for grabs. The only limit to be accepted initially by both Washington and London was on the Pacific coast of what is now British Columbia: there, north of latitude 54°40" north, Russian claims, dating back to the last quarter of the eighteenth century, were recognized by both sides.

This explains the slogan "fifty-four forty or die," which, with the encouragement of leading members of the Democratic Party became a rallying cry for patriots in the early 1840s. If they had had their way, the British would be entirely excluded from the North American west coast. It was not to be. A key political question at this time was who would succeed the Whig, John Tyler, as president in 1845. The most immediate issue facing the new president would be the incorporation of Texas—upon which, as so many Democrats claimed, Britain had its own designs—into the Union. Although this question belongs to chapter 4, it is now to be noted how the Democrats, by linking Oregon with Texas in the months leading up to the presidential election of 1844, portrayed the Whigs—who had no enthusiasm for "fifty-four forty"—as being also opposed to the acquisition of Texas. To counter such allegations, the Whig candidate, Henry Clay, in his "Alabama letters," stated that he was in favor of the annexation of Texas, "slavery and all, if it could be done without dishonor or war."[37] In the election Clay's concession on slavery meant that the critical state of New York was lost to the Democratic candidate, James Polk, by a margin of only 5,106 votes.

Polk was a dark-horse candidate, adopted at a late stage only when the Democratic Party failed to agree on any of the leading contenders for nomination. A southerner from Tennessee, he could be relied upon to favor Texas' admission to the Union: his first act as president, in March 1845, was to endorse the invitation to Texas—the product of a joint resolution of the US Congress—made by President Tyler as one of his last acts while still in office.

The new president, James Polk, still had to resolve the Oregon boundary question with many of his own supporters committed to "fifty-four forty or die." Settling this was the third of four great measures mentioned by the president— just after he took up office—to his secretary of the navy. The fact that it was from the beginning completely overshadowed by the fourth of these measures, the acquisition of California, helps explain why it was resolved as early as Polk's second year in office, 1846. The process which took just over a year, from June 1845 to June 1846, would have been much shorter and considerably less embittered had not the British minister in Washington, Richard Pakenham—acting on his own initiative—rejected the opening American proposal to settle the boundary along the forty-ninth parallel of latitude. This led the British foreign minister, Lord Aberdeen, to run a press campaign supporting this proposal. Its success—in spite of considerable popular opposition—enabled Aberdeen to make the same proposal to Washington, with the proviso that the whole of Vancouver Island should be British. This enabled the Oregon Treaty to be signed on June 15, 1846, to be ratified by the Senate on the same day[38]—the futility of the War of 1812 had been avoided.

On this day, therefore, the northern boundary of the continental United States, from the Atlantic to the Pacific Ocean, was agreed upon definitively. Described "as a milestone in what was to be an era of lasting peace between the two great English-speaking countries,"[39] it has to date remained unchanged, and indeed unchallenged, for more than 170 years. Given Polk's commitment, before his election, to "fifty-four forty," it is worth asking how he was able to disown it with such little difficulty. One answer is that common sense triumphed both within Polk's cabinet and in the Senate—and for that matter in London, where Sir Robert Peel, the British prime minister, was able to ensure that the compromise solution was accepted.[40] At the same time, the cause of "fifty-four forty" gained its strongest support among northern Democrats—mainly from New York state—who, being sympathetic to the abolition of slavery, welcomed any expansion of American territory into new lands where this institution had little chance of being established. In particular, a group known as the Barnburners were regarded as extremists within the Democratic Party: Polk, coming from Tennessee, a southern state, had no difficulty about repudiating their cause.[41]

The president's commitment to the acquisition of California—which seemed every day more certain to involve war with Mexico—was much more important. Washington could not afford to risk war with Britain, which would be a much more formidable enemy. California was a cause even more popular among members of the Democratic Party than "fifty-four forty"—and one also to which Abraham Lincoln, who later in the year would be elected to Congress as a Whig, was steadfastly opposed.[42] As a Whig he was certainly opposed to "fifty-four forty," but he never needed to take a public stand on this issue. Somewhat oddly—in 1849—after he had been defeated for reelection to Congress in 1848, Thomas Ewing, interior secretary in the cabinet of the new Whig president, Zachary Taylor, offered him the governorship of the Oregon territory, which—for reasons both personal and political—he refused.

After 1846, the United States had little reason to be involved with Britain. All outstanding issues had been resolved, while at the same time the focus of American politics was on the future of the new states, and the territories adjacent to them, west of the Mississippi. It was above all what happened there in the 1850s that was decisive for the future of the United States and for shaping the thinking of Abraham Lincoln—as chapters 7 and 11 will make clear.

BRITAIN AND THE CIVIL WAR

The end of the road was the Civil War and here US relations with Britain once more played a significant part. Although after the outbreak of war in 1861 the European powers recognized the Confederates as belligerents,[43] the key question was whether, and in what circumstances, they were prepared to grant full diplomatic recognition to the Confederacy of the Southern States, as it was established in 1861. If, as proved to be the case, the US Navy would successfully blockade the south, then the Lancashire textile mills—whose contribution to the British industrial economy was critical—would be deprived of cotton, their essential raw material. If, on the other hand, the Confederate states were able to fight the war to a conclusion in which they would be established as an independent sovereign state, the southern plantations, still committed to slave labor, would continue to be Lancashire's major supplier of cotton. On this basis Britain, and the other major importers of American cotton, had a persuasive economic reason for supporting the south. What is more, if trade with the south were no longer subject to blockade by the Union, then it could become a major importer of British manufactured goods. In short, if southern diplomacy was to succeed in London, then it must appeal to British economic self-interest.

Neither London nor Washington were blind to the strength of this appeal. Nonetheless it never won over the British government in spite of the fact that Lord Palmerston, prime minister during the whole period of Abraham Lincoln's presidency, had little respect for America—as was shown in the early 1840s by his opposition, as foreign minister, to the terms on which the western frontier between Canada and the United States was finally settled in 1846. An event in October 1861 was sorely to try his patience and that of the British people. In the late summer, James Mason of Virginia and John Slidell of Louisiana were appointed to represent the Confederacy respectively in London and Paris. Escaping the Union blockade, they succeeded in reaching Cuba, then still part of the Spanish empire; there they boarded the British steamship *Trent*, to cross the Atlantic to take up the posts to which they had been appointed. The *Trent* was then intercepted by a Union frigate, the USS *San Jacinto*, and the two would-be ambassadors were taken prisoner, to end up behind bars in Fort Warren in Boston harbor.

The fury of the British became clear from a letter written to Charles Sumner, chairman of the Senate Foreign Relations Committee, by the Duchess of Argyll (whose husband was in Palmerston's cabinet) in which she called the capture of Mason and Slidell "the maddest act that ever was done, and unless the [US] government intend to force us to war, utterly inconceivable."[44] The crisis came to a head on December 23, 1861, when Lord Lyons, the British ambassador in Washington, presented a formal demand for the release of Mason and Slidell and the delivery of an apology from the US government within seven days: if these conditions were not met, the embassy would be closed and Lord Lyons would leave Washington. At a cabinet meeting on Christmas Day it was accepted that rejection of the British demands could mean war with Britain[45] and by the end of the day Lincoln had become convinced that what was "gall and wormwood" to at least one member of the cabinet[46] still had to be accepted. On the day after Christmas, a reply accepting the British demands drafted by the secretary of state, William H. Seward, was endorsed by the cabinet "with expressions of regret but without dissent."[47] Significantly, during the whole train of events, Lincoln—although at one stage wanting to talk face-to-face with Lord Lyons—was always one level removed from negotiations.

To some degree, the fact that dealing with foreign diplomats, even when they spoke the same language, was—for Lincoln—best left to others, reflects a cultural isolation born of his life as a frontiersman. Although he understood hardly a word of any language but English, with his only glimpse of a foreign country being that small part of Canada visible from the American side of Niagara Falls (which he visited in the summer of 1848), Lincoln's approach to life owed much to the English language and literature. His favorite leisure-time activity was going to the theater, with a particular attachment to Shakespeare—so much so that evening after evening he read aloud to his secretary, John Hay, from "Hamlet, King Lear, the histories, and especially, Macbeth."[48]

Lincoln's Emancipation Proclamation of January 1, 1863, also had an important diplomatic purpose, which was to discourage Britain and France from proceeding to recognize the Confederacy.[49] The immediate foreign reaction was not encouraging because many in Europe feared that granting freedom to the slaves laboring on the southern cotton plantations would make the supply of cotton to the textile industry even more problematic. When, however, the news spread among the British populace, vast crowds gathered in London and other British cities to celebrate the proclamation, making clear to Lord Palmerston's government that outraged public opinion would rule out any support for the slaveholding Confederacy.[50] Lincoln himself then turned his hand to public relations in Britain. Helped by Sumner's many good contacts he composed messages intended for the Manchester and London working classes, attributing the shortage of cotton not to the Union blockade but to "the actions of our disloyal citizens."[51] In the words of the president, the British workingmen represented "an instance of sublime Christian heroism which has not been surpassed in any age or any country." The force of Lincoln's popular diplomacy was not lost on the south, and when, in the course of 1864, the tide of war turned decisively in favor of the Union, the Confederate president, Jefferson Davis, sent a wealthy Louisiana planter, Duncan Kenner, to offer emancipation of the slaves in return for British and French recognition. Some in the South were even willing to enroll negroes in the Confederate Army,[52] but these were desperate measures taken at a time when the southern cause was beyond repair.

4

Spanish America: Independence and the Monroe Doctrine

SPAIN IN NORTH AMERICA

When—at the end of the 1780s—the United States was finally constituted as an independent sovereign nation, almost the whole of the remaining territory of North America—except for Canada (including the vast domain of the Hudson's Bay Company) and Alaska (which belonged to Russia)—was part of the Spanish Empire. The same was true of Central America (except for a small British outpost in Honduras), and of all of South America, with the exception of Portugal's considerable empire in Brazil and three small European Guiana colonies. In addition, two important islands in the Caribbean Sea, Cuba and Puerto Rico, together with half of a third island, Santo Domingo, belonged to Spain. Although most of this empire had—following Columbus' discovery of America in 1492—been Spanish for some 300 years, the greater part of its territory in North America had been ceded by France, in 1764, at the end of the Seven Years' War. This was the Louisiana territory, which, once regained for France by Napoleon in 1803, was immediately sold to the United States—as related in chapter 1.

Until the presidency of James Monroe (1817–1825) the US government had no great problem in coming to terms with the existence of Spanish North America, even though it comprised a very substantial part of the continent, extending from the Atlantic coast south of Georgia, to the largely unexplored Pacific coast—first reached overland by the Lewis and Clark expedition in 1805—and included the entire coastline of the Gulf of Mexico except for the Mississippi delta, which, with its great port of New Orleans, was part of the Louisiana Purchase. This part of imperial Spain comprised three major territories: Florida, as a Spanish colony, comprised the whole of today's state of the same name, together with the Gulf coastline as far as the Mississippi delta; west of the delta this coastline was part of Texas, a vast area, extending hundreds of miles inland, bounded on the south by the Rio Grande and the north by the Red River, a tributary of the Mississippi; on the other side of the continer California extended far inland from a long Pacific coastline. Between Tex

California was a great territory known as New Mexico, which, consisting largely of desert and mountain, was populated mainly by a remarkable collection of Indian tribes.

In contrast to their colonies south of the Rio Grande—and extending to the most southerly point of South America and to the three Caribbean islands—Spaniards had hardly settled, let alone developed, any of their territory in North America. For the most part the Spanish presence consisted of occasional Catholic missions—some of which, such as those in St. Augustine, Florida, and Santa Fe, New Mexico, were extremely old—and military outposts. If men of European, though not necessarily Spanish descent, exploited the economic potential of Spanish North America, it was as fishermen along its coast, or as trappers and prospectors inland. For the most part, however, it was effectively the very diverse tribes of Native Americans who called the shots. While it was the missionaries' purpose in life to convert them, and the soldiers' to defend against their depredations, the trappers and prospectors were left to come to terms with them as best they could. Their situation was often precarious, for many tribes, such as notoriously the Seminoles of Florida, were little disposed to deal with them. Although this was one reason why Spain did little to open up its lands in North America, the inhospitable nature of most of the terrain—whether it was swamp in Florida or desert and mountains in Texas and California and almost everywhere in between—was a much more important factor. What is more, with very few navigable rivers, travel and communication were always problematic.

In the opening years of the nineteenth century, Spain's whole mainland empire in the Americas fell apart as successful revolutions brought into existence one new nation after another. Throughout the eighteenth century the Spaniards, "rather than consolidating their hold on what they had already gained, and diversifying the colonial economy, had simply gone on conquering,"[1] failing to realize that the great days of imperial Spain had long passed. By the eighteenth century the empire could only survive with free trade, and this implied local political autonomy;[2] if this was a lesson that the Spanish government in Madrid never learned, it was not lost on the settler populations themselves, which "as they gradually developed their own sense of identity, came increasingly to believe that political autonomy was the only form under which their ambitions could be realized."[3] By the early nineteenth century this conviction was t   into action, and over a period of some twenty years one successful fter another led to the Spanish empire on the American mainland by some thirteen-odd[4] independent sovereign states. Of these ing the whole of the extensive former Spanish viceroyalty, final success of its revolution in 1821—the United States' or. As heir to all the territory that had previous belonged to imperial Spain, Mexico could rightly claim that its northern boundary was defined by the southern and western limits of the Louisiana Territory. In the 1803, the year of the actual Louisiana Purchase, this was hardly disputed in Washington, but then this territory still belonged to Spain.

This was also the status of Florida, where no revolution by local settlers ever threatened Spanish sovereignty. One reason for this was that the land comprised in Spanish Florida—which until 1810 included a strip along the Gulf Coast, bounded by latitude 31° north and extending right up to the Mississippi—was almost worthless, as can be seen by the fact that its total population was less than 20,000. Consisting of pine scrub, swamps, and lakes and rivers infested by alligators, it was far from being the valuable real estate that it became in the twentieth century. As home to unfriendly Indians, smugglers, and fugitive slaves, it was inevitably seen by Washington—in the early years of the nineteenth century—as a nuisance rather than as a prize worth having. In 1805 President Thomas Jefferson—minded to solve the problem by negotiation, backed up by the offer of money to Spain—sent James Monroe, his minister in London, to Madrid armed with a Congressional appropriation of two million dollars. The mission was unsuccessful: Spain was resolute in holding on to the whole of Florida.

After James Madison became president in 1809, US involvement in Florida was chaotic. Madison, on October 27, 1810, proclaimed that part of Florida west of the Perdido River was a part of the United States as a consequence of its belonging to the Louisiana Purchase. In making good this claim—which was denounced by both Spain and Britain—he was helped by the fact that a group of West Floridians had revolted against Spanish rule, occupied Baton Rouge, and declared their independence.[5] Although Madison condemned the revolutionaries he still sent US forces into West Florida with orders to advance to the Perdido. Confronted by Spanish garrisons in Mobile and Pensacola, they stopped short and moved no further than the Pearl River, some 120 miles to the west of the Perdido. Faced by British protests, Congress, on January 15, 1811, secretly authorized Madison to take control of East Florida—preferably with Spanish cooperation but if necessary by force—if ever it faced the danger of foreign occupation (which given the political lineup of Europe at that time could only have been by Britain).

In April 1812, when Louisiana joined the Union as the eighteenth state, Congress added that part of West Florida west of the Pearl River to its territory. A month later it proceeded to add the land between the Pearl and the Perdido rivers to the Mississippi Territory, disregarding the fact that this was controlled by Spain.

While all this was happening, small, irregular American forces, by sea and over land, did their best to destabilize the of East Florida by supporting local revolutionaries. Sebastian Kindelan, the Spanish governor, held firm, with the support both of black soldiers—who well knew that they would become slaves if ever Florida became part of the United States—and Indians, a combination which proved too powerful for US state militias trying to take over Florida on their own initiative. One result, indeed, was to set Georgia and Tennessee (which had no frontier with Florida) against each other.

While all this was going on, James Monroe, Madison's secretary of state, agreed with Kindelan to withdraw all US forces from Florida provided an amnesty was granted to the American insurgents. This was not sufficient to bring peace, for lawless bands of Americans continued to loot and burn. In May 1814, the British Admiral Cochrane—whose exploits are described in chapter 3—intervened, with the intent of encouraging negroes and Indians into British service: his legacy, in Florida, was a fort on the Apalachicola River, "well stocked with weapons and ammunition and garrisoned by blacks and Indians."[6]

This was all too much for the White House. By the end of Madison's second term in office in 1817, a US force under General Andrew Jackson—the hero of the battle of New Orleans in 1815—was ready to march into East Florida to "subdue the Indian and stop the escape of fugitive slaves." By this time Spain, losing control of almost everything else it held in mainland America, had little alternative to calling it a day in Florida. By the Adams-Onis Treaty of 1819, East Florida was ceded to the United States in return for Washington assuming some five millions dollars in claims made by American citizens against the Spanish government. The part of West Florida between the Pearl and the Perdido rivers was divided between two states that had comprised the Mississippi territory—Mississippi, admitted in 1817, and Alabama, admitted in 1819. East Florida became a territory, only to be admitted to the Union as the present state of Florida in 1845.

In 1823, fo   ars after the end of Spanish imperialism on the American mainland,   Monroe, in his annual message to Congress, proclaimed the doctr·   ears his name—that the Western Hemisphere is closed
                        , so that the Untied States would regard any attempt
                        tend its system to the Western Hemisphere as "the
                        'ly disposition towards the United States": at the
                        ild not interfere in European affairs. Although
                        la up until 1819, as recounted in this chapter,
                        m the perspective of Washington—for this
                        ism throughout Latin America, brought
                        as a much more significant factor. In
                        trine could be construed as mainly

a warning to Britain, but when later, in 1863, Napoleon III of France—taking advantage of the American Civil War—installed the Austrian Archduke Maximilian as ruler of Mexico, Abraham Lincoln, concerned about possible French support about the Confederacy, held back from any counteraction.[7]

THE TEXAS SAGA

The 1820s also witnessed the emergence of Texas as a field of conflict between Americans and Mexicans. Mexico, recognized internationally as one of the new independent states of Latin America, had the same rights to Texas as imperial Spain. On this basis the government in Mexico City was entitled to regard Texas as part of its domain. This followed from a provision in the Adams-Onis Treaty of 1819,[8] which laid down the boundary line between Spanish Mexico and the American territory comprised in the Louisiana Purchase: critically, the eastern boundary with Louisiana was defined by the Sabine River (which flows south into the Gulf of Mexico some 150 miles west of the Mississippi delta)—so conceding territory that could reasonably have been claimed by Washington as belonging to Louisiana.[9] However that may be there was little in the early history of the United States—during the era (1789–1825) of the first five presidents—that gave US citizens any rights to Texas beyond a relatively narrow strip of land bounded on the east by the Sabine and on the west by the Neches River. Nonetheless, by 1820, not only was the whole of North America east of the Mississippi and south of Canada part of the United States—with much the greater part of it belonging to states already admitted to the Union—but the same was also true of the vast territories comprised in the Louisiana Purchase, although at this time only Louisiana itself was a state of the Union. In the territory conceded to Spain in the Adams-Onis Treaty, Texas included the whole of the Atlantic seaboard as far south as the mouth of the Rio Grande River, which then—up to El Paso, far inland—defined its southwestern boundary. The treaty also recognized the Red River up to longitude 100° west as the northern boundary: given that the river is a tributary of the Mississippi—so that land on both sides of it was part of the Louisiana Purchase—this also represented a concession to Spain: this was the more so, given that everything west of longitude 100° west, and as far north as the Arkansas River, was also conceded. There was also room for dispute about the short eastern boundary of Texas, north of the Sabine and south of the Red River, which was defined by the treaty as a straight north-south line—in length about a hundred miles—just west of longitude 94° west.[10]

Geographically Texas can be seen as tilting from the northwest, far inland, to the southeast, where the whole Atlantic coastline between Louisiana and

Mexico is part of it. One natural result of the lay of the land is to be found in the way the major rivers, from the Rio Grande through the Nueces, San Antonio, Colorado, Brazos, and Trinity, to the Sabine, flow southeast into the Gulf of Mexico. Up to a distance of some 200 miles inland these rivers flow through a low coastal plain well suited to both agriculture and ranching; the same is true in much of the high country further inland, but this becomes increasingly barren as the distance from the coast increases—to the point that in the north and west mountains and desert predominate.

In spite of quite considerable geophysical advantages the Spaniards did little to develop Texas: looking at their final years of empire they seem almost to have given up on it—so much so that in 1800 the total population, apart from Indians who could not be counted, was only 5,000.[11] Of these a thousand or more lived in three major settlements, of which San Antonio—the seat of Spanish administration in Texas—was much the most important. The rest of the population, scattered across small villages, farms, and ranches, was left to its own devices, but for the most part a good living was to be found in the settled territory. The more remote a settlement, the more vulnerable it was to be raided by Indians, of whom the Apaches and Comanches were reckoned to be the most fearsome. Both church and state were present in the occasional mission and military outpost, but the rule of law, such as it was, owed little to a government in Mexico City whose decrees and regulations were unenforceable. What is more, when it came to commerce with the outside world, Louisiana, to the east of Texas, had much more to offer than the Mexican heartland. Both overland and by sea, trade routes led north and east to territory of the new United States, much more than they did to any part of Mexico: this was a matter of pure geography.

Texas, as it was in the years leading up to the end of Spanish rule in 1821, was, in spite of its small population, remarkably heterogeneous and cosmopolitan.[12] Not only Hispanics, but odd Frenchmen, Irishmen, Germans, Dutchmen and Englishmen joined negroes, mulattoes, and occasional Indians in carrying on any number of trades and professions, with support, according to circumstances, from a relatively large number of domestic servants, indentured laborers and even slaves. Except in the final days there were few Americans, but then, from the 1820s onwards, everything was going to change.

There were two reasons for this: first, the United States, having consolidated its hold on everything east of the Mississippi, was beginning to open land for settlement in the territory west of the river comprised in the Louisiana Purchase; second, Mexico in 1821 became an independent state. For Americans moving west of the Mississippi, Texas, in spite of the fact that it was part of Mexico, offered much the same economic opportunities to prospective settlers as they had known east of the river. Mexico, in turn, had every reason to welcome settlers—wherever they came from—in a remote, sparsely populated region far from its own heartland. In a rational world, American settlement could have proceeded on terms acceptable to both sides, but Mexico in the years following independence was chaotic, with constant and often violent changes in those who claimed to govern it, so that policy—as it related to American settlers—was never stable. A commitment made in one year could well be repudiated in another, simply because new people could be in power at any level, national or local.

One man who discovered this the hard way was Stephen Austin, who throughout the 1820s and on into the 1830s was the driving force behind American settlement in Texas. The original initiative came from his father, Moses Austin, who in the winter of 1820–1821 gained first the approval of Antonio Martínez, the Spanish governor of Texas, for his settlement project, and then that of a much more important figure, Joaquín de Arredondo, who from the city of Monterey, far south of Rio Grande, commanded Mexico's Eastern Interior Provinces. Moses Austin, having been received by Martínez in San Antonio, then the capital of Texas, waited there during the long winter months for Arredondo's favorable reaction to his project. This, when it came, granted the right to introduce 300 American families into an area of 200,000 acres. Such key questions as the location of this land, together with its subdivision and allocation to settlers, being left unanswered by the terms of the grant, were, according to Moses Austin's own interpretation, left in his hands. This was sufficient reason for him to return to Potosi, his American base in what in 1821 would become the state of Missouri—a story told in chapter 7. Once back home he would, as he believed, have little difficulty in finding three hundred families only too ready to move to Texas at a time when Washington was demanding too high a price for public land on the frontiers of its jurisdiction. Having persuaded his somewhat reluctant son, Stephen, to join him, he sent Stephen ahead to Natchitoches in western Louisiana, just short of the frontier with Texas. There, in the summer of 1821, Stephen Austin learned of his father's death: nonetheless he decided to go ahead, provided that Martínez allowed him to take over the grant made by Arredondo.

Martínez not only confirmed the grant, but helped Austin work out the details. There would be 640 acres of land for every head of family, with an additional 320 acres for each of its members and 80 acres for each slave. Austin's responsibility for the good behavior of the settlers—effectively as governor of their colony—extended to his being required to organize a militia to protect them against Indians. Having settled these terms, Martínez then authorized Austin to explore the coastal plains between the San Antonio and Brazos Rivers, to choose the best site for settlement.

If, with his choice falling on the rich bottom lands on the San Antonio and Brazos Rivers, the future of American settlement seemed assured, Austin was in for a rude shock: on a visit to Martínez early in 1822 he learned that revolution had overthrown the Spanish government in Mexico—as it had already throughout Latin America. Although Martínez, by declaring his loyalty to the new revolutionary government, stayed in office in San Antonio, he had to inform Austin that its provisional representatives in Monterrey did not recognize the grant made by Arredondo. By this time Austin had been back to the United States to publicize the grant—with such success that American settlers were already arriving in Texas. Some indeed were already there by the time he himself returned. Martínez had to inform Austin that they would either have to leave Texas or move to San Antonio, to wait until the new Mexican Congress—which in principle favored new settlement—passed a general colonization law. As a concession to the settlers Martínez agreed to delay enforcing the decision made in Monterrey, provided Austin himself went to Mexico City to persuade the new government to overrule this decision and confirm the original grant.

Austin, committed to the interests of Americans who had settled in Texas on his advice, felt himself constrained to accept this challenge. At the end of March 1822, he left on a journey to the distant capital of a country he did not know—apart from Texas—whose language he did not speak, and where law and order had completely broken down. After a month of travel—disguised as a beggar to avoid being robbed in a notoriously inhospitable land—Austin arrived in Mexico City on April 29, and managed to make contact with the congressional leaders. Although they were favorably disposed, this hardly helped Austin's case, since three weeks later, on May 18, the Mexican Congress—overthrown as a result of a coup d'état—was replaced by a junta headed by Agustín de Iturbide. During the reign of the junta any number of foreign entrepreneurs—American, British, German—had joined Austin to plead for a general colonization law, and this was finally approved by Iturbide on February 18, 1823. Austin, streetwise after nearly a year in Mexico City, bided his time there, to become a witness to the fall of the junta on March 19, followed by the restoration of the Congress—which immediately nullified everything enacted by the junta. Austin, who had diplomatically maintained his ties with its members, was almost immediately favored with a special contract in accordance with the law that they had just annulled, and on April 11 this was signed by the acting president of Mexico. Austin himself was recognized as the *empresario* responsible for its performance—which included the enforcement of law and order. This was all that he needed to return to Texas, but before his departure from Mexico City he translated the US Constitution into Spanish at the request of a committee of the restored Congress: this was then the basis of the Federal Constitution of the Republic of Mexico finally adopted on October 4, 1824. The event was important historically since, in the tumultuous years that followed, Mexican politics was polarized between two groups, the Federalists, who based their legitimacy on the Constitution, and Centralists who rejected it. Predictably American settlers in Texas supported the former, even though a federal act of May 1824 had consolidated Texas and Coahuila, a Mexican state of the other side of the Rio Grande, into one single state, Coahuila y Texas, with its capital at Saltillo, a city far from Texas and relatively close to Mexico City. This was a reform almost certain to cause problems in Texas sooner or later.

On returning to his Texas colony, Austin found it despondent as a result of what had happened during his long absence: seed and essential supplies had failed to reach the settlers, drought had led to crop failure, and Karankawa Indians had been stealing livestock. Many settlers had simply given up and returned to the United States. Austin, to retrieve the situation, had land titles issued as soon as surveys were completed, and by the end of the summer of 1824, 272 out of the 300 titles provided for in the contract had been allotted.

With the number of allotments finally reaching 297, these first American settlers came to be known as the Old Three Hundred. They organized a militia to deal with the Karankawas, signed a treaty with the less threatening Tonkawa Indians, cleared fields, harvested crops, built homes, organized local government, and even established a town, San Felipe de Austin, on the Brazos River—complete with stores, grist mills, a cotton gin, and a newspaper. Mexican government officials, who had seen nothing like it, were amazed. Compared to the Americans the few Hispanic settlers were nowhere. What is more, Austin's success was certain to attract new settlers from the United States—in spite of the fact that Mexican law required them to take up citizenship and convert to Roman Catholicism.

The future, however promising it was for American colonists, was inevitably clouded by the constant political upheavals in the country where they had been required to become citizens. What Austin had experienced during his first year-long visit to Mexico City was no more than a foretaste of what would later come his way. Even so, until the end of the 1820s, settlement flourished on the model established by Austin. He himself became the *empresario* of three additional colonies, while others—including a native Mexican, Martín de León—founded new colonies on the same scale, bringing in hundreds of new families as settlers. With roads, ferries at river crossings, cotton gins and grist mills, and new townships, Texas was fast becoming a civilized state. It was not entirely egalitarian: cotton and sugar plantations, worked by slaves brought in from the southern United States and with owners living in elegant mansions, were also part of the Texas scene.

The success of the American colonists inevitably became a concern of the government in Mexico City, and in 1827 it sent an agent, Manuel de Mier y Terán to investigate and report on what was happening in Texas. Terán, after crossing the Rio Grande into Texas in February 1828, reached Nacogdoches, close to the frontier with Louisiana, in June. The fact that he took some four months to cross Texas gives some idea both of its size and of its poor communications; on the other hand his long, slow journey allowed Terán to obtain a very accurate view of the way colonization was going. Noting particularly the diversity of the population, and the increasing dominance of Americans as he got ever closer to the United States, Terán was concerned that Texas could "throw the whole nation into revolution." Once back in Mexico City, Terán recommended as countermeasures the creation of a separate political department of Nacogdoches, combined with the settlement of more industrious and progressive native Mexicans.[13]

While Terán did not explicitly oppose American immigration, he arrived back in the capital city shortly after a friend of his, Anastacio Bustamente—leading a Centralist Party opposed to the constitution of 1824—had seized power following a coup d'état. In opposition to Bustamente and his supporters a new Federalist leader emerged: Antonio Lopez de Santa Anna, who, in the coming years, would play a leading part in the affairs of Mexico. Terán, however, as a result of his friendship with Bustamente, was appointed commander of Mexico's Eastern Interior Provinces—which included Texas. He had a difficult remit, for the Centralist government had passed the Law of April 6, 1830, which placed an embargo on new American immigration into Mexico while at the same time it canceled all *empresario* contracts. It also provided for convict soldiers to man new military garrisons in Texas, with the promise of land for settlement once they had served their term.

Although the law, from the perspective of the American settlers, both actual and prospective, was drastic, everything depended upon how it was interpreted locally. Here the outlook was not unfavorable, because Austin had taken the trouble to establish good relations with Terán, who in a letter to him had once written, "The affairs of Texas are understood by only you and me, and we alone are able to regulate them."[14] Terán prudently restricted the cancellation of the *empresario* contracts to colonies with fewer than a hundred settlers, so leaving the way open for Austin and other substantial *empresarios* to continue colonization. To satisfy American settlers who resented both the closure of the frontier and Mexico's new military presence, Terán ordered local commanders to restrain their soldiers from annoying them. Terán's moderate stance certainly succeeded in buying time, allowing Austin to convince the settlers that they should be patient even though many of them—as a result of the Law of April 6, 1830—were contemplating war against Mexico. At the same time a heterogeneous collection of new colonists—not subject to the restrictions of the law—arrived from Ireland, Germany, and other parts of Europe.

While all this was going on in Texas, the Federalists in the Mexican heartland, led by Santa Anna, were in revolt against Bustamente. In Texas, a local militia formed by American colonists to free two attorneys—imprisoned after they had tried to secure the release of some runaway slaves—while biding its time on the Turtle Bayou, close to the prison, adopted the Turtle Bay Resolution, declaring not only their constitutional right to resist tyranny but also their support for Santa Anna. This reflected the prevailing sentiment in Texas, where so many Mexican soldiers deserted to join Santa Anna south of the Rio Grande that little was left of the garrisons established under the Law of April 6, 1830. In Matomoros, the Mexican coastal town just south of the river, the local forces fighting the revolution—fearing a general American uprising in Texas—agreed to a truce, and under the leadership of the Federalist General Mexía crossed into Mexico—fortuitously accompanied by Austin who was returning home from business in Saltillo. Once in Texas Mexía found overwhelming support for his cause: at a gala banquet held in his honor at San Felipe, Santa Anna was toasted, and the Turtle Bayou Resolution was read out, with cheers for Federalism and the Constitution of 1824.

Mexía returned to Mexico with his army to join the tide of opposition to Bustamante, whose resignation at the end of 1832 signaled the end of the Centralist government. With Santa Anna now in power, the Americans in Texas not unreasonably found the time ripe to protest against the Law of April 6, 1830. Accordingly a general convention, attended by fifty-eight delegates from sixteen Texas municipalities, assembled at San Felipe in October 1832 to draw up petitions to be sent to the central government in Mexico City. The most important, needless to say, was for the repeal of the Law of April 6, 1830, but there was also one for establishing Texas as a separate province as it had always been under imperial Spain. The local representative of the central government, Ramón Músquiz, although broadly in agreement with the substance of the petitions, refused to forward them on the grounds that any such approach should originate from his office, at the same warning the petitioners that their convention was "a disturbance of good order."[15] A second convention, held at San Felipe on April 1, 1833, agreed to requests substantially the same as those contained in the 1832 petitions, but also appointed a new member, Sam Houston,[16] chairman of a committee to draft a constitution for Texas. This, together with the petition for statehood, would then be submitted directly to Santa Anna in Mexico City by a specially appointed committee of three men; of these only one, Austin, actually set off for the capital city. Full of optimism he left in late April to arrive in July—to discover political chaos as great as that he had encountered on his first visit ten years beforehand.

This was all the doing of Santa Anna, who although elected president of Mexico in January 1833, in April refused to be inaugurated. Instead his vice president, Gómez Farías, was left to put through a series of liberal reforms relating mainly to strengthen the position of the church and the army in the Mexican state. Every move by Farías led to a conservative uprising, which Santa Anna, "escaping" from his self-imposed exile, was consistently able to put down at the price of compromising his own position. By "running with the hare and hunting with the hounds" Santa Anna had contrived to ensure that both sides—however bitterly opposed to each other—combined to enhance his own power. Such was his success that in May 1834 he drove Farías into exile, dismissed the cabinet, dissolved Congress, repudiated all the liberal reforms and went on to disband all state and municipal administrations which had supported Farías—his own chosen vice president. By April 1834 Santa Anna had effectively become dictator of Mexico.

As for Austin, the way this chain of events unfolded meant that after he arrived in Mexico City he had to deal with Farías. Making little progress, he wrote a letter to the local administration in San Antonio, suggesting that it take the lead in establishing Texas as a separate state. This letter was hardly on its way, when Santa Anna—after dealing successfully with the first challenge to Farías—took up the presidency in July 1833. For some four months he appeared receptive to Austin's proposals, repealing the Law of April 6, 1830 but denying the petition for statehood. Austin was so pleased that he decided to return to Texas: he had got as far as Saltillo in December when he was summarily arrested. His letter had been sent on from San Antonio, through the various hierarchical stages of Mexican government, to reach Farías just he was, once again, taking over the presidency from Santa Anna. In an extremely precarious political situation, Farías read the letter as a precursor to revolution, and had Austin placed in solitary confinement.

Santa Anna, taking over as dictator in April 1834, had Austin transferred to a city jail, and in December he was released on bail. Finally, in July 1835, he qualified for release under a general amnesty. This was more than two years after Austin had first set out on his mission to Mexico City, but during this time the American settlements in Texas had prospered—largely as a result of the arrival of thousands of new settlers following Santa Anna's remission of the immigration restrictions becoming effective in May 1834.

Until the end of 1834 American settlers in Texas conducted their lives on the basis that they would not be affected by political upheavals beyond the Rio Grande. If it was convenient to assume that Santa Anna was on their side, then this was a rash assumption. As with dictators throughout history Santa Anna's main preoccupation was to remain in power, and here—inevitably, given the state of Mexican politics—he was being challenged. The Federalists—who if down were by no means out—were particularly active in the regions furthest from the capital city, including the state of Coahuila y Texas. There Santa Anna, by granting the petition for a new capital at Monclova—a city much closer to the Rio Grande than Saltillo—succeeded in polarizing the state between Federalists based on Monclova and Centralists based on Saltillo. Although Santa Anna in December 1834 recognized the Monclova government, at the same time he appointed as governor of the Eastern Interior Provinces his brother-in-law, Martín Perfecto de Cos—who fatefully supported the Centralists at Saltillo. To enforce his writ throughout the state, Cos led a small army to capture Monclova on June 8, 1835, but failed to prevent the Federalist forces, led by Ben Milam, from retreating northward across the Rio Grande, to establish themselves at San Antonio. In this way Texas became a battlefield in the Mexican Civil War, so that American settlers, sooner or later, would have to take sides—an unwelcome prospect for many, if not most of them. The result, during the summer months of 1835, was for some to join a peace party, supporting Santa Anna, while others joined a war party set on armed resistance and even a declaration of independence from Mexico.[17]

Cos, refusing the offer of peace made by two committees in San Felipe and Columbia, inevitably strengthened the hand of the war party; the Columbia committee, faced by quite unacceptable demands made by Cos, sent out a general call for delegates to be elected to a General Consultation at Washington-on-the-Brazos in October 1835 to consider Texas' position in the Civil War. Before this could take place, Austin had in the last week of August 1835 finally returned to Texas, where, in a speech made in Brazoria, after first endorsing the call for the Consultation, went on to report upon the political situation in Mexico—which he had witnessed firsthand—and ended by declaring, "War is our only recourse."[18]

Only Cos could retrieve the situation, but his chosen course of action was certain to lead to war. Actual fighting started when the Mexican commander at San Antonio, Colonel Domingo de Ugartechea, sent a hundred dragoons to recover, by force, a cannon that in 1832 had been given to the American settlers in Gonzales for defense against Indians, and which they refused to surrender. Battle was joined across the Guadalupe River, some four miles above the town, where the lieutenant commanding the dragoons, confronted by an American volunteer force, ordered a retreat after one of his men was killed in the first round of fire.

The battle of Gonzales set a pattern that was to be repeated, as Mexican forces, suffering their first casualties, abandoned one position after another. At Goliad, on October 9, the American volunteers, reinforced by troops brought by Ben Milam in his successful retreat from Coahuila, not only acquired valuable military supplies (including lead and powder) but also effectively denied Cos access to the coast. By this time Austin, having reached the volunteer camp at Gonzales, was unanimously elected commanding general: on October 12 he led his forces out to capture San Antonio, and on October 28 the Misión Concepción, just outside the city, was captured. Meanwhile Cos had arrived in San Antonio with 400 soldiers: these—together with the men under Ugartechea's command and recent reinforcements from Coahuila—constituted a force of some 1,200 men. With this force Cos was resolved to defend San Antonio at all costs: he had little alternative if he was not to lose Texas.

The Consultation finally opened at San Felipe on November 3, 1835. By this time Austin, with second thoughts about his plea for war, became the principal spokesman for the peace party, which on November 6 carried the day, with thirty-three against fifteen votes for the Independence Party. On November 7 the Consultation declared its support for the Mexican Constitution of 1824, and went on to provide for a framework for a provisional government. Before adjourning on November 14 it ordered all land operations to be halted, commissioned Austin to lead a delegation to appeal for aid in the United States and appointed Houston to command all troops except for those at San Antonio. There Austin handed over his command to Edward Burleson, who, left to his own devices, was ready to lift the siege, as agreed at the Consultation. At the last moment, however, the Texan prisoners, led by Samuel A. Maverick, escaped from San Antonio, to report that supplies were short and morale low among the men under Cos' command. This news led Milam to disregard the order to lift the siege: instead he led a force of volunteers to attack the city, and Burleston had little choice but to join. Fighting opened at dawn on December 5, and after four days of intense fighting from house to house—during which Milam was killed—Cos surrendered. According to the truce terms Cos agreed not to interfere with the restoration of the 1824 Constitution and further to withdraw all his troops across the Rio Grande. This he did on Christmas Day, leading an army with only such arms as were necessary for defense against Indians, and leaving behind a number of his men who had taken the opportunity to switch their allegiance to the Federalists. It was an ignominious defeat, and within a few days the Mexican troops left all the remaining small garrisons in Texas.

With victory the American volunteer forces fell to pieces, as different groups pursued quite irreconcilable, and often reckless, strategies. Some, intoxicated by the defeat of Cos, wished to invade Mexico via Matomoros—a harebrained scheme roundly condemned by Houston, who foresaw that Santa Anna would pay any price to recapture San Antonio. What is more, the city would be indefensible against the thousands of soldiers under Santa Anna's direct command. Faced by this prospect, the government of Texas decided to abandon San Antonio, and sent William Barrett Travis to organize its evacuation. Instead, with only a small force under his command, he decided to defend the city which had been "so dearly won." The vanguard of Santa Anna's Mexican army was first sighted on February 23, 1836—far earlier than anyone in San Antonio had expected. Commanding thousands of men, many of them seasoned soldiers, Santa Anna entered the city, where the Texans organized their defense in an old fortress known as the Alamo. For nine days Santa Anna bombarded it with artillery, while waves of infantry were turned back by deadly accurate rifle fire. A dawn attack on March 6 finally breached the walls of the Alamo, and by the end of the day every one of its defenders—finally numbered at 187—was dead. Santa Anna ordered their bodies to be stacked and burnt in a vast funeral pyre. He had himself lost some 1,600 men. A similar atrocity followed a month later after some 250 Texans, retreating in the face of much greater Mexican forces, surrendered after being surrounded in the battle of Coleto Creek, just outside Goliad, a major settlement between San Antonio and the gulf coast. José Urrea, the Mexican commander, whose advance ran parallel to that of Santa Anna, brought his prisoners to Goliad and asked his commanding general for clemency. Santa Anna refused, and on Palm Sunday, March 27, the Texans were massacred by Mexican soldiers. This, the last in a chain of defeats suffered by scattered and poorly coordinated Texan forces, effectively lost the whole of south Texas to Santa Anna's army.

At the very beginning of the disastrous month of March 1836, a convention, summoned to resolve the future of Texas, opened at Washington-on-the Brazos. On March 1 it passed a resolution declaring for full independence from Mexico, and the formal Declaration of Independence was adopted the next day. Its next business was to form an interim government to prosecute the war, and on March 4 this appointed Sam Houston as supreme commander of all the Texan forces. The convention finally adjourned on March 17, having produced an excellent constitution for the new Republic of Texas: given the series of defeats suffered by its modest forces its future was extremely problematic. Only Houston's small army could save it.

In its opening stages Houston's defense of the republic depended upon a series of strategic withdrawals, with one river line after another being abandoned. Although this led to hundreds of his men deserting, new volunteers replaced them. At the same time panic set in among the settlers, leading thousands of them to flee their homes to seek refuge in the United States. Life was made even harder as constant rain, driven by cold north winds, drenched both soldiers and refugees, while at the same time rivers overran their banks and roads turned to quagmires.

These conditions made life even more difficult for Santa Anna, who was intent on bringing all his forces across the Brazos River. There, at Harrisburg on the left bank, the new republic had established its interim government. Unable to get the mass of his army, with its heavy equipment, across the swollen river, he crossed it himself at the head of a small force of fewer than 600 men. The Texans abandoning Harrisburg withdrew to New Washington on the coast, with Santa Anna's Mexicans at their heels. From Harrisburg a company of fifty dragoons raced to the coast, while the rest of the army set fire to the town. At New Washington the last contingent of the Texan government, including its president, left by rowboat, under fire from the dragoons, for a schooner anchored in the bay, which was waiting to take them to safety on Galveston Island. Then, after first resting for a day at New Washington, Santa Anna led his force along the coast to establish a camp on relatively high ground near the confluence of Buffalo Bayou and the San Jacinto River. Meanwhile Houston, informed by scouts of Santa Anna's movements, moved his force first to the smoldering ruins of Harrisburg, and then on to a hollow along the bayou where they established a line of defense opposite the Mexican encampment. The result was that two forces, each numbering about a thousand men, were set for battle. This came in the afternoon of April 20 when Houston, choosing a time when the exhausted Mexican troops were resting, let loose all his troops—both infantry and cavalry, supported by two heavy guns—on Santa Anna's lines. The Mexican soldiers, taken by surprise, and hearing a Texan soldier cry out "Remember the Alamo, remember Goliad," disintegrated and broke into a rout. The so-called battle of San Jacinto had lasted eighteen minutes: more than 600 Mexicans lost their lives, but only nine Texans.

The following day, April 21, Santa Anna was captured, fleeing from the scene of battle in the uniform of a private soldier. Fearing the justice that might overtake him after the atrocities he had committed at the Alamo and Goliad, he agreed to order all his armies to leave Texas—all this in spite of the fact that only a relatively small number of his soldiers had fought at San Jacinto, leaving the remaining forces under his command intact. Santa Anna's generals nonetheless obeyed his instructions and withdrew their troops across the Rio Grande. Sam Houston had won the day and Texas its independence.

Hearing the news of victory at San Jacinto, David Burnet, the interim president of Mexico, moved his administration from its refuge on Galveston Island back to Velasco on the mainland at the mouth of the Brazos River. There, on May 14, 1836, he negotiated two treaties with Santa Anna, who had become his prisoner. By the first of these Santa Anna, accepting that hostilities between Mexico and Texas had ended, agreed to withdraw all his forces south of the Rio Grande, exchange prisoners on an equal basis, and restore all Texan property destroyed or confiscated by Mexicans. The second treaty, which was secret, allowed Santa Anna to return to Mexico in exchange for formal recognition of Texas with the Rio Grande as its southern boundary.

Nothing came of either treaty: in Mexico, Bustamante, learning of the defeat at San Jacinto, staged a coup d'état, took over the government, and repudiated every act done by Santa Anna during his imprisonment. At much the same time, a local Texas volunteer commander, Thomas Green, acting on his own initiative, recaptured Santa Anna, just as he was about to leave for Mexico on a ship of the Texas Navy. This act did no more than reflect the confusion, almost to the point of anarchy, in the Texan army, now that the land was at peace. What is more, many in Texas faced destitution, for with so many heads of family absent from home as volunteer soldiers too few crops had been planted for the fall harvest. The new republic also suffered a financial crisis, with the interim government's promissory notes nearly worthless, not only in the United States but within its own frontiers. Burnet, knowing that he was not strong enough to rescue the situation, saw the adoption of the Constitution and the election of a new president and congress according to its provisions as the only way forward.

These objectives were achieved in the fall of 1836. Sam Houston, after only agreeing to stand at a late hour, was elected president. Under the new constitution, which proscribed two successive terms, he could, however, only hold office until December 1838. In the course of this year a high-profile candidate, Mirabeau B. Lamar, emerged in opposition to the Houston faction and won the election with a landslide. Houston, at the same time—elected to the House of Representatives from Nacogdoches—led an opposition that was so vigorous and effective that he was reelected president in 1841. By this time his position in Texas was so strong that his chosen successor, Anson Jones, was elected as the republic's final president in 1844. There is no doubt that Houston was the guiding hand of Texas during the nine years that it existed as an independent republic. The end of this period became certain in December 1845, when the Texas Admission Act became part of the law of the United States—an end that Houston had always seen as his major goal. On February 19, 1846, at its new capital at Austin, President Anson Jones lowered the Lone Star Flag of the Republic at the small capitol building and raised the Stars and Stripes.

While the admission of Texas to the Union solved major problems relating to defense and foreign policy—which automatically became the responsibility of Washington under the US Constitution—the new state of Texas was still left with many others. One, in particular, was the final determination of its actual frontiers, for during the whole nine years of the republic Mexico never agreed a peace treaty. The reason here was the fact that the treaties of Velasco had never been signed. This allowed Santa Anna—once released from his second captivity in Texas—not only to return home but, in 1841, to regain power in Mexico and repudiate what he had himself agreed at Velasco. As far as Mexico was concerned, Texas was still part of its territory.

Prospects for a treaty seemed to improve greatly when, in the summer of 1844, Santa Anna was overthrown and exiled, and a new Federalist government—with José Herrera as president—installed in December. Then, in 1845, following the annexation of Texas, the new US President, James Polk, sent John Slidell to Mexico City to negotiate, first, the settlement of long-standing and substantial financial claims that the United States had against the Mexican government, and second, to secure recognition of the annexation of Texas. Slidell was authorized not only to abandon the financial claims in exchange for recognition of the Rio Grande boundary, but also to offer to purchase the rest of New Mexico—and for an additional sum of up to $40, million—California. As already noted in chapter 3, this was the fourth, and most important, of the measures that Polk was intent on realizing during his presidency.

THE MEXICAN WAR

In the summer of 1845, Polk, recognizing Washington's commitment to the defense of Texas once it had become a state of the Union, ordered General Zachary Taylor to move his command from New Orleans to Texas. In Mexico City this was regarded as a very aggressive move, so much so that when Slidell finally arrived in December, Herrera refused to receive him. Unable to withstand the pressure from Santa Anna's faction, in January 1846 he was forced to yield to the violently anti-American Mariano Paredes. Slidell persisted in asking for an interview with the new president, but after several refusals was ordered to leave Mexico in March. Polk reacted to these new developments by ordering Taylor to take up defensive positions along the Rio Grande. At the beginning of April, Paredes—claiming that the land north of the Rio Grande up to the Nueces River belonged to Mexico—ordered these to be attacked, and on April 23 the Mexican Congress declared war on the United States. The next day Mexican troops crossed the Rio Grande to attack a detachment of American dragoons. When news of this reached Polk, he asked Congress to declare war: this was carried by a large majority.

The Americans fought, and won, the war on three fronts. Taylor advanced across the Rio Grande to Monterey and Buena; Winfield Scott, landing his forces from the sea at Veracruz, Mexico's principal harbor, went on overland to capture Mexico City, and Stephen Kearny advanced deep into New Mexico across the Rio Grande to capture, without any fighting, its capital, Santa Fe. At the end of 1846, the first year of the war, following an election held under Mexico's 1824 Constitution, Santa Anna once again became president. As Scott's forces approached Mexico City his government collapsed, and the war effectively was lost. It was only when Herrero was restored to the presidency,

after months of confusion and disorder, that the Americans were able to negotiate the terms of peace. The result was the Treaty of Guadalupe Hidalgo, signed
on February 2, 1848. This recognized the Rio Grande as the boundary of Texas
and provided for the cession of all the territory west of the river, in New Mexico
and beyond, occupied by Kearny. Since this included the whole of California,
the gain to the United States was very considerable: a nominal payment of
$15 million was made to Mexico, together with an American commitment to
honor certain Mexican claims on American citizens, but all this was far from
recognizing the true value of the land lost by Mexico. The results, for the United
States, were fundamental changes—geographical, economic, demographic and,
above all, political—in the whole character of the Union.

While these changes are the subject matter of chapter 9, this chapter ends
with a short discussion of what the annexation of Texas meant for the United
States. First and foremost it enormously extended the settlement frontier, with
land cheaper than in any other part of the United States being a great attraction
to new immigrants—so much so that the population increased fourfold in the
fifteen years between annexation and the Civil War.[19] Although Texas extended
south to the Rio Grande, very few Americans settled beyond the Nueces River.
(While this in the early days was home to thousands of wild longhorn cattle
it would later become the center of American cattle ranching.) Where north
of the Nueces and right up to the Red River (the northern boundary of Texas)
original settlement was concentrated mainly in the coast plain, the settlement
frontier moved steadily westward into territory that became steadily drier and
less productive. Even so, new immigrants continued to arrive, not only from
the United States but also, if to a lesser extent, from Europe; they were a restless
population, continually moving from one homestead to another—repeating
the pattern of migration familiar in the northern states with such families as
that of Abraham Lincoln.

There was, however, one key difference, which would soon prove critical for
the status of Texas within the United States. From the very earliest days, in the
1820s, a significant minority of new settlers brought slaves with them—which
was no more than was to be expected, seeing that most came from southern
states. Although under Mexican law slavery was illegal, it was always tolerated
in Texas, and inevitably, once Texas was independent of Mexico, its legal status
would be unquestioned—the more so after annexation, seeing that it was
protected by the US Constitution.

The fact that some 30 percent of the population of Texas in 1860 were
slaves[20] shows how important they were as labor: most slave owners—always
a minority in Texas—made their living as subsistence farmers, with the
advantage over those who owned no slaves that they could operate on a
notably larger scale. In the basic agricultural economy, with labor, next to

land, the most important factor in production, this meant a proportionate increase in the area that could be cultivated—so much so that it was quite generally accepted that acquiring slaves was an essential first step to economic advancement. Texas plantations, as those in other southern frontier states, produced export crops, notably sugar and cotton, for the world market. The combination of steadily increasing demand, particularly for cotton, in the quarter century following Texas' independence from Mexico, with abundant new land available for planting, inevitably led to the extension of the slave-based plantation economy established east of the Mississippi across the river into Louisiana, Arkansas, and, above all, Texas. President Tyler's secretary of state, John C. Calhoun, in a letter to Sir Richard Pakenham, the British envoy in Washington, made clear that this was an essential justification for annexation: in his own words "what is called slavery is in reality a political institution, essential to the peace, safety and prosperity of those states of the Union in which it exists."[21] This principle, which Calhoun also proclaimed during his many years as senator for South Carolina, remained, even after his death in 1850, a powerful force in southern politics; as Lincoln much later came to realize,[22] Calhoun never doubted that disunion—as he called it—was the only alternative to the abolition of slavery.

Given the influence of men such as Calhoun, it is not surprising that many in the northern states saw a conspiracy of southern slave owners behind the Texan war of independence. This was the theme of a tract—*The War in Texas*—published by an abolitionist leader, Benjamin Lundy, in 1836. It became historically important because it was adopted by the Whig Party, which was opposed to the admission of Texas to the Union. Although this proved to be a lost cause, the theme revived when, in December 1847, President Polk, backed by the prospect of acquiring New Mexico and California, asked Congress for additional funds, noting that he was about to win a war started by Mexico "invading the territory of the State of Texas, striking the first blow, and shedding the blood of our citizens on our own soil."[23]

This claim to the moral high ground was too much for the Whigs in Congress, and Abraham Lincoln, who was one of their number, led the verbal assault on the president, which ended in a vituperative attack at the beginning of January 1848 accusing a "bewildered, confounded and miserably perplexed man" of being led into war by his desire for "military glory—that attractive rainbow that rises in showers of blood—that serpent's eye, that charms to destroy." These intemperate words, where noted by press and public, were generally condemned, even in Lincoln's home district in Illinois; he was warned that if Whigs persisted in opposing all territorial annexations as a result of war, they would continue to be "the minority party for a long time."[24] "The Whigs certainly had little future in Texas, which for some hundred years and more remained a Democratic stronghold. On the other hand Lincoln's words do reflect an attitude of non-interference that, even in the early years of the Civil War, characterized his thinking about the abolition of slavery in the states where it was established.

After victory in the Mexican War the question was crucial when it came to establishing, definitively, the boundaries of Texas. James P. Henderson, the state's first governor, claimed all land in New Mexico east of the Rio Grande, together with a strip of land extending the Texas panhandle north to the Arkansas River and beyond, to latitude 42° north—level with the northern boundary of California. This was about half the territory allowed to Spain under the Adams-Onis Treaty of 1819, to which Mexico—at least as claimed by the Texans—succeeded on becoming independent in 1821. In the late 1840s there was no way such a vast territorial claim—which would include Santa Fe, the capital of New Mexico—could succeed. The American military government, which had first been established by Stephen Kearny after his successful campaign at the beginning of the Mexican War, was strongly opposed, as were also the citizens of Santa Fe—in spite of the fact that the Texas Congress had established Santa Fe County as part of the state. Texas encountered not only local opposition but that of President Zachary Taylor who—having succeeded Polk in 1849—encouraged New Mexico to hold its own constitutional convention with a view to statehood. The result was for New Mexico to claim a large part of Texas (although statehood had to wait until 1912).

Texas' boundary controversy was tied up with a much more important issue, the admission of California as a free state. With the gold rush, which followed almost immediately after the end of the Mexican War, bringing thousands of new immigrants, the US Congress could hardly refuse the petition for statehood submitted by California. Even so, there was nearly a year of bitter debate before the vote was carried to accept a compromise proposed by one its elder statesmen, Senator Henry Clay of Kentucky, under which California—as related in chapter 9—was admitted as a free state on September 9, 1850. The compromise also settled the boundaries of Texas: on November 25, the state gave up its New Mexico claim for $10 million, of which half was retained by the United States in exchange for assuming the Texas "revenue debt" incurred during the days of the republic. With the loss of New Mexico, Texas was reduced to its present boundaries,[25] which still left it as much the largest state in the Union until the admission of Alaska in 1959.

After the events of the 1840s related in this chapter—culminating, in 1850, in the admission of California as the thirty-first state of the Union, and the definitive settlement of the boundaries of Texas—the whole of imperial Spain's territory in continental North America, as it was at the beginning of the century, had been lost to the United States. At the end of 1850 this comprised three states, Florida, Texas, and California, and the vast Utah-New Mexico territory inland which would only be divided into new states of the Union after the end of the Civil War, in a process which ran parallel to the division of the Louisiana Territory such as it was at the same time.

Effectively Texas was the last slave state, though the reality of this was not accepted by the southern states at the beginning of the 1850s: during this decade the historical crisis only became more acute, but the action was no longer in Texas. In the whole historical process, starting with the cession of Florida in 1819, the losers, inevitably, were the negroes in Florida and the Indians of the southeastern states. Although the lot of the former was slavery, that of the latter—who were forcible removed from their ancestral homes—was in the end just as terrible. Their cause had few friends: most of those who knew about their fate were indifferent to it. This was still part of the price paid for Texas joining the United States.

Illinois: Land of Lincoln

FRONTIER ILLINOIS

Illinois was home to Abraham Lincoln for more than half his life: he arrived there—in March 1830—as a young man helping his father move home from Indiana, and left for the last time in February 1861, when he went to Washington to take up residence in the White House. In this period of thirty-one years Lincoln not only witnessed the transformation of Illinois in almost every possible way—economic, political, demographic—but also played a steadily increasing part in the process. The history of the state was by no means self-contained: as much as, if not more than, that of any other state of the Union, it reflected events and processes in the rest of the country—which, in Lincoln's final ten years as a resident, led him ultimately to Washington. The 1850s, as almost everywhere else in the United States, were years of turmoil in Illinois.

When Lincoln arrived in Illinois in 1830, there were twenty-four states in the Union: of these the most recent was Missouri, admitted to the Union only after the US Congress had agreed to the Missouri Compromise, by which it was admitted as a slave state. As related in chapter 7, the involved history of the compromise became a major concern of the states neighboring Missouri—including most notably Illinois on the other side of the Mississippi River. The result of Illinois becoming the twenty-first state on 1819 was that the number of free states was one more than that of slave states. The balance was set right by the admission of Alabama in 1819, but this meant after the admission of Maine—inevitably as a free state—the balance could only be restored by admitting Missouri as a slave state. The result for Illinois was that for a period of more than forty years it was bounded by two slave states, Missouri to the west across the Mississippi and Kentucky to the south across the Ohio. Until Iowa was admitted to the Union in 1846, Indiana, to the east of Illinois across the Wabash River—a tributary of the Ohio—was the only free state bordering Illinois. Although this was still the state where many of the new settlers in Illinois came from, many of these—including the Lincoln family—were southerners by origin, as were, needless to say, those who had crossed directly over from Kentucky. Whatever the origins of such settlers, they were ready to accept that there would never be slave owners in Illinois, but then few of their families had owned slaves south of the Ohio River.

The important point, historically, is that the settlement of Illinois was a process that started in the south of the state, to move gradually northwards in the course of time. This chapter describes not only how and why this happened, but also the long term consequences of this process.

First, however, one must take a closer look at the geography of Illinois. Although almost its entire territory is part of the Mississippi drainage basin, intensive lobbying by Nathaniel Pope, its delegate to the US Congress before the grant of statehood, led to a northern frontier some sixty miles north of the line laid down by the Northwest Ordinance of 1787.[1] The result, critical for the future prosperity of Illinois, was that it acquired a shoreline of some sixty miles along Lake Michigan. In addition to the three rivers, the Mississippi, Ohio, and Wabash, defining, respectively, its western, southern, and eastern boundaries, any number of their tributaries—and tributaries of tributaries—cut through the state, flowing mainly from north to south. Of these the Illinois River, which joins the Mississippi just north of St. Louis and its confluence with the Missouri, is much the most important. This was the route by which French seventeenth-century explorers, coming down from the Great Lakes, first discovered the Upper Mississippi, and of these the greatest, the Sieur de La Salle gave his name to the city which, on the upper Illinois, marks today's starting point for navigation by steamboat down the river. The city of La Salle, critically not only for its own future but also that of the state, was less than a hundred miles from Lake Michigan; what is more, the land separating the two was flat open prairie. As a project in civil engineering, building a canal linking the lake with the river would be no great problem. The fact that it would transform Illinois' access to the outside world—even though the Great Lakes were frozen in winter—was overwhelmingly in its favor. As early as 1822, the Second General Assembly of the state of Illinois petitioned the US Congress for authorization for the construction of the Illinois and Michigan Canal. Not only was the right of way across federal lands granted, but in 1827 a donation of such land was made to help finance construction.[2] Already, in 1825, a company had been incorporated to dig the canal; the completion of the Erie Canal in the same year—as recounted in chapter 2—was almost a guarantee of the Illinois canal's profitability. Although Illinois—as a result of financial problems during the 1830s—only completed construction in 1848, this soon proved to be the case. Even so, the mere prospect of the canal meant that Chicago, where it would enter Lake Michigan, was already Illinois' largest town in 1837, even though it had only been incorporated four years earlier.[3]

Inevitably the direction of flow of Illinois' rivers means that the elevation of the state declines from north to south. That of both Lake Michigan, and of Rock Island on the Mississippi almost due west from Chicago, is just under 600 feet. That of Cairo, located in the extreme south of the state at the point where the Ohio River joins the Mississippi is just over 300 feet. St. Louis, approximately halfway between Rock Island and Cairo, has an elevation of 450 feet. While elevations such as these are sufficient to ensure a strong downstream current in the rivers—so that navigation upstream is relatively slow—it also reflects the general absence of rapids, let alone waterfalls. An average slope to the south of about a foot per mile means that the change in elevation—in the absence of other topographical factors—is hardly noticeable, except to river traffic. Although a visitor to the Illinois prairies is immediately struck by the extreme flatness of the countryside, it is broken up by river valleys significantly lower than the land surrounding them. Where this is open prairie, with grass as the natural vegetation, the river valleys are noteworthy for the woodlands along their banks—which can stretch several miles inland. The south of the state, on the other hand, is for the most part natural woodland, which meant that southerners settling there—such as the Lincoln family—could farm the land according to their traditional practices. In the early days of settlement the low bottom lands in the area known as Egypt at the confluence of the Ohio and Mississippi, which continued northward for quite a distance along the east bank of the great river, were seen as particularly promising—so much so that Cairo became a significant political and economic center. The promise was however deceptive: in an era when such diseases as cholera and malaria could easily get out of control the land was not only exceptionally unhealthy, but also susceptible to flooding.

Quite predictably the new settlers moved north up the rivers and away from the bottom lands. Although they still had the advantage of a dependable supply of wood from the river valleys—essential for building houses and making much of the equipment needed for agriculture—shortage of land soon constrained them to take up the challenge of prairie farming. This was not easy: the deep roots of the prairie grass made the soil difficult to plow—particularly in the years before 1837, the year in which John Deere invented his steel plow. At the same time the flatness of the land made it difficult to drain, while drinking water was in short supply. But then, if the prairie was broken, it was—after the introduction of the McCormick reaper during the 1830s[4]—extremely productive, so that above all wheat could be harvested in quantities far beyond the consumption needs of a farming family. To achieve this, however, not only were better tools needed, but a better transport infrastructure. All this would be helped by new markets. In the early days, agricultural exports went down the rivers to the southern states—this was why Abraham Lincoln, in 1828,[5] first traveled down the Mississippi to New Orleans, the harbor city at the center of the south's exchange economy.

More than any other factor, the grant of federal land—whether to new settlers, canal and railroad companies, public institutions or whatever—influenced the transformation of Illinois in the forty-two years between the grant of statehood in 1819 and Lincoln becoming president in 1861. In the territories later to become states—such as Illinois—almost all land belonged to the federal government, simply because of the very small number of early settlers who had established land titles. The grant of statehood by Congress did not change the federal ownership of land, so that if new titles were to be granted it had to be by Washington. In 1812 the General Land Office was created to dispose of public domain lands in the midwest and west, and in the course of time it transferred titles to more than a billion acres.[6] This operation would have been impossible without local land offices set up whenever and wherever new titles were to be granted on large tracts of federal land. In the course of the nineteenth century the legal principles upon which they operated became steadily more complex: this was not only the result of the increasing number of settlers attracted by steadily improving economic prospects, but also of the fact that this development depended on, and indeed encouraged, the vast expansion of the state's transport infrastructure. In the early years of statehood this was reflected in the rapid growth of steamboat traffic on the Mississippi and its tributaries—of which the Illinois River was critical for opening up the state—but then water transport took a new turn with the opening of the Illinois and Michigan Canal in 1848. By this time (as related in chapter 8), the first railroads were being built. By the end of the 1850s they comprised several lines across the state from east to west, and the most important of all—the Illinois Central—covered the much greater distances between Egypt and the northern part of the state, from Galena, close to the Mississippi, to Chicago, on the shore of Lake Michigan. Significantly, at the beginning of the 1850s, there were still 22,822 square miles of federal land—some 41 percent of the total area of the state; of all this only 156 square miles remained at the end of the decade. During the same period railroad mileage increased from 15 to 2,867,[7] of which more than 70 percent was constructed in the four years 1853 through 1856. Needless to say the two processes were closely linked, but before considering how and why this was so, something must be said about the history of land grants from the federal domain, starting at a time before the canal and railroad era.

THE RIGHT TO LAND

When in 1816 the Lincoln family moved north of the Ohio River, land in the Northwest Territory was being sold for two dollars an acre, with titles secured according to the Congressional Survey System; the land, divided into one-square-mile sections, was sold in quarter-section lots, which meant each had an area of 160 acres. A new settler could then make a claim on any unsold lot, and arrange for its purchase with the local Federal Land Office. This was in principle a simple, rough-and-ready system, avoiding the controversies over land titles common in Kentucky and other states south of the Ohio which—having been admitted to the Union before 1812—were outside the Congressional Survey. It was just about good enough for Abraham's father, Thomas Lincoln, as he moved, successively, from one home to another, first in Indiana and then, after 1830, in Illinois.

By 1830, however, the system was beginning to fall apart. Quite simply it failed to fit the agricultural economy of the state, as new settlements moved steadily northward, out of the woodlands—common both to its southern part and to Kentucky on the other side of the Ohio River—and into the prairie. New lots open to settlement were then for a time confined to the wooded river valleys, where settlers—if they attempted to break the prairie—would still have access to the wood essential for their traditional way of life as subsistence cultivators. In Illinois—as also in much other territory—the position was complicated by the dedication of a vast area as a military tract.[8] In Illinois the tract—some 3.5 million acres in extent and representing nearly 10 percent of the total area of the state—took up all of the land between the Mississippi and the Illinois Rivers south of latitude 41°30" north. In principle this land was reserved for grants to soldiers who had fought in the War of 1812, and other earlier wars, together with their heirs and successors, but this class—with more than half a million members—was so numerous that relatively few ever took up the land to which they were entitled. Of the majority who did not do so, each member was issued a warrant for 160 acres of government land. This was an open invitation to graft and speculation, so it is hardly surprising that warrants for a total of 840,000 acres of land ended up in the hands of congressmen;[9] this represented 24 percent of the entire military tract, and the congressmen were by no means alone in profiting from the measures which had set up the entire system.[10] In the five years from 1847 through 1852 successive acts of Congress so extended the right to claim government land that after that of March 22, 1852 almost anyone who had served in war in pay of the federal government was entitled to a warrant for 160 acres. In Illinois the result was that within three years—during which time the Federal Land Offices were extremely busy—almost all government land had been disposed of.

Although, at a final count, some 551,193 ex-soldiers, or their successors in title, were entitled to warrants, the majority preferred to sell them—at prices ranging from 50 cents to $1.15 an acre—rather than take up government land. The result, in Illinois, was that by 1855 more than a quarter of the entire area of the state—with a total value not far short of $10 million—had become the property of speculators.[11] With little left over for prospective small farmers seeking 80 or 160 acres, by the end of the 1850s, in one area after another, the once busy Federal Land Offices were closing down—simply for want of business. In any case the officials gave first consideration to the speculators looking for large blocks of land. In part this was because, with far fewer blocks to deal with, it much simplified the administration, but politics inevitably played a part at a time when federal patronage was a major factor at the grassroots level. At the state level, however, the politicians, with strong support from local newspapers, constantly complained about the way prospective settlers, unable to afford the prices charged by speculators, moved on across the Mississippi to states such as Iowa—or north to Wisconsin—where new land was still affordable.[12]

The so-called military bounty acts were not the only provision for the disposal of government land: in particular a specific grant of nearly 300,000 acres was made for the construction of the Illinois and Michigan Canal, and of another 2,595,000 acres for what was to become the Illinois Central Railroad. The rationale was that the land would underwrite, in one way or another, the development of the transport infrastructure of the state; with the prospect of being close to a canal or a railroad, land was specially valuable for commercial use—as opposed to the traditional subsistence farming.

Given the way in which until the mid-1840s land grants (mainly of wood-lands) moved gradually northward up the major river valleys, the later land grants (mainly of prairie) moved southward, taking up either the space between the rivers or that along the proposed route of the Illinois and Michigan Canal. In this process, the lower south of the state—including Egypt and its main city, Cairo, at the confluence of the Mississippi and Ohio Rivers—was left with a population which came originally from Tennessee and the Carolinas. To the north, in the upper south, the settlers were mainly from Kentucky. At the other end of the state, in the area inland from the Michigan lakeshore as far as the Mississippi River, the settlers were Yankees from New York, Pennsylvania, and Ohio: critically this area contained Chicago, the city which by the 1860 had become the undisputed hub of the transport infrastructure linking the upper Mississippi and the Great Lakes.

The way that settlement gradually extended northward can be seen from how Illinois was organized into counties at successive stages in its history. The state started off in 1819 with only nineteen southern countries, of which all but three lay along the Mississippi, the Ohio or the Wabash, close to, if not actually part of, Egypt. By 1826 a further twenty-six counties had been organized so as to comprise the whole of the military tract, and a substantial area bounded on the east by the Indiana state line. Ten years later the whole state was organized so as to comprise sixty counties, which by further subdivision, mainly of the new northern counties, came to number a hundred by 1854: this is substantially the state of Illinois as it is now. The result of this process was a relatively large number of small, comparatively backward counties in the south, set against much more populous, larger, and richer counties in the north of the state. Needless to say, the process engendered endless political conflict, as parties—notably the Democratic—in the south of the state had to suffer a secular loss of power to parties, such as the Whigs—and later the Republicans—which were strong in the north.

At the same time, the development of commercial agriculture—based mainly on wheat[13] and entirely dependent upon both state-of-the-art farming equipment (such as the John Deere steel plow and the McCormick reaper) and the rapidly developing railroad and canal system—meant that the general level of rural prosperity was significantly higher in the north of Illinois than in the south. This related also to the fact that the new Yankee settlers had more money to invest.

As to the settlers in the midlands of Illinois, they were a mixture of both north and south, together with numerous immigrants from overseas.[14] The area was divided in two by the Illinois River, which was the eastern boundary of the military tract; the area to the east of the river, and extending to the Indiana state line, was more important, both politically and economically. It included all but a small part of both the Seventh Congressional District (which Abraham Lincoln represented in Washington during the Thirtieth Congress 1847–1849) and the Eighth Judicial Circuit, where, from 1837, he carried on his law practice. Springfield, which became the capital of Illinois in 1837, belonged both to the district and to the circuit. (Significantly the previous capital, Vandalia, was some fifty miles further south.) In the course of the 1850s, as the settlement of the state became largely complete, this midland area represented a sort of microcosm of a nationwide conflict of any number of different interests, political, economic, and religious.[15] Demographically speaking, a new dimension was added, from the 1830s onward, by a constant stream of foreign immigrants. In Illinois many of these were Germans who, after landing at New Orleans, had come upriver by steamboat, preferring not to set up home in states which allowed slavery.

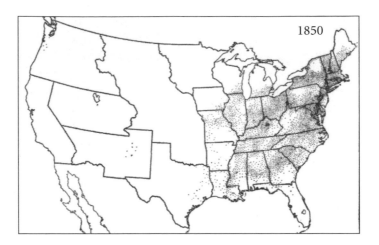

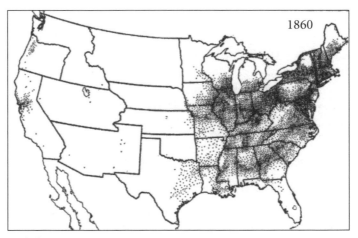

Each dot represents 25,000 acres

Improved land 1850–60.

CHANGING ORIENTATIONS IN ILLINOIS

The history of Illinois during the Lincoln years also reflects a fundamental change in the orientation of the United States from north-south to east-west. In 1820 the Missouri Compromise affirmed what was then regarded as the essential balance between north and south; in 1850 the admission of California to the Union foreshadowed—in a way that was unmistakable for politicians from both sides—the end to this state of affairs. The writing was already on the wall. Illinois, in particular, was at the center of this transformation. Nothing reflected it better than the way in which new railroad companies were formed to build lines running east-west across the state, challenging the Illinois Central's predominant north-south orientation.

One of the most important of the new lines was that of the Chicago and Rock Island Railroad Company, the first to link Chicago, on Lake Michigan, with the Upper Mississippi. Significantly the line of rail ran almost exactly east-west, across the seemingly endless flat prairie, cultivated mainly in wheat, of northern Illinois. This was land devoted to what is now known as industrial farming. The first passenger train ran on October 10, 1852, but could go no further than Joliet, some forty miles away from Chicago, which was then the end of the line. The line finally reached Rock Island on February 22, 1854, but by this time its directors had already incorporated, in Iowa, the Mississippi and Missouri Railroad Company, to link Davenport, on the Mississippi opposite Rock Island, with Council Bluffs on the Missouri. Its line of rail, crossing the whole state from east to west, cried out for a bridge across the Mississippi at Davenport, to link it with the Rock Island Railroad on the other side of the river.

No sooner said than done, the bridge, whose cornerstone was laid in Davenport on September 1, 1854—only seven months after the railroad had reached Rock Island—was open for the first train to run on April 21, 1856,[16] long before the railroad in Iowa had been completed. To meet the needs of steamboat operators—who had long protested that the bridge would be a hindrance to navigation—it was built with a drawspan which could open to let boats through. Two weeks after the opening, the *Effie Alton*, the fastest side-wheeler on the Mississippi, after clearing the bridge on an upstream journey, suddenly veered out of control and drifted back to hit the drawspan—which had by then been lowered—leading not only to its own loss by fire but, by the end of the following day, to the destruction of the whole bridge. Delighted steamboat captains blew their whistles, and John Hurd, the owner of the *Effie Alton*, sued the Rock Island Railroad Company in the Federal District Court in Chicago for $50,000.

In the history of Illinois the most notable fact about the trial was that the defendant corporation was represented by Abraham Lincoln.[17] Hurd claimed that the bridge was a hazard to navigation, while the railroad claimed that the suit was a deliberate attempt—not only on Hurd's part but on that of other steamboat proprietors—to have the bridge destroyed. Much more was at stake than responsibility for a single accident. If bridges could not be built across the Mississippi, the role played by railroads in the development of the American west would have been gravely impaired. At its deepest level the question before the jury was whether in the United States an east-west orientation should prevail over a north-south one. In other words, was the jury ready to accept that the future lay with railroads rather than with river steamboats.

Although it was his experience with railroad cases that led to Lincoln being chosen as the attorney to represent the Rock Island Railroad, the high profile of the case ensured that his reputation—already well established in Springfield, the capital of the state—extended to Chicago, its largest city. At a critical stage in his political career he became known statewide as a great trial lawyer. Significantly also, the cause that he represented before the court was essentially "northern." The issue was one which split the state. The first jury in *Hurd* v. *Rock Island Railroad Company* disagreed and was discharged, but then after a second trial the court ordered the bridge to be removed. The case finally reached the Supreme Court in 1862, which then handed down an opinion establishing railroads' rights to bridge navigable streams. By this time the appellant railroad's attorney was in the White House where the experience gained from the case served him well.

Inevitably the settlement of Illinois, in all the stages related above, had a critical political dimension. This, as elsewhere in the United States, reflected the balance between the established political parties, which, in 1830, with Andrew Jackson in the White House, was changing quite radically—largely as a result of the way in which he ran his successful campaign for the presidency in 1828. In the following thirty years this process of change would continue to the point that in the mid-1850s people throughout the nation would have to choose between the Democratic Party—which was that of Jackson—and the new Republican Party, which first put forward a presidential candidate in 1856. This meant the end to the Whigs, a party that between 1841 and 1853 produced four presidents—W. H. Harrison, Tyler, Taylor, and Fillmore[18]—and to which Abraham Lincoln belonged during his two years (1847–1848) as a congressman.

In the America of his day, Jackson had all the makings of a popular hero: a native of Tennessee, a southern state but one west of the Appalachians, he was able to present himself as a man of the frontier, ready to take up any challenge to advance the interests of the common man. The fact that this category in his terms inevitably excluded both Indians and negroes only helped his cause. Few held against him the cruelty involved in banishing the Indians of the southern states to reservations beyond the Mississippi—an event now remembered as "the Trail of Tears."[19]

Until the end of the 1820s Jackson's chances as a presidential candidate were blocked by the way in which the House of Representatives, voting by states—in a system which ensured that no candidate had a majority of the electoral votes—had to choose between the candidates with the largest number of votes. In 1824 this meant a choice between Jackson, John Quincy Adams (son of the second president, John Adams) and secretary to the treasury, William H. Crawford—the man preferred by Congress insiders. Although Jackson led in number of votes, with two Jackson electors and one Adams elector from Illinois, the state's sole representative in Congress, Daniel Cook—swayed both by his own personal preference and the persuasive voice of Henry Clay of Kentucky—voted for Adams, who secured the nomination and went on to be a disastrous president. The people of Illinois saw this as betrayal, and in the 1828 elections it became clear that no one opposed to Jackson would be elected to any sort of office. Jackson was elected president with overwhelming support nationwide, and his Democratic Party was firmly entrenched in Illinois.

Jackson's election marked the end of a patrician era in American politics, with four presidents, Washington, Jefferson, Madison, and Monroe, substantial Virginia landowners—and as such, inevitably, slave owners as well—and two from Massachusetts, John Adams and his son, John Quincy Adams, both of whom had represented the United States abroad at the highest level. In early nineteenth-century politics, as already related in chapters 1 and 4, Jefferson, Madison, and Monroe, each of whom served two terms, were notably more successful than Adams, father and son, both of whom were defeated after one term. It was Jackson's defeat of the younger Adams—who had had little success as president—in 1828, that introduced a new populist era into American politics. Significantly Adams, continuing his political career in the House of Representatives after 1829, became a noted supporter of the abolition of slavery. This was never a part of Jackson's agenda, but it lost him little popular support. In so far as Jackson claimed a political inheritance, it was that of Jefferson, and in time the Democratic Party—as it was formed out of amorphous political mass[20] at the end of the 1820s—claimed both presidents as founding fathers.

Jackson shared with Jefferson a deep antipathy to banking, rooted above all in their mistrust of paper issued by out-of-state banks such as notably Philadelphia's powerful and privileged Bank of the United States. In 1833, Jackson said to James Polk (who later became US president), "Every one that knows me does know that I have been always opposed to the U. States Bank, nay all Banks."[21] Jackson's attitude was an essential part of his popular appeal both to frontiersmen west of the Appalachians and to working men in eastern cities. While experience had led both classes to mistrust the way banks granted credit, the westerners, anxious to finance the purchase of cheap land from the federal domain, welcomed small local banks over which they would have some control, while the easterners, "seeking economic democracy, fought the whole banking swindle . . . tooth and nail."[22] It was part of Jackson's genius as a popular leader that he was able to exploit the discontent of both sides, so as to create a party which was strong both in the north and the south—as it continued to be until well into the twentieth century.

Jackson's strong support of the convention system also strengthened his own party. Illinois well illustrates the system's advantages. Until 1834 the state had no effective Democratic Party, so that any number of people (even including some who endorsed a United States Bank) stood for office claiming to be Jacksonians—allowing opposition candidates to be elected on a split vote.[23] With the formation of the state's Democratic Party during the years 1834–1836 a candidate for office could only stand as a Democrat with the support of the convention at the level—county, district, state or whatever which he sought to represent. In practice the system well suited Jackson's bent for cronyism, which, once in the White House, he extended to federal government appointments—laying the seeds of the system of patronage long characteristic of American politics.

THE AGE OF STEPHEN DOUGLAS

In Illinois the successful introduction of the convention owed much to Stephen Douglas, a young Democratic politician, who—in 1833, at the age of twenty—had settled in Jacksonville as a penniless immigrant from Vermont. Elected to his first state office in 1835, the Democratic convention held in the Illinois First Congressional District (in the north of the state) chose him as its candidate for the US House of Representatives in 1838. A narrow defeat meant that electoral success had to wait until 1842, in which year Douglas was elected to represent Illinois' Fifth District in the Twenty-eighth and Twenty-ninth Congresses. Then, in 1846, after being chosen as Democratic candidate by a statewide convention, Stephen Douglas was elected to the US Senate, where he served until his death in 1861. His "fierce willingness for political battle at any time and at any odds, his strong partisan spirit and his deep patriotism" made Stephen Douglas "the idol of millions of his countrymen."[24] With these attributes he was an almost perfect Jacksonian. His success in Illinois was equaled by only one other politician, his near contemporary, Abraham Lincoln. This, however, only became clear at a very late stage: throughout the greater part of the 1840s and 1850s Stephen Douglas, as a Democrat a member of much the strongest party—not only in Illinois but in the nation at large—dominated the politics of the state. What is more, the part Douglas played, as a US senator, in bringing to an end the Missouri Compromise in 1854, helped set the stage for the conflict between north and south, that—as related in chapter 12—would in the end be fatal to his own political career.

The Whig Party emerged during Jackson's second term in the White House as a coalition of forces opposed both to his leadership style and his policies. The use of the word "Whig," after its first appearing on New York City ballot papers in 1834, spread rapidly throughout the Union. The party appealed on one side to men of ambition, enterprise and a spirit of independence in business and the professions, and on the other to farmers who resented the Jacksonian opposition to federal government concern for internal improvements. Whigs were elitist in their distrust of semi-literate city rabble and rural backwoodsmen.[25] In its early days they found in Henry Clay, a Kentucky senator, a charismatic leader, whose "American system" called for "internal improvements,[26] protective tariffs and a national bank"[27]—all policies abhorrent to Jacksonians. (Although tariffs, essential for raising public revenue, were imposed by the first US Congress in 1789, congressional Democrats consistently ensured low-level tariffs, favoring the south, until 1861.)

Significantly time would be on the side of the Whigs, but only after their party had been dissolved. In particular, after 1861, the need to fund the vast expenses of fighting the Civil War strained the fragmented US banking structure to the breaking point. The solution found by President Lincoln's treasury secretary, Salmon P. Chase, was for the US Treasury to issue banknotes, which by force of law enacted by the US Congress[28] were to be legal tender throughout the Union. This was the origin of the famous "greenbacks," still issued by the US Treasury in various denominations from a dollar upwards. Central banking, in the form of the Federal Reserve System, had to wait until 1913.

In national politics the Whigs produced only two presidents, William Henry Harrison, elected in 1840, and Zachary Taylor, elected in 1848. Both were compromise candidates, sharing—with Andrew Jackson—the advantage of a reputation acquired as generals victorious in battle. Harrison's victory was won at Tippecanoe, north of the Ohio River, in December, 1811; his defeated enemies were Shawnee Indians led by their charismatic chief, Tecumseh.[29] Even in 1840, the victory was remembered for making safe for American settlers the territory that by then had become the states of Indiana and Illinois. Taylor's victories—in Mexico—were, however, much more recent, and, in the 1840s, made him, much more than Harrison, a popular hero of the day.

If both Harrison and Taylor were compromise candidates, this was even more true of their vice presidents, James Tyler and Millard Fillmore, both chosen to offer voters a balanced ticket. The choice, in both cases, was critical, since both Harrison and Taylor died in office, leaving it to their vice presidents to take over the White House. Harrison died only a month after his inauguration so that Tyler, who came from Virginia, served nearly a full term—at the very end of which (as recounted in chapter 4) he signed the bill admitting Texas to the Union, contrary to the wishes of Whigs such as Abraham Lincoln. This made him to many in his party something of a "wolf in sheep's clothing."

Taylor died in 1850, leaving the White House to Fillmore—a dark horse candidate from New York, who proved to be a much weaker president. By this time, however, the two parties, Whig and Democratic, were difficult to distinguish at the national level, while representatives of different and conflicting policies were to be found in both of them. During the 1850s this led to crisis in both parties, mainly as a result of the strains to which the Missouri Compromise of 1820 was subjected.

Their causes, as well as their drastic outcome, are related in chapter 11. Here it is sufficient to note the part played by opposing reactions to what is known to history as the Wilmot Proviso. David Wilmot was a Democratic congressman from Pennsylvania, who, as a passionate defender of the rights of labor, saw himself—as many others did also—as a thoroughgoing Jacksonian.[30] Although in 1844 a supporter of the annexation of Texas, in August 1946 he moved an amendment to an appropriations bill required by President Polk to cover the costs of the Mexican War that would exclude slavery in all territories that might be acquired as a result of it. In moving the amendment Wilmot declared, "I would preserve for free white labor a fair country, a rich inheritance, where the sons of toil, of my own race and color, can live without the disgrace which association with negro slavery brings upon free labor". The amendment failed, but in February 1845 it was reintroduced as the Wilmot Proviso by Representative Preston King of New York with the words, "The time has come when this republic should declare by law that it will not be made an instrument to the extension of slavery . . . If slavery is not excluded by law, the presence of the slave will exclude the laboring white man."[31] In the words of the historian Arthur M. Schlesinger, noting the failure of the proviso to pass in the House of Representatives, "the free soil issue was now formulated and laid before the country in terms which invoked deep Jacksonian sentiments."

The proviso was far from being dead and buried, as chapter 9 makes clear. It is time, however, to look at how the opposition between Democrats and Whigs developed in Illinois. The rule that the allocation of congressional districts to the various states of the Union was governed by the census taken at ten-year intervals, meant that Illinois, from its admission as a state in 1819 until the Twenty-third Congress (1833–1834), had only one representative in the US Congress. This was always a Democrat. In the Twenty-third Congress—with the allocation of districts based on the 1830 census—this increased to three, and, of these, one in the third (and northernmost) district of Illinois was consistently a Whig. With the Twenty-eighth Congress—with allocation based on the 1840 census—the number increased to seven, but of these only one, elected to the Seventh District, was consistently a Whig, and in the Thirtieth Congress, this was Abraham Lincoln. That he only served one term was the result of an agreement made between the leading Whig politicians in the district shortly before it elected its first congressman in 1842. This committed them to the principle of rotation in office, with each successive representative serving only one term—an arrangement also adopted in many other states. In

Illinois it meant that Lincoln was third in line in the Seventh District, which brought him to Washington for the two years, 1847–1848.

There was no question of the consistent Whig success in the Seventh District extending to the rest of the state. Statewide Democrats had a comfortable majority in Illinois, which never voted for a Whig candidate for president, nor elected a Whig governor or US senator.[32]

THE CHALLENGE OF ABRAHAM LINCOLN

Although this was the position throughout the 1840s, during the 1850s it began to fall apart, with the Democrats dividing on the issue of slavery, and the Whigs losing their identity completely in the new Republican Party, which first contested elections in 1854. It deliberately based its appeal on the way its members were united in their opposition to the Kansas-Nebraska Act of 1854, which had been sponsored in the US Senate by Stephen Douglas, Illinois' most prominent Democrat. It derived its strength from the strong popular reaction to the Act—which to many foreshadowed the extension of slavery not only into Kansas where it already had a foothold, but into Nebraska, where it did not. (For this reason those opposing the act were commonly known as "anti-Nebraska" men.) After Iowa and Maine—two states regarded as Democratic strongholds—were lost to the Republicans, Douglas, with every reason to fear that Illinois would go the same way, campaigned vigorously in favor of the act. Lincoln, with equal vigor, campaigned against it, starting with a speech made on October 4, 1854, at a large, well-attended meeting in Springfield.[33]

In the northern states the November elections were disastrous for Douglas. With a total of eighty-eight representatives in Congress, New York, Ohio, Pennsylvania and Indiana only elected eight Democrats. Even in the Democratic stronghold of Illinois—with nine districts as a result of the 1850 census—five were won by anti-Nebraska men. Just as critical for the future of Illinois was their prospective control, by a small majority, of the state's General Assembly. Abraham Lincoln immediately set his sights on his being chosen as US senator to succeed a Democrat, James Shields, whose six-year term would expire in 1855.

Lincoln, however, faced a number of obstacles even before the General Assembly would have to make its choice. For one thing the anti-Nebraska majority was not only slim, but fragmented: in the early days the best Lincoln could do was to appeal to the Whigs among it for their support. Even if that proved strong enough for him to be chosen to oppose Shields, the state senate, where the Democrats retained their majority, could prevent his election by insisting that the choice be made by a joint session. He also had the problem that the Sangamon County voters had reelected him to the state legislature in 1854, so that he might have the deciding vote in the senate election at the end of January 1855, in which case propriety would require him to abstain, if not vote for his opponent. Faced with this dilemma, Lincoln declined to accept his election to the state legislature: this left the anti-Nebraska voters in such disarray that just before Christmas 1854 a Democrat won the special election held to replace Lincoln as representative of Sangamon County—a result which one of Lincoln's opponents called "the best Christmas joke of the season."[34]

The result, in any case, was to leave Lincoln free to pursue his US Senate ambitions. The problem he then faced was that the radical anti-Nebraska men were no longer Whigs, but members of the new Republican Party, which in its 1854 convention had included in its platform both the exclusion of slavery in all national territories and the repeal of the 1850 Fugitive Slave Act. To Lincoln's embarrassment this convention had also made him a member of its Illinois central committee. While repudiating his membership would alienate voters whose support he needed, affirming it would alienate the conservative Whigs in his own backyard in central Illinois.

Lincoln solved the problem by accepting his membership of the Republican central committee, while making clear at the same time that it was as a Whig, and not as a Republican—let alone an abolitionist—that he could be counted as an anti-Nebraska man. Although he hated slavery he conceded that he "would consent to the extension of it rather than see the Union dissolved."[35] He supported neither its elimination in the national territories nor the repeal of the Fugitive Slave Act.

Lincoln had only a month to rally the essential support in the Illinois legislature after it assembled on January 1, 1855. A complicating factor was the emergence of the new Native American Party, whose main appeal was to native-born Protestants who resented—at a time of economic setback—both the increasing number of immigrants (who competed in the labor market) and the Catholic Church to which many of them belonged. Because of their secrecy, when questioned about the party to which they belonged, its members became known as "Know Nothings," not only in Illinois but in other states where they were powerful.

When the General Assembly met, Lincoln realized that Shields could count on forty-three (out of a hundred) members who were Douglas Democrats, and Douglas made it clear that if Shields were defeated the blame would rest with the Know Nothings—who for Lincoln and others opposed to Douglas were somewhat dubious allies. Although Lincoln started off strongly—winning over all "the extreme Anti-Slavery men"[36]—at a critical stage three Whigs deserted him, in one case at least because of his connections with the Know Nothings.

With this his only hope rested with a small group of anti-Nebraska Democrats who had broken with Douglas. As was clear to Lincoln, none of them could ever vote for a Whig: in the event they chose to support—from their own number—Lyman Trumbull from Alton in southern Illinois, who was known for his hatred of slavery. Eventually the Democrats, realizing how difficult it would be to muster more than forty-five votes for Shields, found a new candidate: Illinois Governor Joel A. Matteson—a wealthy public works contractor, who in public had supported the Kansas-Nebraska Act while privately expressing his misgivings, and who had considerable legislative support as a result of favors he had given to assemblymen from the districts along the Illinois and Michigan Canal. After six ballots the Democrats abandoned Shields for Matteson, who could then count on forty-seven votes; at the same time Lincoln's vote was down to fifteen, while Trumbull's was up to thirty-five. At this critical moment Lincoln directed his fifteen hardcore supporters to vote for Trumbull, who was also his friend. On the tenth vote Trumbull was elected to be the new senator for Illinois.

Although this was a bitter disappointment to many, including Lincoln's wife, Mary, it was far from being a complete disaster. In the US Senate Douglas' life would be made miserable by having an anti-Nebraska Democrat as the other senator from his own state. At the same time the anti-Nebraska men promised to support Lincoln in the next Senate race in 1858. Then Lincoln would run against Douglas himself, a contest with far-reaching repercussions for the future not only of Illinois, but of the United States.

This, in 1855, was three years ahead. By the end of that year it was clear to many that the Whig Party had no future. Illinois had to follow many other northern states in organizing a new party which would provide a home to all opponents of the extension of slavery. This was achieved on May 29, 1856, at a "state fusion convention" held at Bloomington. Its result was the emergence of the Illinois Republican Party, whose platform was broad enough to accommodate conservative Whigs—like Lincoln himself—anti-Nebraska Democrats, Know Nothings, German immigrants and abolitionists, all of whom were represented in the slate of officers nominated by the convention. On slavery the platform, while not including abolitionist demands, contained a declaration that Congress had both the power and the duty to exclude it from the national territories. The congress ended with an extemporaneous speech by Lincoln, regarded by those present as the best he had ever made. Slavery was explicitly identified as the cause of the nation's problems. As Lincoln's law partner, William Herndon, recalled later, "His speech was full of fire and energy and force . . . it was logic; it was pathos; it was enthusiasm; it was justice, equity, truth, and right set ablaze by the divine fires of a soul maddened by the wrong; it was hard, heavy, knotty, gnarly, backed with wrath."[37]

The Republican Party held its first national convention, in Philadelphia, from June 17 through 19. The most important business was to nominate its own candidate in the presidential election due in November. Against Lincoln's advice the convention chose California's first senator, John C. Frémont, widely known as the "Pathfinder of the West" on account of his explorations beyond the Rocky Mountains. On the final day the Illinois delegation tried hard to rally support for nominating Lincoln as vice president; their attempt had come too late, and although Lincoln received 110 votes, his opponent, William L. Dayton received 253. Even so the support for Lincoln was regarded as very significant. Indeed, if he had beaten Dayton, then, with his name on the ballot papers, the Republicans could well have carried Illinois for Frémont. The state, however, went to the Democratic candidate, James Buchanan of Pennsylvania, because the new "American" Party—as the Native American Party had renamed itself—by choosing the former Whig president, Millard Fillmore (1850–1853) as its candidate, gained the votes of almost all the old anti-Nebraska Whigs. At the very start of the campaign Lincoln had predicted that "with the Frémont and Fillmore men united, here in Illinois, we have Mr. Buchanan in the hollow of our hand, but with us divided . . . he has us."[38]

The way was now open to Lincoln to campaign against Douglas for election to the US Senate in 1858. This was a battle that Lincoln saw a good chance of winning, but everything turned on winning the Illinois legislature. In spite of Lincoln's steadily increasing popularity in the state, this was extremely problematic. According to the Illinois constitution, thirteen members of the state senate were not up for reelection in 1858, and, of these, eight were Democrats. This meant that Lincoln would need a majority of at least three in the state house of representatives; here the problem was that the division of the state into districts was based on the 1850 census. This was a considerable advantage to the Democrats who were strong in the south of the state—where the population had remained more or less stable in the intervening eight years—while in the northern districts, which were strongly Republican, the number of voters had greatly increased. This was particularly true of Cook County, which included Chicago and much of the Michigan lakeshore.

At the Republican convention held in the statehouse at Springfield on June 16, 1856, Lincoln was chosen by acclamation as the party's candidate in the forthcoming Senate election. He had long realized—as Douglas had also—that the future of slavery in the United States was the only issue that counted with voters. What his involved became clear in his acceptance speech:

> We are now into the *fifth* year, since a policy was initiated, with the *avowed* object, and *confident* promise, of putting an end to slavery agitation.

Under the operation of that policy, that agitation has not only *not ceased*, but has *constantly augmented*.

In *my* opinion, it *will* not cease, until a *crisis* shall have been reached and passed.

"A house divided against itself cannot stand."

I believe this government cannot endure permanently half *slave* and half *free*.

I do not expect the Union to be *dissolved*—I do not expect the house to *fall*—but I *do* expect that it will cease to be divided.

It will become *all* one thing, or *all* the other.

Either the *opponents* of slavery, will . . . place it where the public mind shall rest in the belief that it is in the course of ultimate extinction; or its *advocates* will put it forward, till it shall become alike in *all* the States, *old* as well as *new*—*North* as well as *South*.[39]

The theme of a "house divided" is one that not only Lincoln, but other leading politicians, had adopted on previous occasions; after all, it originated in the New Testament,[40] as almost all of Lincoln's contemporaries must have recognized. The extreme black-and-white terms of the last paragraph can be seen as a reaction to Chief Justice Taney's judgment given in the US Supreme Court in the Dred Scott case[41]—as it is related in chapter 11. Plainly the lines of battle were being drawn for a massive conflict, but it was still one which Lincoln hoped to avoid.

Following his adoption as Republican candidate, Lincoln's campaign against Douglas in the second half of 1858 was unprecedented in the history of American politics. Douglas' campaign had to wait until July, when he returned from Washington to his home in Chicago. In Washington he had to his credit the defeat, in the Senate, of Kansas' Lecompton Constitution[42]—which, if adopted as the basis for admitting the territory as the thirty-fourth state, would have committed it irrevocably to slavery. In Illinois politics this was a hostage to fortune that Douglas could not afford, but the Republicans missed no chance in pointing out how, in this matter, he had disregarded the policy of both President James Buchanan, and the Kansas territorial governor, Robert J. Walker.

Douglas opened his campaign with a speech delivered from the balcony of the Tremont House Hotel in Chicago, and the next night Lincoln reacted by speaking from the same balcony. For some weeks he pursued this strategy, following in the footsteps of Douglas from one place to another in Illinois, but in the end his advisers persuaded him that this was counterproductive. Instead he challenged Douglas to a series of seven debates, one in each of the state's congressional districts, with the exception of the second (which contained Chicago) and the seventh (which contained Springfield) where both candidates had already made major speeches. Douglas reluctantly accepted this challenge, knowing that he had more to lose by associating with his lesser-known opponent.

The debates (whose content is considered in detail in chapter 12) took place in every corner of the state; they attracted vast crowds, arriving over considerable distances by every means of transport—including the railroad trains that now traveled throughout Illinois. According to the Republican *New York Times* they made the state "the most interesting political battleground in the Union,"[43] but they were only a part of the campaigns fought by both sides. Douglas made more speeches, and covered greater distances, but Lincoln was not so far behind, having covered in the four months leading up to the November election day 3,400 miles by train, 600 by carriage and 350 by boat. Those covering all seven debates found that although Lincoln was relatively weak in the first three, the impact he made became steadily stronger. This became clear in the final debate in Alton on the Mississippi, a town with strong southern sympathies with the slave state of Missouri on the other side of the river. In his speech Lincoln, as he had at the Republican convention, recognized a controversy "on the part of one class that looks upon the institution of slavery *as a wrong*, and another that *does not* look upon it as a wrong . . . It is the eternal struggle between these two principles—right and wrong—throughout the world."[44]

The debates were significant for the fact that they focused almost entirely on slavery, as if other important issues did not count. Douglas' strategy was to put the slavery question in the context of self-government, which, as he told his vast audience in his final speech at Alton, he cared for more than "all the negroes in Christendom."[45] For Lincoln there were certain inalienable rights—to life, liberty, and the pursuit of happiness—enshrined in the US Constitution, which counted for more.

It is doubtful how much the debates changed the outcome of the election. Although statewide the Republicans had a small majority of votes, the results, in party terms, were much the same as those of 1854 and 1856. As Lincoln had foreseen, the final lineup in the state legislature was against him; in the balloting on January 4, 1859, he only received forty-six votes to Douglas' fifty-four. Douglas returned to the Senate, but his stand against the majority of his own party on the Lecompton Constitution made his prospects as the Democratic presidential candidate in 1860 very problematic. Lincoln, on the other hand, had in his own words, gained nationwide "a hearing on the great and durable question of the age." After 1858, his political arena extended far beyond Illinois to embrace the whole nation.

As for Illinois, during the 1850s the state, as much as the rest of the nation, had been transformed in any number of ways, not just politically. Its population, and particularly that of its largest city, Chicago, had greatly increased. Particularly in the north of state, the cities, where many more people lived, banished the livestock that in the first half of the nineteenth century had crowded their muddy streets; these were then improved by paving and gas lighting, drains, and piped water—with the control of diseases such as cholera and malaria as an additional benefit. Transport within cities was by horse-drawn trolley, between them by train or stagecoach on the new all-weather highways. The great cities of the eastern states could be reached in a day or two, or within minutes by the electric telegraph. Prairie agriculture not only produced wheat and corn for the whole nation and much of the world outside it, but created a vast new market for new local industry, such as Chicago's McCormick Harvesting Machine Company or Moline's John Deere Company at the other end of Illinois' Rock Island Railroad—both enterprises born out of inventions, one of a reaper and the other of a steel plow, made in the 1830s. On any count, this was not a world that had any place for slavery.

King Cotton

THE WORLD BUILT BY SLAVES

If today the cotton plantation, as it developed in the deep south in the first half of the nineteenth century, is regarded as representing the most characteristic and traditional southern lifestyle—with overtones of decadence and family intrigue—in its heyday before the Civil War it was much more than that. Cotton, which was unrivaled in its contribution to the American export economy, and the economic system governing its production—with its complete dependence upon slave labor—had a political and social dimension that defined the place of the southern states in the nation as a whole in a way that they would fight to preserve at any cost.

Although in the Union, as it was finally constituted in 1789, only two states, Massachusetts and New Hampshire had already outlawed slavery, the institution as such was, by the beginning of the nineteenth century, in decline throughout the north; even so, the process of abolition was only complete in 1850, when slavery was finally outlawed in Pennsylvania. This, however, was far from being the whole story: in the Northwest Territory beyond the Ohio River—which would eventually be divided into six new states—the Northwest Ordinance of 1787 banned slavery.[1] This meant that the whole succession of northern states admitted after 1790 were always "free." Even the five original states—Connecticut, New Jersey, New York, Pennsylvania, and Rhode Island—whose legislatures had yet to abolish slavery, were, for good reason, both political and demographic, counted as "free." The figures speak for themselves: while in the first half of the nineteenth century there was a more than fourfold increase in the total population of the northern states, not only was there a decline from 3 to 2 percent of those who were negroes, but after 1840 those who were still slaves numbered only a few hundreds. Significantly the greatest decline took place during the 1820s, with the number of northern slaves falling from 18,000 to less than 3,000. In economic terms, at least, abolition would make little difference.

The trend of public opinion, at least in the north, was already unmistakable when Congress, in 1807, voted to terminate the international slave trade in the United States from January 1, 1808. By this time two new "free" states, Vermont (1791) and Ohio (1805), together with two new "slave" states, Kentucky (1792) and Tennessee (1796), had joined the Union. The result, therefore, was that there were nine "free" to eight "slave" states. With Louisiana being admitted as a "slave" state in 1812, the balance was restored.

Economically there was only ever one reason for establishing slavery as the form given to labor as a factor of production. Ever since the British colonial settlers in Virginia in the seventeenth century first chose to establish an agricultural economy based on the cultivation of tobacco, this was labor-intensive farming—of a staple crop destined for sale in open markets—of a kind which had no precedent. Since the British colonists only discovered tobacco after it had been introduced to them by local Indians, such agricultural practices and marketing strategies as they had known on the other side of the Atlantic were of little use in organizing its cultivation. Once the tobacco habit crossed the Atlantic to the old world, the consequent demand for the product could only be met by large-scale production; the bottleneck was labor. The answer here was the Atlantic slave trade, which brought hundreds of thousands of Africans to be sold as slaves in the new world. The demand went far beyond the needs of Virginia tobacco planters; the scale of their operation was small in relation to that of the Europeans—French, Dutch, Spanish, Portuguese, as well as British—who planted sugar. This crop, however, was only suited to the soil and climate of the North American mainland in a few restricted areas, of which the most important was in Louisiana—which until 1803 belonged to either France or Spain.[2] Sugar was preeminently the plantation crop of the islands of the Caribbean, and a long stretch of the South American coastlands from the Guianas through Brazil.[3]

In the North American colonies rice and indigo were more important, but they never rivaled tobacco. In colonial times Virginia, with Maryland some way behind, was the largest producer—if only because there was considerably more land available for cultivation. In the nineteenth century Virginia retained its lead, but Kentucky, followed by Tennessee—two states in which major settlement only began in the late eighteenth century—overtook Maryland. North Carolina (which in the twentieth century became the leading producer) and Missouri were also substantial producers—as were the three free states of Ohio, Indiana, and Illinois,[4] and the Canadian province of Ontario. The states of the deep south, South Carolina, Georgia, Alabama, Mississippi, and Louisiana were never much interested in tobacco. Their soil, climate, and infrastructure were much better suited to another crop, cotton, for which the demand increased by leaps and bounds up until the Civil War.

The history of cotton was quite different from that of tobacco, or for that matter, any other crop. A cotton plant, after flowering, is left with a boll, in which seeds are wrapped in fibers; these, if they can be separated from the seeds—by a process now known as ginning—can be spun into a yarn well suited for weaving into textiles. So much was known in tropical regions, in both the old world and the new, as long as 5,000 years ago. In Europe, where only the lands of the Mediterranean had the right climate, the cultivation of cotton only took off in the fourteenth century, when the fibers could be exported to the Netherlands for spinning and weaving. There skilled craftsmen could adapt to cotton spinning wheels and looms developed for wool. Even so, ginning remained a laborious process, and one which wool, by its nature, never required. What is more, wool came mainly from Britain, which was much more accessible to the textile industry of northern Europe; the same, incidentally, was true of two important vegetable fibers, flax and hemp.

Once the production drawbacks have been overcome, cotton fibers, because of the way they interlock, are easily spun into a yarn which looms can turn into cloth which, for consumers, is often superior to any alternative.[5] By the end of the eighteenth century a British invention, soon adopted in the United States, enabled cotton to be spun by water-powered spinning machinery. By this time, also, Americans had discovered how well suited the soil and climate of the southern states were for cotton cultivation. The key technological breakthrough came with the invention in 1793, by Eli Whitney, an American, of a mechanical cotton gin, to separate the fibers from the seeds in the boll. This was just the right time for the British textile industry, when the development of a comprehensive canal network, followed by the introduction of steam-powered machinery, opened the way to producing cloth, from any suitable fiber, on an industrial scale. On the supply side, the United States had not only the right land for growing cotton, but also in slavery a system of organized labor that had developed since the seventeenth century to satisfy the needs of plantation agriculture. If, in the time of the founding fathers, this meant mainly the cultivation of tobacco, by the beginning of the nineteenth century planters were beginning to realize that cotton could be a much more lucrative crop. The critical importance of slave labor to the American export economy was enormously enhanced at a time when otherwise it might have declined. This was certainly the opinion of one southern politician, for, as told by Abraham Lincoln in the summer of 1860,[6] Representative Preston Brookes of South Carolina[7] had declared that "when this Government was originally established, nobody expected that the institution of slavery would last until this day." He said at the same time that "the framers of our Government did not have the knowledge that experience has taught us—that experience and the invention of the cotton-gin have taught us that the perpetuation of slavery is a necessity. He insisted, therefore, upon its being changed from the basis upon which the fathers of the Government left it to the basis of its perpetuation and nationalization."

This line of reasoning lay behind the principle, widely accepted in the southern states, that *slavery* was "natural" for terrain to which cotton was better suited than any alternative plantation crop; in other words, the states in which cotton cultivation was the mainstay of the market economy could not exist without slavery. This principle, if consistently applied, could have meant that slavery would never extend to new states where cotton could never be a profitable crop;[8] if this had been accepted by the south, all the trials of Kansas, as related in chapter 11, would have been avoided.

As slavery became ever more deeply entrenched in the southern plantation economy, there emerged (as already mentioned in chapter 1) an increasingly powerful movement—driven by a number of factors, based on principle as much as expediency—for the abolition of slavery in every state, both north and south. This became notorious in 1833, when its most prominent leader, William Lloyd Garrison, organized the American Anti-Slavery Society. In his publication, *The Liberator*, Garrison famously described the clauses in the Constitution permitting slavery as a "covenant with death and an agreement with hell." Although this extreme position was widely condemned in the north—with Garrison being nearly murdered by a Boston mob in 1835—the survival of slavery inevitably became the key issue dividing the two sides, north and south, and making parity between them in electoral terms a matter of principle.

The critical demographic dimension was implicit in the way the federal regulations allocated seats in the Senate, on one side, and the House of Representatives on the other. As to the Senate, with two senators coming from every state, both large and small, it was sufficient for maintaining the balance between north and south that each would comprise the same number of states. Given not only the need for all legislation to pass the Senate, but also its special powers in approving such matters as foreign treaties and appointments to the federal judiciary, the principle of parity went a long way in guaranteeing southern rights, of which the most important were those relating to slavery.

When it came to the House of Representatives, with districts allocated to the separate states according to their populations, as measured by a national census taken every ten years, the northern states always had a considerable majority—which throughout the century consistently increased. Given the rule that 60 percent of a state's slave population counted in determining the size of its representation in Congress, this trend was less disadvantageous for the south than it might otherwise have been.[9]

To a considerable extent the cultivation of cotton began at the end of the eighteenth century as a substitute for tobacco and other plantation crops in

Virginia, the Carolinas and, marginally, Georgia. It could hardly have been otherwise, since the Atlantic coast of the United States extended no further south than Georgia. It is true that the Mississippi Territory, bounded on the east by Georgia and on the west by the Mississippi River, belonged to the United States, but the presence of the Spanish in Florida and Louisiana made access to the sea somewhat problematical. Even so, navigation rights on the Mississippi granted by Spain were sufficient to encourage pioneers in Tennessee to turn to cotton even before the introduction of Eli Whitney's cotton gin—and at a time before it had been granted statehood. Cotton was planted near Nashville as early as the 1780s with such success that when Tennessee was admitted to the Union in 1796 the cotton plant was incorporated into the great seal of the state.[10] The Cumberland River—a major tributary of the Ohio—defined the essential transport infrastructure for what would always be an export crop. However long the journey downstream, the fact that it ended at the great seaport of New Orleans was enough for the Tennessee planters. In the late 1790s, realizing how the Whitney cotton gin[11] would transform their fortunes, they petitioned the state legislature to purchase the patent rights, and for three critical years, 1804–1807, its inventor was granted an agreed royalty of 37.5 cents for every gin sold in Tennessee. The impact was unmistakable: production increased threefold between 1801 and 1811. At this time cotton was best sent downriver by flatboats, moving with the current, to be broken up at their destination; for planters this meant returning home overland, and for those in central Tennessee, following the Natchez Trace—connecting the lower Mississippi with Nashville, the state capital—meant a journey that was shorter by several hundred miles.

Where Tennessee led, the territories along the lower Mississippi were, sooner or later, bound to follow, but here the way ahead was much more uncertain. Until 1803, when the whole territory west of the river, and the coastal area to the east of it, belonged to Spain, plantation agriculture was devoted mainly to sugar. Both land and climate were suitable, while Spain's whole Caribbean economy—as could be observed in Cuba, Puerto Rico, and Santo Domingo—was based on sugar, as was that of Britain, France, and the Netherlands. With the Louisiana Purchase (as related in chapter 1) in 1803 the position changed entirely: the whole of the lower Mississippi, except for a small corner of Florida[12] became American territory. By this time cotton plantations were already developing upriver from Baton Rouge, but expansion inland was blocked by Indian territory, which, although taking up only a relatively small corner of southwestern Mississippi, covered more than half of Alabama and a considerable part of western Georgia.

In 1811, the Shawnee chief, Tecumseh—whose exploits north of the Ohio River are related in chapter 3—came south to visit the Creeks, who were the dominant Indian tribe in the Mississippi Territory (which within ten years would become the two states of Mississippi and Alabama) and encouraged them to defend their rights against American settlers. In the summer of 1813, Creek warriors, having been subjected to a surprise attack by a small mixed force of local Americans and a mixed-blood militia, emerged victorious from the so-called "Burnt Corn Fight" in southern Alabama,[13] and went on to capture Fort Mims, an ill-guarded American stronghold close to Burnt Corn—where they set the buildings on fire and murdered most of those present. The victims were both soldiers and civilians, but the lives of the Negro slaves were spared, with many of them departing with the Creek warriors from the scene of battle. With many alleging previous collusion with the Indians, the actual event led to a wave of hysteria in the American settlements along the Indian frontier threatened by a "red-black" alliance.

The man chosen to make the whole territory safe for American settlement was one of the most remarkable in American history. In 1787 Andrew Jackson (1767–1838), a young lawyer from North Carolina, came to Nashville after being appointed prosecuting officer in the Superior Court of what was then the Western District of the state. When in 1796 this became the state of Tennessee, Jackson was elected as its first congressman; a year, later the state legislature elected him as one of the two senators. After only one term in Washington he returned home to serve as a judge of the Tennessee Supreme Court, being elected at the same time—on the strength of his record in the Revolutionary War—a major general of the state militia. All these appointments still left him time to become a successful cotton planter and slave owner on his estate outside Nashville; as such his concern for shipping cotton down the Mississippi put him in contact with one of the wealthiest planting families—that of Thomas and Abner Green—of the lower river. This was the result of Jackson's setting up a small trading post at Bruinsburgh, near the mouth of the Bayou Pierre, and close to the Greens' vast Springfield Plantation. There, in the house of Thomas Green—who would later become Mississippi's first congressman—Jackson met and married his wife. Such is the background of the man sent by Tennessee governor Willie Blount—whose family also came from North Carolina—to defeat the Creek warriors decisively. A lawyer, politician, and planter, he turned out to be a great general. In the spring of 1814, commanding some 3,300 soldiers—much the largest force ever to be deployed against Indians in the American south—he confronted the Creeks, in the heart of their own territory, at Horseshoe Bend, a narrow peninsula of about a hundred acres in the Tallapoosa River. Supported by Cherokees and Creek Indians opposed to those defending the stockade at Horseshoe Bend, Jackson overcame a fierce defense of the Indian position, leaving dead on the field 1,800 Creek warriors together with countless women and children. In the days that followed, Jackson's forces devastated some fifty Creek towns and villages. By the treaty of Fort Jackson, imposed upon the Creek chiefs, some 23 million acres—about half of all the Creek lands—were ceded to the United States, a loss shared even by the Creeks who had fought with Jackson. This was all open to settlers, and they would not wait long in planting cotton. Mississippi became a state of the Union in 1817 and Alabama in 1819, the year in which Spain, by ceding Florida to the United States (as related in chapter 4), also provided the new state with an outlet to the sea. Mobile, at the mouth of the long, navigable Alabama River, became, after New Orleans, the major seaport for the export of cotton.

The economic geography of the southern states was transformed. Along the Atlantic seaboard, South Carolina and Georgia—the states most suited for the cultivation of cotton—lacking the great navigable rivers of tidewater Virginia, had problems shipping cotton down to harbors such as Charleston and Savanna. The Mississippi River, together with any number of its navigable tributaries, provided a far more extensive transport infrastructure—which, as related above, the Tennessee planters were already exploiting. New Orleans, close to the mouth of the Mississippi, was already a port that handled considerably more traffic than any of its rivals, and Mobile, where the Alabama River reached the sea, would soon outrank both Charleston and Savannah. At the same time the introduction of steamboats—already well underway by 1820—enormously enhanced the economic potential of the whole area.

THE HEYDAY OF THE PLANTATION ECONOMY

With all the developments related above, the cotton plantations rapidly extended westward across a wide band of territory—some distance inland from the Gulf of Mexico and known as the Cotton Belt—where soil and climate were ideal. East of the Mississippi, western Georgia, Alabama, and Mississippi joined Tennessee as major producers of cotton, followed, in due course, to the west of the river, by Louisiana, Arkansas, and Texas. The new settlers, for historical reasons which they appreciated only too well, were subject to one critical limitation: they could only work with negro slaves.

Economically speaking, this was both a logistical and a demographic problem. As to the former, moving a household was a much more complicated operation when it included slaves; as to the latter, the actual number of slaves available, by reason of the ban on foreign trade, was in principle dependent on natural increase of the existing population.[14] There was no essential reason why supply, on this basis, should keep level with demand, particularly when the overseas market for American cotton, which in the early stages consisted mainly of the Lancashire cotton mills in Britain, expanded to include much of continental Europe. To a degree the shortage of slaves was mitigated by illegal importation from the Caribbean,[15] but this was always problematic, particularly after the British government abolished slavery in its colonies in 1833. At the same time, the overall population of the United States was continually increasing as the result of European immigration,[16] which far from being restricted was positively encouraged; the south had little room for such immigrants, who in turn had no wish whatever to come to terms with slavery. The result, throughout the nineteenth century and beyond, was a southern white population mainly of British descent. This meant in turn that it was well established and extremely conscious of its political rights. As related in chapter 3, the institutions which would enforce them were created by men of British descent, and operated according to British legal and political principles. What is more, when it came to cotton planters, who soon came to constitute the southern elite,[17] the market for their products was mainly in the English-speaking world. With the emergence of the American textile industry in the early nineteenth century, this meant Massachusetts as well as Lancashire.[18]

Once again, the demographics are essential for understanding the historical process in the critical first half of the nineteenth century. Where, during this period, the total population of the south increased by a factor of 3.4, that for the north was 5.2, much the greater part of which was accounted for by the new states north of the Ohio River and west of the Appalachians in which slavery was outlawed. In other words, the population consistently increased most rapidly precisely in that part of the United States where there was little or no history of slavery. Although some of the new settlers, such as the family of Abraham Lincoln, came from southern states, to most of them the prospect of a state without slaves was no hindrance. In any case, just as many—and in the long run a majority, came from northern states, and, significantly, from Europe.[19] Although the main impact of the demographic process did not come until after 1820, already by that year it was clear to both north and south what the future had in store. The year is important because it is that of the Missouri Compromise. Although this is the subject of chapter 7, it must be noted here, that not only did the admission of Missouri as a slave state maintain parity between north and south in the US Senate, but it also left the way open to a substantial slave population in a state that otherwise would have counted as part of the north. One result was that cotton—if only on a small scale—came to be planted in the relatively unfavorable climate of Missouri. If this meant that the majority of slaves brought to Missouri by settlers from east of the Mississippi were never intended for labor on cotton plantations, the same was always true of many, and often the majority, of the slaves in the states they had left behind.[20]

The Cotton Belt, however, employed its slaves mainly in the cultivation of cotton, and it was in the states which comprised it—Alabama,[21] Georgia, Louisiana, Mississippi, and South Carolina—that the proportion of the population consisting of slaves was highest, to the point, even, that in Mississippi and South Carolina, it was more than 50 percent.[22] Only tobacco ever reflected the same trend, with other states, such as Virginia and North Carolina, pre-eminent. The scale, however, was lower, with the total market value of the crop at a level less than a quarter of that of cotton. In any analysis, cotton dominated the southern economy, and imposed its own demographics and transport infrastructure on the regions involved in its cultivation. Indeed, in the earlier years of the nineteenth century, cotton also came to dominate the US export economy.[23] What then did this involve in the first half of the nineteenth century?

The plantation, long regarded as the basic production unit, was defined in terms of the minimum number of slaves employed, generally set at twenty. The secular trend was not only for production and the overall area cultivated to increase, but for the proportion attributable to plantations to do so, too. Even in the very earliest days there were people with capital, such as the Green family of Natchez, who saw planting cotton as the most profitable way of investing it.[24] This prospect was shared by hundreds of small farmers, who, accompanied by their families and slaves, cultivated cotton in small patches, where they treated it as a garden plant.[25] Experience, born out of trial and error, led to better practice and higher yields—which also followed after about 1805 as a result of replacing the ordinary "Tennessee green seed" with "Mexican" cotton. Inevitably in such a process the big planters rather than the small farmers led the way. At the same time the farmers were much less able to withstand the occupational hazards inherent in growing cotton: the boll attracted its own pests,[26] whose destructive work could vary, as could that of the weather, from one year to another or from one district to another. In the lower Mississippi Valley, floods were a constant threat to plantations on both sides of the river, with that of 1849 being exceptionally destructive.[27] Rains could also fail, so that drought blighted some years, as did also frost and wind storms.[28]

The health of a farming family, as that of its slaves, was critical to its success in producing a good crop.[29] Cholera was the most frequent and widespread affliction, with a particularly severe epidemic coinciding with the great flood of 1849.[30] Yellow fever, however, was "the most dreaded scourge of the nineteenth century South"[31] even though epidemics—of which the worst erupted in New Orleans in July 1853—were less frequent.

Planters who successfully withstood the ravages of storm and sickness still faced the problem of selling a crop destined for an overseas market. In principle, growers sold via professional factors, who, with their own trade organization, had exclusive access to representatives of Liverpool or New York in New Orleans, and the other lesser seaports shipping cotton. Chronically indebted small farmers, who in any case had difficulty in making up sufficient bulk to interest factors, sold to local merchants, who, in return for advancing money on the crop, paid much lower prices, while planters were able to consign their crops to the ports, to be sold by the factors at a standard commission of 2.5 percent.[32] There was no doubt who got the better bargain.

Inevitably small farmers faced by debt had to sell out to their more fortunate competitors, generally losing their slaves as well as their land. The alternative, commonly adopted when the frontier was continually being extended, was simply to move on, say to Texas—where land was abundant—leaving unpaid creditors behind in Alabama. The trend always was to fewer and larger units, which meant not only the transfer of land, but the sale of slaves—a quite distinct operation with its own dealers, whose dominant presence at slave auctions, gave their occupation a bad name, even in the south. Where in the eighteenth century, before cotton became dominant in the southern agricultural economy, factors imported slaves and, as often as not, sold them on credit, by the nineteenth this occupation was regarded as too disreputable, although factors still lent money to enable planters to buy from dealers. In the planter aristocracy, as it developed in the first half of the nineteenth century, the factor could claim to be a gentleman, a class closed to dealers—however successful they might have been in business.

The social consequences of the development of a plantation-based economy were unmistakable. The small farmer, whose family was likely to be at least as numerous as his slaves, lived and worked in a household where differentiation between different tasks was based largely on age and sex. The effect of including slaves was to extend the household's productive capacity by an amount that represented a positive return on the investment they represented. This at least was the principle, which a modern economist would regard in terms of marginal return on capital. In practice slaves were a considerable hostage to fortune, which they had to pay for, when hard times came, by seeing their families broken up as they were sold by auction. The common result of such a sale was life on a plantation, where the community of slaves would be organized, more or less rationally, as a factor in production. This involved a hierarchy of authority among slaves, with those who had acquired skilled crafts at its head. As can be seen from dealers' advertisements, a high price was expected for the most highly qualified slaves.[33] The result was that the plantation, like a large country estate, became a self-contained unit, with the work of the field hands being supported by blacksmiths, carpenters, and other craftsmen.

In the richest cotton planting regions, the fact that there was no room for any unit smaller than the plantation meant also the exclusion of the society of the common man, with its characteristic village life. The extent to which, on a plantation, the number of slaves could far exceed that of the white residents is made clear by the census figures for the counties of Mississippi and Louisiana, on both sides of that stretch of the Mississippi river where it constituted the boundary between these two states. By the 1850s the proportion of slaves to the total population was between 80 and 90 percent.[34] This reflected the fact that a single white overseer was sufficient for a plantation with hundreds of slaves. From the perspective of their employers, overseers were often far from satisfactory; one planter is on record for denouncing them as "a nuisance to be abated as soon as possible."[35] In addition to general incompetence and inability to supervise negroes, their possible shortcomings included excessive alcohol consumption and familiarity with female slaves.[36] With hundreds of slaves to supervise, even a good overseer—and there were many—relied on "drivers" recruited from their negro field hands—in principle according to merit. Drivers were a much more stable factor in the plantation workforce, often enjoying greater confidence from the owners.[37] The wealth they—together with the slaves subordinate to them—created for their owners can still be seen in the splendid mansions of Vicksburg and Natchez, on the east bank of the Mississippi.

The final question to ask about the elite economy of the large plantations is how it related to politics in the different southern states. The distinction to be made here is between the "old" south, defined by the Atlantic states, from Georgia to Delaware, which were original members of the Union, and the "new" south, consisting of the states along the Gulf Coast and Lower Mississippi, of which the first to join the Union was Kentucky, in 1792, and the last, Texas, in 1845. Leaving aside the four border states of Delaware, Maryland, Kentucky, and Missouri—which in 1861 were to remain loyal to the Union—one is left with the eleven states that were then to secede. Of these, two, Virginia and South Carolina, had established a patrician way of government in which the large land and slave owners dominated the state government, while the broad mass of citizens had to be content with a limited franchise. In South Carolina, in particular, "the voice of democracy was but faintly heard [while] the elite exercise[d] complete political domination throughout the entire antebellum period."[38] Political representation, both at state and national level, was almost entirely confined to the planter elite.[39] That this was acceptable to the rank and file of white South Carolina related to the fact that the 402,406 slaves in its population constituted the highest percentage (57.2) among all the southern states. This was not, however, decisive, for in Mississippi, where the percentage, at 55.2, was nearly as high, popular representation in government was much broader, with most of the richest planters content to stay out of politics. Some indeed, such as Josiah Winchester of Natchez, stayed loyal to the Union even after Mississippi seceded in 1861.[40] Mississippi, only admitted to the Union in 1817, was a much more open society where both rich and poor tended to be recent immigrants—simply by virtue of the historical reasons stated in chapter 1. This meant also that a number of plantations were established by, and remained the property of, wealthy northerners, who therefore had ties to both north and south. This was never the case within the enclosed society of South Carolina, whose original colonial constitution dated back to the seventeenth century. Nonetheless, whatever the historical background, South Carolina and Mississippi were joined together in the vanguard of the southern cause, which was tied inextricably to planting cotton and exploiting slave labor. It was a senator from the former state, James Henry Hammond, who, on March 4, 1864, famously declared on the floor of the Senate, "Cotton is king." Charleston, its leading harbor, was where the Civil War began—to immense popular acclaim—while Mississippi gave the Confederacy its only president, Jefferson Davis.

COMMUNITY AND ECONOMY OUTSIDE THE PLANTATIONS

Given that in the main Cotton Belt states—from South Carolina to Louisiana—slaves were always more than a third, and in two of them, more than a half of the total population, their concentration in the actual cotton-growing counties could only mean that a steadily increasing number of white citizens were left with almost no part to play in the most profitable sector of the economy. Some, it is true, could continue as small farmers, working with no more than a handful of slaves, growing cotton on the margins of the great plantations, but in all the states of the Cotton Belt there was also a considerable acreage which, being unsuitable for cotton, was farmed with other crops or, in many areas, livestock. In both cases aggregate production actually exceeded that of the northern states, but somewhat paradoxically the southern states produced relatively little surplus for markets outside their own boundaries[41]—to the point even that the plantations consistently imported cereals and livestock from the north. Nonetheless there were a few counties in such locations as Virginia's Shenandoah Valley or the southern reaches of the Appalachians in Georgia and Alabama with substantial exports of staples—including cotton.[42]

One explanation of the dominance of plantation agriculture—and of the cultivation of cotton in particular—is to be found in the slow, piecemeal development of the south's transport infrastructure outside the considerable natural waterways. When, from the end of the 1840s, railroads were built, their most lucrative traffic was cotton, whose cultivation then extended to areas ill-served by the riverboats.[43] Once again economic development favored a single sector, dependent upon slaves. The railroads did have the advantage of providing new employment for white Americans, at the same encouraging the growth of towns—such as notably Atlanta—in a part of the country where there had been remarkably little urban development. Inevitably the labor force engaged in actual railroad construction consisted of slaves.[44] Although, next to railroads, mining, light industry, transport and livestock raising were all part of the southern economy,[45] the majority of white Americans were still left to survive, as best they could, by farming the areas unsuitable for plantation crops. Some employed slaves, but for many—probably the majority—slaves represented an investment not justified by any returns that might come from it, even if it could be afforded. Indeed when cotton prices were high, the dealers, in turn, ensured that higher prices were paid for slaves. In such circumstances the optimal strategy for a small farmer who did own slaves was often to sell them, and then move westward onto new land. The slaves, needless to say, would almost certainly end up on a plantation.

None of this was open to the landless non-slaveholders—so numerous in the extensive areas of marginal hill farming as to constitute half the local populations while owning barely 3 percent of the regional wealth.[46] Most of these farmers were tenants, often of poor land that local slave owners could not profitably devote to cotton or some other staple. The result was often an estate with some parcels of land worked by slaves, and others let to subsistence tenant farmers—materially no better off that their negro neighbors. Indeed they sometimes worked the fields together under the supervision of an owner or overseer.[47] In 1815 this was the strategy adopted by Thomas Jefferson at Monticello.[48] Although the result of all this was the emergence of a degraded and despised class of poor whites, whose lot—as anyone could see—was no better than that of negro slaves, the two sides never found a common cause. If there were few abolitionists among the poor whites, many of them, when faced with the choice in the winter of 1860–1861, were loyal to the Union rather than the Confederacy. This was particularly true of the border area of Tennessee and North Carolina, and the western counties of Virginia—which, as related in chapter 12—formed the new state of West Virginia in 1863.

The Missouri Compromise

THE MISSOURI CONTROVERSY

Outside Abraham Lincoln's own state of Illinois, nowhere in America counted for more in his political life—and that of many of his contemporaries—than the neighboring state of Missouri. When Illinois became a state in 1818, with Missouri following three years later in 1821, both had attracted much the same sort of settlers—consisting mainly of families from slave states, such as notably Kentucky (where Lincoln himself was born) and Tennessee. There was—at least in principle—a critical distinction between Illinois and Missouri: those who settled in Illinois had chosen a territory in which slavery was banned,[1] while there was no such restriction in Missouri. In practice a number of the early settlers in Illinois, including the state's first two US senators, brought slaves with them, while Missouri also attracted settlers who were not and never had been slave owners. Even so, when the United States was confronted with the question of admitting Missouri as the twenty-fourth state, one-sixth of its population of 66,000 were slaves—a far greater proportion than in Illinois. In practical terms this was a very powerful reason for admitting Missouri as a slave state: what otherwise—as its citizens never ceased to point out—would happen to its negro population? Even so, as a matter of principle, there were very strong objections—maintained throughout the northern states—to admitting what would be the first new state entirely to the west of the Mississippi River as a slave state. There would then be, for one thing, a precedent to apply to other new states to be formed out of the Louisiana Territory—purchased from France in 1803. While there were few problems in admitting Illinois as a free state in 1818, or Alabama as a slave state a year later, the future status of Missouri proved to be the most divisive issue of that time.

The whole balance of power between slave and free states was at issue. The Missouri Compromise, as agreed by members of the US Congress in the years 1819–1821, not only opened the way for the admission of Missouri in 1821 as the twenty-fourth state of the Union, but also, and much more critically, established a formula that would preserve the lineup between the states into the indefinite future.

The United States was from the beginning founded on compromise: every one of the thirteen original states—in the process of ratifying the constitution in the years 1787 to 1790—had made key concessions relating both to rights and property, and to representation in Congress. Whatever concessions were made, the principle of the rights of individual states remained sacrosanct. In particular this meant that questions of citizenship were for each individual state to decide upon. These were crucial for two classes within the American population, Indians and negroes.

Provision was made for both classes in the Northwest Ordinance of 1787, which was adopted by the constituent states of the union even before the constitution was ratified. As the name suggests, the primary purpose of the ordinance was to regulate the government of the Northwest Territory, which had accrued to Britain as a result of the terms agreed with France by the Treaty of Paris at the end of the Seven Years' War (1756–1763)—which, not for nothing, is known to American historians as the French and Indian War. Geographically the territory extended south to the Ohio River (which was also the northwestern frontier of Virginia), west to the Upper Mississippi and north to the Great Lakes. Where, however, the British colonial governors—acting in the interests of the substantial and politically important Indian tribes—had restricted white settlement of the territory, the Northwest Ordinance plainly envisaged settlement, as can be seen from the fact that it laid down the process by which territories would qualify for statehood.

As for Indians, the ordinance provided that "the utmost good faith shall always be observed towards the Indians; their lands and property shall never be taken from them without their consent." This provision was honored more in the breech than the observance: from the 1790s onward American frontiersmen fought any number of battle against Indians, with victory in every case leading to the cession of Indian territory—so much so that as early as 1805 Ohio, which was part of the Northwest Territory, became the seventeenth state of the Union. One principle stood firm: Indians were not—and would never become—American citizens.

As for negroes, slavery was banned in the Northwest Territory. At the end of the eighteenth century such a ban added up to very little: there was little prospect of plantation agriculture, which was always the main purpose for which Africans had been brought as slaves to America. On the other hand there were decisive political implications, which in the course of time would become steadily more critical.

The resolution of one much-disputed question, relating to the way in which the slave population of the separate states could be counted for the purpose of allocating seats in the House of Representatives, is described in chapter 1. Then, although the provision for three-fifths of the slave population of any state to count in determining its representation in the House of Representatives substantially increased the power of the southern states in Congress, this was not sufficient to give them a majority. This was all the more reason, therefore, for the south to do everything possible to extend slavery to any new state admitted to the Union.

Following the grant of statehood to Alabama in 1818, the US Senate had forty-four members, equally divided between north and south, while the House of Representatives had 186, of whom eighty came from southern states. Although sectionalism in the United States went back to colonial times, the main conflict of interests was then between New England and the south, with New York, New Jersey, and Pennsylvania largely uncommitted. At the same time, the US Constitution, as finally adopted in 1789, resolved definitively a number of disputed questions, such as the conflicts of interest between small and large states, and those with and those without western lands.[2] Other disputed matters, such as negotiating with Spain navigation rights on the Mississippi River, did however lead to the three middle states siding with New England, but nonetheless proved to be unimportant over the course of time—in this particular case simply as a result of Spain's loss of Florida to the United States (as related in chapter 4). Even so, when it came to slavery—the one matter which, more than any other, threatened to be decisive—there was considerable reluctance in the northern states to take a stand on an issue which, in principle, should be left to the individual states. This left the way open for one northern state after another to ban slavery in the years after 1789, so that by 1804 every single one of them had taken some steps toward achieving this result,[3] with three New England states going the whole way.

THE BALANCE OF POWER

Somewhat paradoxically, as the emancipation of slaves gained ground in the north, the balance of power in the nation at large shifted in favor of the south. In the years up to 1800 power rested with eastern Federalists, whose mind cast was conservative, and interests, commercial and industrial. This reflected their power base in New England, so that the Virginian, Thomas Jefferson, was able to complain that "we are completely under the saddle of Massachusetts and Connecticut, and ... they ride us very hard."[4] Jefferson's answer was to establish a new broad-based Democratic Party, representing "southern planters, Western frontiersmen and Eastern farmers and mechanics," and with its support he was elected president in 1800, in succession to the Massachusetts Federalist John Adams. When Jefferson was inaugurated in 1801, he became the first of three patrician presidents from Virginia—being followed by James

Madison (1809–1817) and James Monroe (1817–1825); during the twenty-four years the Virginians were in office the strength of the Democratic Party—with southern members also occupying key positions in Congress—was sufficient to maintain the southern ascendancy. Given that Jefferson, in 1800, was elected with only a majority of nine electoral votes, without the benefit of the three-fifths rule he would have been defeated. As John Quincy Adams (who would succeed Monroe as president in 1825) noted in 1804, "slave representation . . . will forever be thrown into the Southern scale, and must forever make ours kick the beam."[5] Ironically, as another commentator noted in 1812, "the negroes turned the majority and actually put in the President."[6]

The Federalists, who had a majority in both houses in the Sixth Congress (1799–1801), steadily lost ground in the first two decades of the nineteenth century; this was largely the result of losing touch with a population which was growing rapidly in areas, such as the new states created out of the Northwest Territory, where their party had never been strong. Their prospects in the Louisiana Territory were even less promising, but then, in the first quarter of the nineteenth century only the relatively small state of Louisiana was admitted to the Union—inevitably as a slave state. The Federalists' half-hearted support for the War of 1812 (as described in chapter 3), and their reluctance to abandon the property qualifications still required of voters in the states where they were strong, made it even more difficult to turn the tide in their favor—so much so that by 1819 Massachusetts was the only state they still controlled.

Although the steady loss of ground by the Federalists to the Democratic Party did not of itself reflect either popular support for, or opposition to the extension of slavery—the majority of northern residents being content to mend their own fences[7]—it did, for a minority, present an opportunity to take a stand on a matter of principle, which could also earn political capital. The first sign of opposition to the admission of Missouri as a slave state came on April 4, 1818—a day after a committee of the House of Representatives had reported an enabling act—when Arthur Livermore, a New Hampshire Democrat, proposed a constitutional amendment prohibiting slavery in any states that thereafter might be admitted to the Union.[8] This was essentially preemptive, since nothing was said about slavery in the petitions for statehood submitted from Missouri. The general assumption, however, was that slavery would be permitted; before its purchase by the United States in 1803 there had never been restrictions on slavery in the Louisiana Territory—of which Missouri was a part—and many of the new American settlers had brought slaves with them.

There was something of a diversion later in 1818, when John Tallmadge Jr., from New York, opposed the admission of Illinois as the twenty-first state—where the Northwest Ordinance had previously ruled out slavery—on the grounds that its constitution did not "sufficiently" prohibit it. Even though

Tallmadge never stood a chance, when it came to a vote he was supported by thirty-three other congressmen. Illinois was admitted to the Union as a free state before the end of the year, by which time also, the Speaker of the House—Henry Clay from Kentucky—presented a memorial from the people of Missouri asking permission to adopt a constitution and form a state government. At much the same time—December 1818—delegates from anti-slavery societies in New York, Pennsylvania, and Delaware, meeting in a convention in Philadelphia, appointed a committee to prepare a memorial to Congress, to be signed by American citizens, requesting that "slavery be prohibited in all territories established in the future as well as in any states erected from such territories."[9]

The question, as it affected Missouri, came to a head in February and March 1819—during the final session of the Fifteenth Congress—when a committee of the whole House considered bills enabling the people of both Alabama and Missouri to form state governments. Tallmadge, moving once more to prevent the extension of slavery, presented an amendment which would exclude—in categorical terms—this possibility in Missouri. By doing so he precipitated, more than anyone else, the famous Missouri Controversy.

Although Tallmadge, in presenting his case in Congress, stressed the moral objections to slavery, he also conceded that he had political reasons for opposing it in Missouri. These went back to the three-fifths provision mentioned above, which, if applied to Missouri, would eventually add to the number of its representatives in the US Congress. These, coming from a slave state, could then be counted upon to support the south. This argument was somewhat flawed as a result of the fact that the American slave population showed little sign of increase, so that, for instance, the 10,000 slaves already in Missouri were lost to the states from which their owners had brought them. Tallmadge, however, claimed that 14,000 slaves had been smuggled into the country in 1818—a number likely to increase as slavery extended further west.[10] He also pointed out that the three-fifths clause in the constitution had been conceded as "a compromise and benefit to the Southern States which had borne part of the Revolution"[11]—an argument unlikely to impress anyone from these states. From a historical perspective, the south was clearly intent on remaining as powerful as it had been when the constitution was adopted at the end of the 1780s.

To many in the north the conservative southern position was quite unacceptable for political as much as for moral reasons. As related in chapter 6, for some twenty years the plantation economy of the south had continually expanded to meet the increasing demand, mainly from England, for cotton, while, at the same time in Washington—under three successive Democratic presidents from Virginia—the south had a near monopoly of high government offices.[12]

By 1819, a year of crisis for northern industry, this had become intolerable for many northern Democrats. In Congress southern Democrats had consistently blocked the introduction of protective tariffs, being content, in the words of one newspaper,[13] to "uphold this pernicious system [of dependence on foreign manufactures]," while according to another the north was "a prey to English cupidity and Southern *plantation* avarice".

The north was also hurt by the position taken first by President James Madison (1809–1817), and then by his successor, James Monroe (1817–1825), that the Constitution did not allow for roads and canals—the so-called "internal improvements"—to be constructed at federal expense.[14] Although the original bill providing for federal funding was proposed by Senator John C. Calhoun of South Carolina, New York was hit hardest by the presidential veto. The state would have to complete the Erie Canal—its major public works project, and one which would transform the communications infrastructure of the whole nation—without outside aid.

In New York, where the dynamic governor, DeWitt Clinton, had long been the driving force behind the Erie Canal, Judge Matthias Tallmadge accused the Monroe administration of being "decidedly opposed to the Repbn. Prosperity of N.Y.," with his brother in Congress complaining to President Monroe in similar terms. The Clintonians split the Democratic Party in the north: allied with the small number of Federalists—and with just sufficient support from Ohio, Indiana, and Illinois, the states created from the old Northwest Territory—they succeeded in carrying the Tallmadge amendment in the House of Representatives. This success owed everything to the strength of feeling in the north for restoring the balance of power with the south, which had steadily been eroded ever since Thomas Jefferson became president in 1801.

In the Senate the vote to strike out the two clauses of the Tallmadge amendment to the Missouri bill was certain to be carried. Although there were in 1819 eleven free states and eleven slave states, reflecting a balance between north and south, the two senators from Illinois—both slave owners—voted with the south to strike out both clauses, as did a handful of other northern senators; the south, on the other hand, was solid, with not a single senator voting to retain either clause of the amendment.

The impasse was unlikely to be resolved by the Fifteenth Congress, whose final session was due to end in March 1819. Even so, in the short time available, one related question—that relating to the status of the Arkansas Territory—was resolved. South of Missouri, on the west bank of the Mississippi, the geographical case for allowing slavery in Arkansas was very strong. The economy of the two states on the opposite side of river, Tennessee and Mississippi, was based on plantations employing slave labor, with Memphis, Tennessee, as the hub of the river traffic in cotton bales. With most of the new settlers in Arkansas coming from across the river, its economy was bound to be an extension of cotton planting. This was accepted in the final days of the Fifteenth Congress, although on one key vote the Speaker of the House had to break a tie by voting in favor of slavery. The debate showed that for many congressmen geographical latitude was the deciding factor governing the question of slavery, whether it related to Arkansas or Missouri. Where in Arkansas, at the same latitude as Mississippi and Tennessee, slavery should be allowed, in Missouri, whose latitude was that of Illinois, Indiana, and Ohio, it should be banned. On this basis the question relating to Arkansas was resolved by the Fifteenth Congress, so one problem was out of the way. This result was achieved by the Massachusetts Federalist Ezekiel Williams casting the deciding vote. As to Missouri, he voted the other way, arguing that otherwise Congress would put an end to the established pattern of dividing the west equitably between slaveholding and free states.[15] (This assumed the eventual admission of Arkansas following that of Missouri, which only took place some seventeen years later, in 1836.) The result, as almost everyone had expected, was that Missouri's future was still undecided when the Fifteenth Congress finally adjourned in March 1819.

THE POLITICAL GEOGRAPHY OF MISSOURI

It is time to take a closer look at the territory of Missouri, as it was in the critical two-year period, 1819–1821, ending up with statehood. The Missouri River, with its source in the Rocky Mountains, flowed into the Mississippi just north of St. Louis. As a result of the steadily increasing steamboat traffic on the two rivers, the city, originally founded by French settlers, was on the way to becoming one of the largest in the United States. It was not for nothing that it became known as the gateway to the west, with the Missouri River, as it crossed the state, providing, for many pioneer settlers, the first stage of the journey overland to the far west. Almost as important for Missouri was the fact that the Ohio, flowing in from the east, joined the Mississippi at Cairo, Illinois, nearly 200 miles south of St. Louis, but on the other side of the river. The fact that Cairo was so far south meant that for most of Missouri's shore on the Mississippi, there were—at least in principle—no slaves to be found on the other side of the river. In practice that part of southern Illinois between the Ohio and the Mississippi, known as Egypt and with Cairo as its main township, had much of the character of Kentucky and Tennessee—both slave states. In 1819, this was also much the most populous part of the Illinois.

American settlement of Missouri, having started along the west bank of the Mississippi, then proceeded up the Missouri. Since much of the land along the two rivers was suitable for intensive agriculture—including in the early nineteenth century the cultivation of cotton—the necessity for slave labor was taken for granted, even by those who did not employ it.

Missouri never developed the plantation culture characteristic of the deep south. In 1820 the culture was that of the American frontier—so much so that according to a letter from one contemporary observer,[16] the population "live somewhat in the stile [sic] of savages, on venison and bare meat, in little smoky huts exposed to the changes of climate, and the inclemency of the weather." As in the whole frontier area, on either side of the Mississippi, settlers had to accept extremes of temperature, both drought and floods, violent storms and even the occasional earthquake. Subject to these hazards, almost the whole territory was well-suited for settlement, with abundant woodland, terrain that could be cleared for cultivation, and ready access to waterways that sooner or later reached the Mississippi.

Missouri was at the center of the American frontier. To the east it touched Kentucky, which had become a state in 1792, and to the west, Oklahoma, which, after being set aside as territory reserved for Indians, only became a state in 1907. The greater part of its western frontier was, however, with the Kansas-Nebraska territory, whose destiny—as related in chapter 11—became critical for the survival of the Union. In 1819, however, the population of Missouri had no doubts about where it stood: one meeting after another affirmed the principle that the abolition of slavery would be "equally contrary to the right of the state and to the welfare of the slaves themselves."[17] In the words of one toast drunk at a Fourth of July celebration, "the Territory of Missouri—with a population of near 100,000 souls—demands its right to be admitted to the union on an equal footing with the original states." The state of Missouri was plainly intent on making its own decision on the question of slavery.

This was then the local background in Missouri when the House of Representatives in, the final days of the Fifteenth Congress, considered the Tallmadge amendment. By this time it was clear from the election results at the end of 1818 that the House—during the Sixteenth Congress—would be no more favorable to admitting Missouri as a slave state. Tallmadge would no longer be a member, but others would take over his cause. In its first session this was John W. Taylor—a Clintonian Democrat from New York—but after he was elected Speaker of the House at the beginning of the second session, John Sergeant, a Pennsylvania Federalist, took over as leader of the antislavery party. Significantly this included Daniel Cook—an outspoken opponent of slavery—who had won Illinois' only congressional district after a campaign in which the future of Missouri was a key issue. Although there was little chance of the position already taken by the House changing during the Sixteenth Congress, there was no prospect of the Senate accepting it. Nonetheless, it was generally agreed that the Missouri question would have to be resolved by the

Sixteenth Congress, which convened for the first time in December 1819. The result was a congressional poker game, with players from the south opposed to those from north, with the strong cards held by the former in the Senate, and by the latter in the House of Representatives.

The first round was played by a House committee appointed by Henry Clay in his last session as Speaker, and chaired by John Taylor. In the final days of December 1819 this produced two possible compromises. By the first the existing ownership of slaves already in Missouri, together with that of their descendants, would be guaranteed, while the further introduction of slavery in all the territory west of the Mississippi River should be prohibited. The second compromise required the Missouri River, perhaps extended by the Kansas River, to become a boundary between slave and free territory west of the Mississippi—a result which would split the state of Missouri in two, with the north banning slavery and the south permitting it. With the committee unable to agree to either compromise, it was discharged at its own request on December 28.

The second round turned on the admission of Maine as the twenty-third state of the Union. Maine had always belonged to Massachusetts but the short Atlantic coastline of New Hampshire separated the two geographically. When the people of Maine found this a good reason for becoming a separate state, the state legislature of Massachusetts, by an act of June 19, 1819, consented, but only on the condition that Maine be admitted to the Union before March 4, 1820. It was never contested that Maine, like Massachusetts itself, would be a free state.

On December 8, 1819, Representative John Holmes of Massachusetts (whose distinct was actually in Maine) presented to the House a petition for the grant of statehood, and the House in turn passed the enabling bill on January 3, 1820. In the Senate the judiciary committee suggested an amendment enabling Missouri to form "a constitution and state government without slavery restriction."[18] As Henry Clay had predicted while still Speaker of the House "Maine and Missouri were to be connected and the admission of the one made dependent on the unconditional admission of the other." After a motion to strike out the amendment was rejected, a proposed antislavery proviso to it had even less success. Illinois Democratic Senator Jesse B. Thomas, who consistently supported the south, then proposed, as an alternative, a proviso prohibiting slavery in the unorganized Louisiana Purchase north of 36°30" north—the latitude contemplated for Missouri's *southern* boundary.[19] Disregarding this proposal, the Senate, on February 16, voted to accept the report of the judiciary committee uniting the Maine and Missouri bills in one containing no mention of slavery. The margin was close, with twenty-three (including both Illinois senators) for and twenty-one (including both Delaware senators) against acceptance; it was only the vote for acceptance of a single northern senator, the Democrat Waller Taylor of Indiana, that prevented a tie.[20]

Senator Thomas then moved to attach his proviso relating to the unorganized Louisiana Purchase as an amendment to the new bill, hoping that by doing so it would become acceptable to the House of Representatives. The amendment read:

> *And be it further enacted* That, in all that territory ceded by France to the United States, under the name of Louisiana, which lies north of thirty-six degrees and thirty minutes north latitude, excepting only such part thereof as is included within the limits of the State contemplated by this Act, slavery and involuntary servitude, otherwise than in the punishment of crimes whereof the party shall be duly convicted, shall be and is hereby forever prohibited: *Provided, always,* That any person escaping into the same for whom labor or service is lawfully claimed in any State or Territory of the United States, such fugitive may be lawfully reclaimed and conveyed to the person claiming his or her labor or service as aforesaid.

On February 23, 1820, the House of Representatives rejected all the Senate's amendments, with the largest majority—of 141—against Thomas' compromise. Instead, with a much smaller margin, it voted in favor of its own Missouri bill, including an antislavery amendment introduced by John Taylor. The Senate then sent its Maine bill to the House, together with non-restrictive amendments relating to Missouri; these too were rejected by the House. The future of Missouri was debated furiously by both House and Senate, with women and negros crowding the galleries. Speaker Henry Clay noted how "the Missouri subject monopolizes all our conversation, all our thoughts and for three weeks at least to come all our time. No body seems to think or care about anything else."[21] Clay also noted how the words "civil war" and "disunion" were uttered almost without emotion.[22] Foreshadowing the war that would come some forty years later, Georgia Senator Freeman Walker envisaged "intestine feuds, civil wars . . . the father armed against the son, and the son against the father . . . a brother's sword crimsoned with a brother's blood . . . our houses wrapt [*sic*] in flames, and our wives and infant children driven from their homes."[23] Walker was not alone: one senator after another—particularly if from a southern state—contemplated bloodshed, and in general the south produced the more eloquent orators.

HENRY CLAY'S COMPROMISES

In the end the crisis was resolved by Speaker Henry Clay, piloting three compromises through the House in 1820–1821. These were contained in the report of a joint conference committee, convened as a result of a Senate initiative with a view to finding a common agreement regarding Maine and Missouri. The report, presented to the House by John Holmes on March 2, recommended: (1) that the Senate withdraw its amendments to the Maine bill, (2) that both houses strike out the slavery restriction clause from the House Missouri bill, and (3) that they add to the latter bill a provision forever excluding slavery from that part of the Louisiana Purchase lying north of 36°30" which was not included within the limits of the new state of Missouri.[24] This was the Thomas compromise, which was essentially—as Horace Greeley wrote in 1860—an offer from the south on this basis: "Let us have Slavery in Missouri, and we will unite with you in excluding it from all the uninhabited territories North and West of that State."[25]

The House considered first the second recommendation, with New Jersey Representative Charles Kinsey, who had earlier voted for restriction, pleading that rejection, as a result of a majority of northern votes, would be "a victory snatched from our brothers . . . an inglorious triumph, gained at the hazard of the Union."[26] With a majority of only three, the House, on March 2, 1820, voted for the recommendation—a result only made possible by fourteen northerners doing so, and the absence of another four. This was followed by a vote of 134 to forty-two in favor of the third recommendation—which contained the essence of the Thomas compromise—with, in this case, thirty-seven southerners voting against. The next day, March 3, the Senate withdrew its amendments to the Maine bill, so that a House vote on the first recommendation was unnecessary. An act of the same day admitted Maine to the Union, and another, on March 6, authorized the people of Missouri to form a constitution and state government without a slavery restriction, while at the same time slavery was prohibited forever outside Missouri according to the geographical terms of the Thomas amendment. The first essential step in establishing what is known to history as "the Missouri Compromise" was complete.

The votes recorded show how, with solid southern support, the act of March 6 passed by a large majority in the Senate, but only by a small majority in the House of Representatives. In neither house was there a northern majority in favor of the compromise. The vote in favor of the act by fourteen northern representatives led to them being referred to as "dough-faces," a term coined by the Virginia Democrat John Randolph—who, it is said, only meant it to refer to the four absentees.[27] In the north the term caught on, and was used to refer not only to all eighteen, but also in the years that followed to any northern supporters of the southern cause, particularly as it related to slavery. The motives of the original doughfaces, whom many in the North denounced as traitors, have been endless analyzed. One common accusation was that they had sold their votes in exchange for patronage from the Monroe Administration, but the historical record is significant for showing how little the president allowed himself to be involved in the whole Missouri controversy.[28]

Although the congressional votes in March 1820 were sufficient to admit Maine to the Union, the admission of Missouri required first a state constitution and a form of government acceptable to the US Congress. The provision in the compromise of March 3 that "the said State, when formed shall be admitted into the Union, upon an equal footing with the original States, in all respects whatsoever," provided that its constitution was "republican and not repugnant to the federal Constitution," justified the assumption that there would be no problem about the US Congress accepting from Missouri a constitution which sanctioned slavery. On the other hand, the fact that there was as yet no such constitution left the way open to northerners opposed to the compromise to fight against the admission of Missouri as a slave state. They would also have the advantage of a stronger presence in the US Congress, the more so with Maine's two seats in the Senate.

Given that the compromise had been established as a result of an act of Congress passed only with doughface support, those in the north who had consistently opposed it had every moral claim—at least according to their own assessment—to fight for its repeal, and they did not hesitate to do so. As in 1819, there was considerable press support for the campaign against slavery in Missouri, and its cause was greatly strengthened when a convention held in Missouri in the summer on 1820 agreed to a constitution with two particularly obnoxious clauses. The first of these made it illegal for free negroes and mulattoes to enter the state, and the second forbade the legislature to emancipate slaves without the consent of their owners.

The Missouri convention adjourned in July 20, while the second session of the Sixteenth Congress would only open on November 13. In the meantime the campaign against the admission of Missouri gathered strength. Those who supported it were greatly encouraged by the election of John Taylor, their champion in the House of Representatives, as its new Speaker. Although this was only on the twenty-second ballot, a fellow New York congressman, Solomon Van Rensselaer, could still write to his wife that "we have received one great victory in the choice of Speaker, which like the Allies over Bonaparte, has given our ranks confidence; and I hope and believe we will put down the *Missouri Constitution*."[29] Southerners in Congress were dejected, and as one of them—Alabama Senator John W. Walker—noted, "the glory is departed."

Taylor proved to be an impartial Speaker, even to the point of appointing pro-southern majorities to key committees. At the end of November 1820, this meant that two out of three members of a select committee appointed to advise on the proposed Missouri constitution, supported the south; this may have been one reason why its favorable advice was rejected by ninety-three votes to seventy-nine, after a long debate in the House.[30] This was the start of a legislative process which was just as agonizing as that which preceded the first compromise in 1820. Once again it was Henry Clay, who had returned to the House as an ordinary member, who resolved the deadlock. By convening a select committee of thirty, with seven members from the Senate and twenty-three from the House—most of whom he had himself chosen—Clay was able to present a resolution for the second Missouri compromise to both Houses of Congress. Missouri would be admitted to the Union on condition that no law could be passed under its constitution to exclude "any citizen of any of the States in this Union ... from the enjoyment of any of the privileges and immunities to which such citizen is entitled under the Constitution of the United States." If then a constitution containing this "fundamental condition" were transmitted to the president of the United States before the fourth Monday of November 1821, he could by proclamation admit Missouri to the Union.

There was never any doubt about this compromise being accepted by the Senate: in the House of Representatives Clay noted that in the committee all the senators were unanimous in its favor, as were also almost all the members of the House. Persuaded by Clay, the House, by eighty-seven votes to eighty-one, passed the compromise on the same day—February 26, 1821—as he reported it from the committee. Two days later the Senate approved it by twenty-eight votes to fourteen. In June the Missouri legislature, with ill grace certain to anger the antislavery press, kept to the promise required by Congress. On August 10, President Monroe proclaimed the admission of Missouri as the twenty-fourth state of the Union.

Henry Clay's role, more than that of any other member of Congress, was decisive, and established him as one of the great figures in American political history. At a public dinner in his honor, Thomas Hart Benton, one of the two new senators from Missouri—who would long play a key role in American politics—described him as the "Pacificator of ten millions of Brothers," while in the opinion of a Pennsylvania congressman, "Henry Clay of Kentucky saved that which *George Washington* of Virginia won, the United Independence of America." In the years to come Clay never forfeited his reputation as a statesman; if anything it was enhanced.[31] When, as related in chapter 17 of *Huckleberry Finn*, the eponymous hero unexpectedly found himself a welcome guest in the Grangerford home in Kentucky, one of the books piled up on the table in his bedroom was "Henry Clay's Speeches." The incident would have taken place some time in the 1840s, when Clay—as a senator—still represented Kentucky in Congress.[32] The most notable of his younger contemporaries, however, was Abraham Lincoln who ranked him higher than any other American politician. In his eulogy, spoken on the death of Clay in 1852, Lincoln—almost alone of Clay's admirers—made clear that he "did not perceive, that on a question of human right, the negroes were to be excepted from the human race . . . he was, on principle and in feeling, opposed to slavery," but recognized that it could not be "at once eradicated, without producing a greater evil."[33] This was the key point upon which those northerners who voted in favor of the Missouri Compromise had allowed themselves to be persuaded by Clay.

THE VOICE OF THE PEOPLE

Except in Missouri itself, where the compromise determined the whole character of the state into the indefinite future, the conflicts leading up to it involved the members of Congress far more than those citizens, whether north or south, whom they represented. The endless debates meant that little effort was made to deal with the economic crisis of 1819–1821. As noted by the Philadelphia *Democratic Press*, "never was representation less representative of the sentiment at home than in this affair. The country is as free from the political fever with which Congress is inflamed, as it is from the deadly distemper prevailing among its members." Newspapers in other leading cities, such as Baltimore, Cincinnati, and Pittsburgh, reflected similar views.[34] There was harsh criticism of the long-winded speeches, as there was also, at least in the final days of the debate, in Congress itself.[35] Such solidarity of sentiment as there was in the north was largely due to the success of the pamphleteers. This fortunately was sufficiently short-lived so as not to jeopardize success of the compromise; otherwise, with the prospect of being consistently outvoted in Congress, the south could well have withdrawn from the Union—as it did, finally, some forty years later. Behind the critical support for the compromise among northern Democrats in Congress lay the conviction that the Federalists and the Clintonians were making political capital out of the Missouri crisis.[36] As noted by one of the most prominent mainstream northern Democrats, the New Yorker Martin Van Buren—who would later become president: "in the Missouri agitation . . . I could not conceal from myself the fact, to which all we saw and heard bore testimony, that its moving strings were rather political than philanthropic."[37]

That is certainly how things were seen in the south—where the impact of the economic crisis was equally severe. In 1819, there was hardly more concern about the future of Missouri than in the north. In 1820, Virginia, not only the most populous state in the Union but also one accustomed to be dominant in the south, saw its position threatened by the antislavery movement. Significantly none of its "aristocrats of liberal views"[38]—including three past and present presidents, Jefferson, Madison, and Monroe—who were in principle opposed to slavery, favored its restriction in Missouri. This is one aspect of the way in which the controversy, as played out in the US Congress, made the "solid south" even more so.

Finally it must be asked what the south and north expected to gain from the compromise in its final form. The extreme southern position is to be found in the words of South Carolina Representative Charles Pinckney contained in a letter published by a Charleston newspaper on March 10, 1820; this hailed the compromise as "a great triumph" for the south, since Missouri, Arkansas and the Floridas would give the southern interest in a short time an addition of six, and perhaps eight, Members in the Senate of the United States, and at the same time described the territory north of 36°30" north as "at present of no moment; it is a vast Tract, inhabited only by savages and wild beasts, in which not a foot of the Indian claim to soil is extinguished; and in which, according to the ideas prevalent here at present, no Land Office will be open for a great length of time". As the northern press did not hesitate to point out, even from the perspective of Charleston this painted a false picture of the free territories implicit in the terms of the compromise. In 1820, the truth of matter was that compared to Missouri, Arkansas, and the Floridas, the northern territories were little known, and certainly no one could accurately foresee how they would eventually be incorporated into the Union—a process that would not be complete until the end of the nineteenth century.

The answer, in 1820, was that only time could tell, and in the event, the Missouri Compromise lasted for thirty-three years. The admission of Missouri as the twenty-fourth state in 1821 left the balance of power divided twelve-twelve between south and north. In that year only Arkansas and Florida were south of the 36°30" North dividing line, with the former being part of the Louisiana Purchase and the latter being acquired from Spain as a result of the Adams-Onis Treaty described in chapter 4. At the same time a quite considerable part of the Northwest Territory, consisting of the future states of Michigan and Wisconsin, together with a part of Minnesota, had yet to be admitted to the Union. Little of this territory fitted the description in Pinckney's letter. There was also Iowa, due north of Missouri, with the Mississippi River as its eastern boundary. What no one foresaw in 1820 was that Texas would first become free of Mexico, and then ten years later, in 1845, join the Union—a process described in chapter 4.

This, in its way, was a happy accident for the continuance of the Missouri Compromise. As things happened, Arkansas was admitted as a state in 1836, and Michigan in 1838, so restoring the balance. Then, in 1845, first Texas, then Florida, were admitted to the Union, with the balance once again being restored by the admission of Iowa in 1846 and Wisconsin in 1848. So far, so good. As chapter 4, however, makes clear, the admission of Texas opened a real can of worms, with, first, war against Mexico, and then, after its defeat, a treaty by which the whole of its vast territory in the American west was ceded to the United States. With the almost inevitable admission of California as the thirty-first state of the Union, the balance, so carefully crafted by the Missouri Compromise, tipped irrevocably in favor of the north. This process continued with the admission of Minnesota in 1858 and Oregon in 1859, but by this time the Missouri Compromise had been repealed. Why this happened—in 1854—and the consequences that then followed, provide the subject matter for the last two chapters of this book. Here I need do no more than quote the final words of Glover Moore's classic study of the Missouri Compromise:[39] "its repeal . . . set in motion the chain of events which culminated in the Civil War and was easily the second greatest tragedy in American history, the greatest being the original introduction of slavery among a people who were, in other respects, democratically inclined."

Railroads

THE FIRST AMERICAN RAILROADS

American railroad development always depended upon the divergent economic interests of the separate states of the Union. Later in this chapter the focus will be on the special case of Illinois—where the planning and construction of the Illinois Central Railroad dominated state politics as much as any other issue during the years that Abraham Lincoln lived in the state capital, Springfield. First, however, it is useful to look briefly at the thirteen original states, each with its own port on the Atlantic seaboard, where geographical factors largely determined the extent to which this had a future as the hub of a railroad network. The key distinction was between harbors such as New York and Philadelphia, which were the gateway to long navigable rivers already well-served by steamboats at the beginning of the railroad age, and others, such as Boston, Baltimore, and Charleston, which lacked this advantage. Such cities, then, had every incentive to support the construction of railroads, to provide transport for their economic hinterland, whereas others, such as New York—based on the island of Manhattan at the mouth of the Hudson River (which was navigable at least as far as Albany, some 150 miles upstream)—had little immediate incentive to do so.

Baltimore, together with the Baltimore and Ohio Railroad (B&ORR), provide the right background for studying how the first American railroads developed. Inspired by the success of the early British railroads, the original directors of the B&ORR, who, having first organized the company in 1827, went on to adapt British technology (including the importation of British locomotives), soon found that established British standards were unnecessarily restrictive in the quite different topography of the hinterland of Baltimore.

First, and above all, was the matter of distance. That separating Baltimore from the Ohio River, the intended destination of the B&ORR, was hundreds of miles greater than the length of any railroad likely to be constructed in Britain. When, in 1832,[1] the B&ORR reached the Potomac River at Point of Rocks,

Maryland—completing the essential first stage on the way to the Ohio—the total length of its track already exceeded the combined mileage of the existing British railroads.

The directors of the B&ORR had no choice but to innovate, so that rails were laid on wooden ties—in preference to the British stone blocks—and railroad cars equipped with wheels with flanges on the inner edge fixed to rotating axles. It was realized, also, that the British insistence on slight gradients and curves would involve prohibitive costs in constructing any line across the Appalachians. The alternative was to build much more powerful locomotives: the local design, adopted by the B&ORR, had its weight evenly distributed over at least four driving wheels, with a swiveling front bogie to enable it to deal with the sharpest curves. The fact that British locomotives were much more economical with fuel counted for little: in contrast to Europe, the first American railroads—constructed at a time when coal-mining was little developed—followed the example of American steamboats and burned wood, which was just as abundant along their lines as it was along the rivers.

Boston, in the very early days of the 1830s, was in the forefront of railroad investment: by 1835 it was already a hub, with three different railroads, each with its own terminus. Of these, one, the Boston and Worcester Railroad, after linking up with the Western Railroad of Massachusetts, reached the Hudson River at Albany after crossing the Appalachians with what, in its day, was the highest railroad in the world. Although after its opening in 1841 this line operated at a profit, it was in the end a failure. This was in part the result of the intransigence of New York state, of which Albany was the capital. New York was against the line for two reasons: first, any extension to the west would not only threaten the profitability of the Erie Canal—but also in doing so would have to contend with the fallacy that steam could run uphill cheaper than water could run down—and second, in the American export market any eastbound traffic to Boston would be lost to the port of New York. If there were to be railroads in the state, and they were soon constructed, they would have served its interests and not those of Massachusetts. This was an attitude common throughout the United States. Even so, the first rail link between Albany and Buffalo, formed by the New York Central Railroad, only opened in 1853.

Charleston, in South Carolina—a state with few good navigable rivers—in attempting to provide a railroad infrastructure for the plantation agriculture inland, encountered much the same difficulties as Boston had. The best route inland needed to pass through Georgia, which was anxious to protect its steamboat traffic on the Savannah River. South Carolina was left to build its railroads over the Great Smoky Mountains. This was achieved with a deviant five-foot-gauge line whose maximum gradient of 4.8 percent was the steepest in the United States. Although this was within the powers of the newest locomotives, the inland terminal at Hamburg, on the Savannah River, had little share in the lucrative transport of cotton from the plantations that stretched west of the river as far as the Mississippi. Georgia, on the other side of the river, much preferred to ship cotton by steamboat downstream to its own seaport at Savannah.

The favorable economics of transport by water explains also why Georgia constructed the Western and Atlantic Railroad, north into Tennessee to a new terminus at Chattanooga on the Tennessee River, a navigable tributary of the Ohio. In Georgia this railroad started at a town appropriately called Terminus, where its link with the already existing Central Railroad of Georgia meant that the whole of the Upper Mississippi river system, from 1845 onward, was no longer dependant upon the Lower Mississippi for an outlet to the sea in the southern states. When Terminus became much most the most important railroad hub in Georgia, the name of the city was considered much too prosaic. It was changed therefore to Atlanta—recognizing the contribution of the Western and Atlantic Railroad to its prosperity. Atlanta became not only the largest railroad town in the United States, but also the capital of Georgia. Savannah, even with new railroad links to the heart of the United States, never attained the success of Boston, New York, Philadelphia and Baltimore. One reason for this—as already shown in chapter 6—was that cotton, which already dominated the southern economy at the beginning of the railroad age, was most advantageously cultivated on plantations with good access to navigable rivers, such as the Mobile in Alabama and the Mississippi. In contrast to the exploitation of agricultural land in the northern states west of the Appalachians, railroads had relatively little to offer to southern plantations.

This explains why at the end of the 1850s, of the six railroads crossing the Appalachians only one was in the south. Of the remaining five, four[2] were in the United States and one in Canada,[3] a situation reflecting the secular decline of the southern economy in relation to that of the northern states. This was reflected in a length of rail in the north several times that in the south—a factor that proved to be decisive in the Civil War.

Before the war there had also been considerable railroad construction west of the mountains, but—with one or two minor exceptions—east of the Mississippi. When it came to freight, the necessity for such development was somewhat doubtful in the light of the steamboat traffic on the Mississippi and its major tributaries, as described in chapter 2. On the other hand, railroads had already crossed the Appalachians to points on the Ohio where river cargoes could be transshipped for carriage to the east coast states and the Atlantic ports. This traffic was lost to the canals, rather than to the river, but it could only be a question of time before the railroads crossed the Ohio and went on to the Mississippi. The B&ORR was the first to reach this goal, at East St. Louis, Illinois, in 1857; in the next four years both the New York Central and the Pennsylvania Railroad reached Chicago, where the Chicago and Rock Island Railroad—with the first-ever bridge across the Mississippi opened in 1857—continued on to the great river itself. The 1850s, therefore, witnessed the start of the process by which Chicago would become America's most important railroad center.

RAILROADS IN ILLINOIS

The state of Illinois, for geographical reasons, was always certain to play a major part in American railroad history in the years leading up to the Civil War. The potential importance of Illinois to the American transport infrastructure—bounded in its northeast corner by Lake Michigan, to the west by the Mississippi, to the south by the river's most important tributary, the Ohio and to the east by the Wabash, a main tributary of the Ohio—was clear from the state's earliest days. A railroad system—designed mainly for carrying passengers rather than competing with the rivers for freight—that linked Cairo, in the extreme south of the state at the confluence of the Ohio and the Mississippi rivers, with Galena on the upper Mississippi and Chicago on Lake Michigan in the north, was seen as essential to economic development. The Illinois Central Railroad was chartered to construct it in 1851.

The Federal Land Grant Act of 1850 made possible a new solution to the problem of raising sufficient funds. If the federal government in Washington, which—as in most of the new midwestern states—was the largest landowner, could allow the proposed railroad to sell standard-size plots along its lines, then the money raised would pay for its construction; even better, those who bought and developed the plots would themselves generate new traffic, both passenger and freight. The Illinois Central thus became the first railroad to benefit from the land-grant system, which, after the end of the Civil War, would pay for the construction of new lines to the west coast. Illinois, however, could only get congressional approval if a southern state was offered something comparable. The result was the Mobile and Ohio Railroad, linking the port of Mobile on Alabama's gulf coast, with a point on the Ohio, opposite Cairo, Illinois, at the confluence of that river with the Mississippi. Although this established the first north-south rail link between the Great Lakes and the Gulf Coast, the line's success was limited. Other rail links between the Ohio River and the south, such as that of the Louisville and Nashville Railroad, profited more from trading cotton from the south and agricultural produce from the north—the essential economic rationale of all such links.[4]

The history of the Illinois Central's land grants again illustrates the way in which railroad construction was tied up with politics, at both national and

Illinois railroads in the 1850s

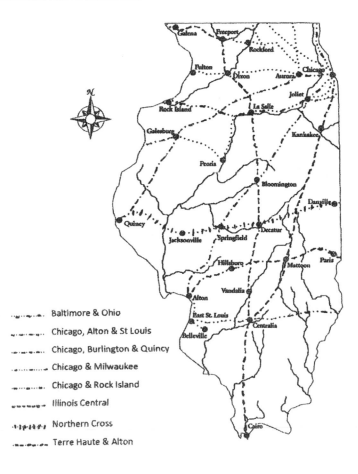

Illinois Railroads.

state levels. The state's involvement meant that in deciding upon the route of the railroad too much depended on its providing for communications within, rather than across Illinois. That this unduly favored the southern region, known as Little Egypt, with Cairo at its main town, was no coincidence. With representation in the state legislature always lagging behind demographic changes—inevitable when a census was only held every ten years—the "Old Settlers," defined as those who had arrived in the state before the Deep Snow of 1830–1831,[5] were disproportionately overrepresented. This explains why the main Illinois Central line led north from Cairo, their political stronghold, to divide at Centralia into a main branch leading to Galena, and a second branch to Chicago. By the late 1850s the need to provide services on two routes in the north of Illinois, where the wooded country of the south gave way to open prairie, led to a critical shortage of wood fuel for locomotives. This led to coal—widely distributed in the prairies—replacing wood, an example soon followed by other railroads.[6]

Much more than the Illinois Central, the other railroads in the state were free to respond to the geographical imperative, which was largely defined by out-of-state economic developments. While the Baltimore and Ohio Railroad constructed its lines due west across Illinois to its terminal at East St. Louis—crossing the north-south Illinois Central lines at Centralia—the other railroads radiated out from Chicago, which had become the terminal of three main lines from the east, the Michigan Central, the New York Central, and the Pennsylvania. These lines crossed Illinois to terminate in towns important for river traffic on the Upper Mississippi, with the Chicago, Alton, and St. Louis Railroad becoming, in 1853, the first to reach the river.

The result of all these developments was that by 1860, Illinois, with 2,799 miles of track, ranked second among all the states of the Union. What is more, Chicago, whose fortune was built on railroads, was already in 1850, with 30,000 residents, not only the largest city in Illinois, but also, with thirteen separate railroads planned to converge upon it, on its way to becoming the nation's leading railroad center. This, significantly, was also the year that California was admitted as the thirty-first state. In Illinois both businessmen and politicians knew only too well that the future of the state's railroads depended upon extending them westward across the continent to access the new wealth of the American west coast.

WEST OF THE MISSISSIPPI

If, during the 1850s, Illinois was the strongest contender in the railroad race to the west, other states were equally determined to enter the competition. The key question was where railroads would be built west of the Mississippi River, and the answer, inevitably, depended first upon what locations would be chosen for terminals on the Pacific Coast. This is turn would play a large part in determining the location where the lines would cross the river.

Although in the course of time—and long after Lincoln's day—lines would end at a number of terminals up and down the Pacific Coast, from Seattle to Los Angeles,[7] in the 1850s, the economic and political dominance of San

Francisco—as a result of the California gold rush—meant that the terminal indicated for any railroad from the east must be in the Bay Area. This was certainly how things looked in most of California, and this view, needless to say, was also that of eastern states, such as notably Illinois, which would profit from any line constructed. From the perspective of Chicago, a railroad to the west coast could cross the Mississippi at any number of locations—from north to south, Rock Island, Burlington (Iowa), Quincy and Alton—to which it was linked by new lines during the 1850s. On the other hand, for connections to the Atlantic states, the Baltimore and Ohio Railroad, with—after 1857—its terminal at East St. Louis, Illinois, had as strong a case as any of the lines from Chicago. This was supported by the state of Missouri, where St. Louis was set to become an important railroad center in the only state west of the Mississippi with, in 1850, advanced plans for a comprehensive railroad network—including a link to the west coast (see chapter 11). The claims of the state were presented, forcibly, by Thomas Hart Benton, who while representing it for thirty years (1821–1851) in the US Senate, had become well-known nationally for his support for settlement in the American west. The drawback to St. Louis was that it was too far south in relation to Chicago; what is more, the Chicago and Rock Island Railroad was ahead in actually constructing a bridge—completed in 1857—across the Mississippi. The problem for Missouri was that the state almost due west of Chicago, on the other side of the river at Rock Island, was Iowa.

While both Illinois and Missouri were busy with proposals for a railroad running due east from San Francisco, powerful representatives of southern interests were promoting alternative routes terminating either on the Gulf Coast or on the lower Mississippi. The most active was California Senator William Gwin, who before moving to the west coast had been a substantial Mississippi slave owner. In spite of California's wealth being concentrated in the north, Gwin—as related in chapter 9—worked hard to make the state an appendage of the American south. For this purpose a southern terminal for the prospective railroad linking California with the eastern states was essential. With this in mind Gwin proposed a resolution in the US Senate almost immediately after taking his seat in 1850. When this failed he submitted a much more comprehensive plan for a railroad, which, after leaving San Francisco, would pass round the southern end of the California Sierras, then to continue east to Albuquerque, New Mexico.[8] From Albuquerque there would be no less than four lines, leading respectively to St. Louis, Memphis, New Orleans and a Texas location on the Gulf Coast. This was successfully blocked by Michigan Senator Lewis Cass on the grounds of cost, which, whatever the route chosen for a railroad to the west, were certain to be very high.[9]

The reason was simple enough: any railroad, north or south, would have to cross hundreds of miles of mountain and desert before it reached the west coast. Even so, a northern route would probably cost less, if only because distances would be shorter. This never discouraged southerners from making their case in Congress, where, as was only to be expected from the party lineup in the two houses, they would face many obstacles. This became clear when Texas Senator Thomas Jefferson Rusk presented a cheaper, revised version of Gwin's bill, whose main interest for Rusk—as seen by northern senators—was that the new railroad would have a very long mileage in Texas. To counteract this possibility three senators, two from Illinois and one from Missouri, tabled an amendment prohibiting the use of any part of the proposed federal government appropriation of $20 million in an existing state.

This was a clever tactical move since southerners had long held that the US Constitution did not allow federal money to be spent within a state. The amendment then had sufficient southern support to pass by a single vote. The north then had the advantage, in the 1850s, that land beyond the western frontier of Missouri the Kansas-Nebraska Territory belonged to the federal government. This led Illinois Representative William Richardson to propose a bill to organize the territory—and so open the way for a railroad. Although in the House of Representatives the bill passed with a substantial majority, southern votes were sufficient to defeat it by twenty-three votes to seventeen in the Senate. Of the southern senators only the two from Missouri voted in favor.[10] The result was a stalemate.

Although Congress was not going to vote for any route, north or south, it did pass a bill authorizing Jefferson Davis, President Pierce's secretary of war, to survey possible routes for a railroad to the west coast. The rationale, conceived in the aftermath of the Mexican War, was that the railroad would be important for national defense. Davis entrusted the survey to a fellow southerner, William H. Emory, chief of the US Corps of Topographical Engineers, who had accompanied General Kearny during the invasion of California in 1846. Emory advised a southern route for the railroad along the Gila River, which, after flowing west across what is now Arizona, joins the Colorado River at a point just north of the Mexican frontier, with California's Imperial County on the other side. After wrongly stating that this would be the shortest route, Emory also claimed that it would avoid both the highest mountains and the winter snowfalls; the absence of any water across hundreds of miles of desert in New Mexico could be cured by sinking artesian wells.

There was, however, a political problem. According to the very recent Treaty of Guadalupe Hidalgo, the land south of the Gila River belonged to Mexico. Secretary Davis found another fellow southerner, James Gadsden, who was only too ready to help resolve this difficulty. Somewhat reluctantly President Pierce was persuaded to send Gadsden to Mexico City to negotiate the purchase of land. The Mexican president, General Santa Anna, agreed to sell some 45,000 square miles, but only because his treasury desperately needed the sum of $15 million offered by the United States. Even this was too much for the US Senate when the deal came up for the necessary two-thirds approval. Iowa Senator Caesar Dodge, furious at the prospect of losing a railroad across his state, linking Rock Island, Illinois, with Omaha, Nebraska, introduced a bill to organize the Nebraska territory. In the House of Representatives, Thomas Hart Benton (who had previously sat in the Senate) described the area to be bought from Mexico as "so utterly desolate ... and God-forsaken that Kit Carson says a wolf could not make his living in it."[11] (Today's residents of places like Tucson, Arizona, no doubt think otherwise.) In the end, after reducing the area purchased to 29,000 square miles and the agreed price to $10 million, together with a number of sweetheart deals offered to northern Democratic senators, the purchase was approved by thirty-three to twelve.[12] Jefferson Davis did not give up the fight, so this was not quite the end of the story—and he went on, as related in chapter 12—to become president of the Confederate States of America. With the Gadsden Purchase, which he orchestrated, the United States of America acquired some real estate but it was still far from getting a railroad to the west coast.

This is the end of the story of the first generation of American railroads, which ended with the Civil War. The railroad network, while comprehensive east of the Mississippi river—particularly in the northern states—hardly extended beyond it.

Finally, the war itself deserves more than a footnote in American railroad history. At the beginning of the war, in 1861, it was clear to the Union generals that when it came to rail transport they had an overwhelming logistical advantage. In 1860 the north had 21,978 miles of railroad, compared to 9,010 miles in the south.[13] The Illinois Central, in particular, played a pivotal role in funneling federal troops and supplies southward to open the Mississippi River to the Gulf. At the same time only nineteen out of 470 locomotives were built in the south, where the railroads, working with several different gauges, were much more disjointed. Then, as the war went on, both track and rolling stock had to be cannibalized by mainly unskilled labor to maintain a skeleton service.[14]

Although it was a Confederate general, Joseph E. Johnson, who first used railroads for tactical purposes, by moving 6,000 soldiers up to the front just before the first battle of Bull Run in 1861, the Union soon learned the lesson, and in the course of the war, US Military Railroads, a new special branch of the War Department, supervised the transformation of the northern lines into "an integrated, efficient, mostly double-tracked and fully standardized network."

Its command of civil engineering was also remarkable, making possible the construction, in forty hours, of a 400-foot-long bridge over the Potomac Creek to bring the railroad to Gettysburg in support of General Meade's army.[15]

The most remarkable incident in the railroad war was the Andrews raid, named after its leader, James J. Andrews, who conceived the underlying plan almost entirely on his own initiative.[16] The concept was born out of the way in which geography forced the war to be fought on two fronts, separated by the great chain of the Appalachian mountains. The war in the east was fought mainly in the southern state of Virginia, home to the Confederate capital, Richmond. The fact that its northern frontier, the Potomac River—with Maryland, and the federal capital, Washington, on the other side—was also the line between north and south, explains why so much of the war, at every stage, was fought there. In the west the field of battle was defined by the Lower Mississippi River, and the southern tributaries of the Ohio River, before it joined the Mississippi at Cairo, Illinois. Of these the most important was the Tennessee River, and on the river itself the most important town, strategically, was Chattanooga, in the southeastern corner of the state of Tennessee. The state was also the scene of many decisive battles, of which that fought at Shiloh—and won by Union forces commanded by General Ulysses S. Grant—was the greatest battle of the whole war.

Chattanooga, the "mountain city," although west of the Appalachians, was the key railroad junction in the supply line—absolutely essential to the Confederate armies—between Virginia and Georgia. The railroad line northeast from the city led to Virginia, following roughly the course of the Tennessee River, while that across the mountains to the southeast—which was much shorter—provided the link with Atlanta, Georgia, the hub of the Confederate railroad system. There were also lines leading north and west from Chattanooga, in the direction of the front line of battle—and for that reason essential to the Confederate supply chain.

By 1862, the second year of the war, the strategic importance of Chattanooga was clear to the Union forces in the west. When, therefore, James J. Andrews—a plausible character with a questionable past—presented a scheme for taking out the link between Chattanooga and Atlanta, which was operated by the Western and Atlantic Railroad, the generals listened to him. The scheme was simple enough: at a convenient station on the railroad somewhere north of Atlanta, Andrews, with a force of some twenty volunteers—including two or three locomotive engineers—would steal a train bound for Chattanooga. Then, as they proceeded north, they would cut the telegraph lines and destroy the track behind them.

The first part of the operation went more or less as planned. Andrews, who himself came from Kentucky, recruited his men, one of whom was English, from three Ohio regiments. Meeting together for the first time on Monday April 7, 1862, at Shelbyville, a Tennessee town just inside the Union lines some fifty-odd miles northwest of Chattanooga, the men, after a briefing from Andrews, split up into small groups to make their way on foot across the Confederate lines to Chattanooga. Appalling weather set them back, but even so all but two arrived in time to take a train—a day later than planned—to travel as ordinary passengers down the line to Atlanta. Their destination was Marietta, twenty miles short of the city, where they arrived to spend the night in a hotel on the evening of Friday, April 11.

Except for two who overslept, the men, as planned, all caught the first train back to Chattanooga—the one they planned to steal—on Saturday morning. They would travel as ordinary passengers to Big Shanty, eight miles north and the first scheduled stop down the line. There would then be far fewer people around to impede the operation, which proved to be the case. The engineer, the conductor, and almost all the passengers left the train to have breakfast at the station, allowing Andrews—with two of his men who were trained engineers—to leave on the opposite side, and uncouple the last three coaches, two of which were for passengers and one for mail. This left a train consisting of a locomotive named the *General*, its tender full of wood fuel, and three empty boxcars. At a signal from Andrews, the two engineers mounted the footplate, while the remaining men stepped out of the passenger coaches, walked a few yards down the track and boarded the boxcars. The line ahead was clear and the much-shortened train moved off without anyone around realizing what was happening. Such was the beginning of the "Great Locomotive Chase."

Although the distance between Big Shanty and Chattanooga was only 110 miles, a long and difficult day was ahead of the men who had stolen the *General*. They had above all to take into account trains coming in the other direction on a single-track railroad. Andrews, having acquired a timetable, knew in advance the stations where trains could pass each other on parallel tracks; in particular, he knew that he would have to wait at Kingston, thirty-one miles out of Big Shanty, for a southbound train. In 1862 running speeds were still very slow, so that the *General*—with a number of stops for minor adjustments to the engine, pulling up the track behind them and cutting telegraph wires—needed two and half hours to cover this distance. At Etowah, fifteen miles out of Big Shanty, they passed, for the first time, another locomotive, the *Yonah*, working a short branch line leading to local iron works. Unwisely the raiders left it alone.

The real troubles started at Kingston. For one thing Andrews had to explain to the station staff the arrival of an odd unscheduled train, with men on the footplate they had never seen before—the regular train crews were known all along the line. Andrews' story was that his train had been organized at short notice to bring urgent supplies to the front line beyond Chattanooga; this was just about credible, because the Union armies had in the previous days captured considerable Confederate territory in Alabama, not far to the west of the Western and Atlantic line to Chattanooga. Although Andrews had gotten away with his story, he was dismayed to see that the scheduled southbound train, when it arrived at Kingston, had a red flag on the last carriage—indicating that a second, unscheduled train was following on behind it. But when the second train arrived, it too had a red flag, so Andrews had to wait for a third train. When he was finally able to proceed north from Kingston, he had been there for more than an hour. This was critical, because sooner or later the railroad men left behind in Big Shanty would organize a pursuit.

The theft of the *General* registered almost immediately to those left behind in Big Shanty. Impetuously, three railroad men, including the train's conductor, William Fuller, ran after it—a measure of desperation that in the end paid off. After two miles they encountered a maintenance and repair crew, with a hand car used for carrying material and equipment—and propelled along the track with poles. Fuller then appropriated this for continuing the chase at a somewhat higher speed, hoping to find the *Yonah* at Etowah. Luck was him, and with the *Yonah* he covered the sixteen miles to Kingston in as many minutes. Even at this breakneck speed he was still too late for the *General*. With the track through Kingston station blocked by the three trains from the north, Fuller had to switch to another locomotive, the *William R. Smith*, which was due to take a train down a branch line to the west of Kingston. This could only take Fuller three-miles-odd to a point where Andrews and his men had broken up the track. Once more there was nothing for it but to continue on foot; this was by no means hopeless, since Fuller knew that a southbound freight train was due to come down the line.

In the meantime, Andrews, with the *General*, had passed this train at Adairsville, some ten miles north of Kingston. Its engineer, with a locomotive called the *Texas*, talked to Andrews, and told him he should wait, along with the *Texas*, for a long overdue, southbound passenger train. Andrews, knowing better, persuaded the engineer of the *Texas* to continue his journey south, so unblocking the line north of Adairsville. Recklessly, Andrews chanced reaching the next station, Calhoun—some nine miles down the line—before the passenger had left it. Traveling at more than a mile a minute, with its whistle blowing almost continuously, the *General* was just in sight of the station as the passenger train was pulling out. The engineer of the latter prudently reversed it into the station, allowing the *General* to pass alongside it into a siding. Once again Andrews had to use his story to persuade the other engineer to continue on south, so that the *General* could leave to the north.

By this time Fuller, running north along the tracks, had met the *Texas* traveling south. Once the engineer heard from Fuller what was up, he willingly joined the chase. Running the *Texas* in reverse, he first shunted all the freight cars into a siding at Adairsville, and then, with only the tender, put on speed so as to catch up with the *General* as soon as possible. Passing the southbound passenger train at Calhoun, the engineer of the *Texas* caught sight of the *General* just as the raiders were preparing to set fire to the long wooden bridge over the Oostanaula River. With no time to do so, the only way open to them was to continue northward without delay. The only alternative for Andrews, with twenty armed men, was to stand his ground at the entrance to the bridge, and if necessary engage in battle with the railroad men on the *Texas*.

The decision not to do so was fatal, just as that taken earlier in the day not to disable the *Yonah*. First, once the *Texas* reached Dalton, some eighteen miles further down the line, it was finally possible to telegraph the news of the capture of the *General* to Chattanooga. This meant that a train was immediately sent up the line to confront the *General*. Second, the *General*, just beyond Ringgold, and only twenty miles short of Chattanooga, ran out of fuel. It had a loaded a cord of wood between Etowah and Kingston, but this would never get the train to Chattanooga. The end was inevitable. Andrews and his men had no choice but to abandon the train, leaving each one of them, on his own initiative, to make it back to the Union lines. Not one succeeded: the men, once captured, were tried and convicted as spies. Andrews and seven others were hanged. Eight of the remaining men, with their fate uncertain, ended up in prison in Atlanta, whence eight eventually escaped, all making it back to the north along a variety of routes. The few left in Atlanta were later freed as a result of an exchange of prisoners. On March 23, 1863, at a ceremony at the War Department in Washington, six of the raiders became the first recipients of the newly instituted Medal of Honor. They then walked the short distance to the White House, to be received by President Abraham Lincoln. Better still, they were all granted sixty days' leave to return to their homes in Ohio. It is appropriate to the theme of this chapter that they traveled by the Baltimore and Ohio Railroad, the earliest in the United States.

Far to the west, two of the best-known generals at the end of the war, William T. Sherman and Ulysses S. Grant both relied on railroads for transporting troops to Vicksburg and Atlanta, where they won decisive battles for the Union. Following his victory at Atlanta—achieved after advancing down the railroad from Chattanooga, which in 1862 had been the scene of the great locomotive chase—Sherman, by concentrating on the destruction of the remaining railroads in southern hands, had found the strategy that led to the Confederate General Robert E. Lee's final surrender at Appomattox in April 1865.[17]

Finally, the secession of eleven southern states made it possible for Congress to pass the Pacific Railroad Act of 1862, making possible the construction of the transcontinental railroad. The route chosen, which was the southernmost one possible within the free states,[18] led up the Platte River Valley from Omaha, which had been designated the eastern terminal of the railroad. This opened the way to Senator Dodge's railroad across Iowa, also allowing a link across Missouri to St. Louis in accordance with Thomas Hart Benton's plans for his home state. Construction did not begin until after the Civil War, so President Abraham Lincoln, who had long favored railroads, never saw the completion of a line which, in the days before the war, had been a major issue between north and south. In considering the causes of the Civil War the prospect of the transcontinental railroad must never be left out of account.

California Strikes Gold

THE ACQUISITION OF CALIFORNIA

The Treaty of Guadalupe Hidalgo of 1848, which contained the terms, dictated by Washington, on which the Mexican War—as related in chapter 4—was ended, extended the United States to the Pacific coast of California, far beyond the limits of the territory comprised in the Louisiana Purchase of 1803. To the north of the vast area of new land, some 529,017 square miles in extent, was the Oregon Territory,[1] whose southern boundary—as agreed between the United States and Britain in 1818[2]—was defined at latitude 42° north; this was also accepted by Mexico, before the treaty of 1848, as its northern boundary. The land lost to Mexico,[3] although mainly defined by the 1848 treaty, was—as related in chapter 8—extended by some 29,640 square miles following the Gadsden Purchase of 1853. This meant effectively that west of Texas the definitive frontier between Mexico and the United States—except for a short stretch of the Colorado River between Arizona and the Mexican state of Baja California—was defined by straight lines, running roughly east-west, as shown by the map on page 11.

California, with its long Pacific coastline, was—by the standards of the mid-nineteenth century—almost the only part of the land ceded by Mexico that offered any prospects to settlers. Although Spain had explored much of this land in the sixteenth century—as can be seen by a number of remarkable buildings such as the church of San Miguel in Santa Fe, New Mexico—very few Spaniards ever chose to settle there. The Catholic Church, set upon converting local Indian populations, established quite a number of missions—mainly in California[4]—and the Spanish military built a number of outposts to maintain some semblance of law and order. Mexico, after gaining independence in 1820, did little to develop its northern territories.[5] As related in chapter 4, Texas was lost in 1836 as a result of the overwhelming presence of settlers from the United States, but California was a quite different case. Whatever its appeal to prospective settlers, access from the United States in the 1840s was extremely problematic. Traveling overland, such Mexicans as were to be found in California had much better access to their own heartland—although the long journey from Mexico City was far from easy.

In spite of the formidable obstacles in the path of settlement, there was by this time some exploitation of California's natural resources by a mixed population of Mexicans, Americans, and Europeans. San Francisco (which American forces captured in 1846) had developed as a useful harbor, particularly for US whalers operating in the Pacific. The ships, coming mainly from the American east coast, had no alternative but to sail around Cape Horn, at the furthest extreme of South America, to reach the Pacific. If this was acceptable to hardened men whose vocation it was to exploit the resources of the ocean—even at the cost of being away from home for two years or more at a time—the long arduous sea journey severely discouraged prospective settlers to California. Panama—then known as New Granada, and a province of Colombia—provided an alternative route, but until the completion of a railroad in 1855 this involved an extremely arduous journey across the isthmus, with no certainty that a ship would be waiting at Panama City to provide transport to San Francisco.

There can be little doubt that with all difficulties involved in travel to California, Mexicans comprised much the greater part of its non-Indian population at the time it was ceded to the United States—and they numbered hardly more than 100,000. With the annexation of the land on which they lived, they became American citizens—provoking an Indiana congressman, William Wick, into stating that he did "not want any mixed races in our Union, nor men of any color except white, unless they be slaves."[6] Before the treaty of 1848 the largest American community in the land lost to Mexico was that established by Mormons in the Utah territory in the latter months of 1847, after persecution had finally driven them from their homes along the Mississippi River in January 1846. On the other hand, the Mormons, if the most numerous and best organized of the pioneers who settled this new land, were by no means alone, and for some years before their epic journey others had followed overland trails to the west, with some ending up in California. The best-known of these pioneers was a born adventurer, John C. Frémont, who was also the son-in-law of the Missouri senator, Thomas Hart Benton—for many years a well-known, and often controversial, figure in national politics.

Frémont played a key part in developing the Oregon Trail in the early 1840s,[7] and the reports of his travels, edited by his creative and well-connected wife, had immense influence on potential settlers of the American west. Among others, the Mormon leader Brigham Young was inspired by Frémont's description of the Great Salt Lake basin, where his community finally settled in the summer of 1848. Nonetheless, a close reading of every report from the western frontier made clear that the land beyond the prairies had little to offer but a desolation of mountains and desert.

In 1848, this led Daniel Webster to tell the US Senate (where he represented Massachusetts) that he could not "conceive of anything more ridiculous, absurd, and more affrontive to all sober judgment than the cry that we are profiting by the acquisition of New Mexico and California. I hold that they are not worth a dollar."[8]

THE GOLD RUSH

Although he could not have known it, the senator was already being overtaken by events. On January 24, 1848—nine days before the treaty of Guadalupe Hidalgo was signed—gold was discovered at the edge of an estate in the Sacramento Valley granted by the Mexican government to a plausible, but hard-working fugitive from justice, Johann Sutter. This was a vast property, intended for agriculture and named New Helvetia by Sutter out of loyalty to his native Switzerland. As in the Illinois prairies described in chapter 5—which were as flat as the Sacramento Valley—shortage of timber was a major problem for prospective settlers. Sutter solved it by exploiting woodland in the foothills of the Sierras some forty miles from his base at Sutter's Fort, where trees growing along the south fork of the American River would meet his needs, while at the same time the flow of water would provide sufficient power for a sawmill.

The contract to construct the mill was granted to a somewhat eccentric American immigrant, James Marshall, a carpenter from New Jersey; his labor force comprised some fifty Mormons who had come down from Utah to earn money fighting Mexicans, only to find that the war was over. For the tailrace essential to the mill, the Mormon laborers dug a shortcut in a bend of the river, and on the morning of January 24, Marshall, while supervising this operation, noticed a small pebble shining under the flow of water. While both Marshall and the Mormons thought this might just be gold, they were still skeptical. On the other hand, Jennie Wimmer, who cooked for them and had worked with gold miners in her native Georgia, knew how to test it for corrosion. Seeing how it withstood the test, Marshall rode forty miles through pouring rain to consult a very surprised Sutter.

After carrying out a range of tests listed in the *American Encyclopedia*, the two men became convinced that Jennie Wimmer was right. The following day they rode together back to the sawmill, where Sutter swore his laborers to secrecy. Inevitably the silence was broken—by Sutter himself, among others—so that by March San Francisco had heard about what had been discovered on the American River. By this time peace with Mexico had left the city (which had been in American hands since 1846) with a mixed band of soldiers and sailors waiting to return home, supported by civilians led by circumstance to this distant frontier. Prominent in this small community was a dynamic entrepreneur, Sam Brannan, who, as a leader among east coast Mormons, had saved some 250 men, women, and children from the fate suffered by Joseph Smith and his Mormon community in Illinois, by bringing them by sea to San Francisco.

Materially Brannan was well-equipped to establish a new community, although he was somewhat dismayed to find the US flag flying over San Francisco when he arrived there on July 31, 1846. Nonetheless, having brought with him a printing press, the parts needed to set up both a sawmill and a flour mill, and tools of every sort, he lost little time in building up a business empire. This included the *California Star*, a newspaper published in San Francisco and—close to Sacramento—a general store outside the walls of Sutter's Fort. All this meant that Brannan was not only one of the first to learn about the claim to discover gold, but also was able to determine the way the news was presented to the public.

To begin with—in March and April 1848—Brannan played down the story. At the same time, as a deputy to the Mormon leader, Brigham Young, he visited the Mormon laborers working on the American River sawmill to collect tithes. The money collected never reached Young in Salt Lake City. Instead Brannan—who had never intended otherwise—used it for his own purposes. He opened a local store near the sawmill, stocked his store in Sacramento with everything an independent gold miner might need, built a hotel there and negotiated exclusive rights to steamboat landings on the Sacramento River. It must have been a busy time.

After two months spent inland Brannan returned to San Francisco with a bottle of gold dust, and there, at the corner of Portsmouth Square, he presented it to the public, shouting out, "Gold! Gold! Gold from the American River!"[9]—orchestrating an event which, needless to say, was well publicized in the *California Star*. In a world in which the most rapid means of transmitting news was by the pony express overland and the sailing ship by sea it could hardly be said that that proclaimed by Brannan spread like wildfire: none the less once men heard it they lost little time in acting upon it. By the end of May, soldiers—some recently discharged at the end of the Mexican War and others deserting their units—together with crews of both warships and merchant-men in the harbor, Mormons brought to California by Brannan, and almost anyone else who was free to go, abandoned San Francisco and Sacramento for the American River. Government (including law enforcement) and business came to a standstill; even the *California Star* had to stop publishing, but by this time it had served its purpose and its owner was well on the way to becoming a very rich man.

The gold rush was not confined to California. Ships leaving San Francisco brought the news to Acapulco, Honolulu, Canton, Sydney, Callao, and Valparaiso, and from every one of these ports ships were chartered to bring prospectors to San Francisco. Inevitably California acquired a population of remarkable ethnic diversity: some, such as hundreds of Chinese from Canton, had deliberately been fed false hopes, and indeed, at the end of the day, the prospects for most new immigrants were not fulfilled. Experience soon taught that serving and supplying the miners was a far better business than joining their company: this, after all, was the lesson taught by Brannon.

The discovery of gold in California made little impact in Washington and the east coast until the end of 1848. The first to bring the news was Kit Carson, already famous as a result of the publicity given to his exploits by John C. Frémont, whose life he had once saved. Leaving San Francisco at the beginning of May, to travel overland to Washington, he arrived there on August 2 with a copy of the *California Star* reporting how Brannan had broken the news in San Francisco. Carson's feat made more impact than the news he brought with him. Washington's apparent lack of interest in gold from California was confirmed on September 18, when a US Navy lieutenant, who had also traveled overland, presented an official report, together with some real gold, to the Navy Department. This led to an interview at the White House, but President James Polk—who had played a key role in acquiring California for the nation—refused to believe the report.

Where the navy failed, the army at last succeeded. A young lieutenant, William Tecumseh Sherman, persuaded California's acting military governor, Colonel Richard Mason, to visit the diggings. Once in the Sierras they not only met both Sutter and Brannon but could see, with their own eyes, how the miners were finding gold. Sherman's report, valuing gold at $16 an ounce, predicted that the new find would pay "the cost of the war with Mexico a hundred times over."[10] An army lieutenant, traveling via Panama, brought this to Washington, together with a tea caddy containing over 200 ounces of gold, but a second messenger, dispatched, like the first, by Mason, but traveling via Mexico, arrived earlier, on November 22.

By this time President Polk was ready to be persuaded, but for reasons that were largely political. In spite of the American victory sealed by the treaty of Guadalupe Hidalgo, the Democratic president—confronted by opponents of the Mexican War such as Daniel Webster and the young Illinois representative, Abraham Lincoln—got little credit for it. All the glory went to the victorious generals: these were all Whigs, and one of them, General Zachary Taylor, had won the presidential election on November 7. With the discovery of gold in California, President Polk, in his last annual message to Congress on December 5, could claim that the war had been worthwhile; in his own words, "the abundance of gold . . . would add more to the strength and wealth of the nation" than any previous acquisition.[11] Two days later the tea caddy finally reached Washington, to be put on display at the War Department. If all this came too late to save the Democratic presidential candidate, Lewis Cass, from defeat by Zachary Taylor, Washington was at last coming to terms with events on the other side of the country which would radically transform the political scene.

The rest of the country was already on the move, and in 1849 the stream of immigrants from the east into California became a flood. In addition to some 40,000-odd who came by sea—most taking the long route round Cape Horn—almost as many came overland, with some 30,000 following the Oregon Trail from its starting points at St. Joseph on the Missouri River. Among these were a number from Illinois' Seventh Congressional District, as Abraham Lincoln was to discover on returning to Springfield after his single term in Washington.[12] Not for nothing did St. Louis—a city close to Springfield, located at the point where the Missouri joins the Mississippi—become the "gateway to the west." Lincoln's interest in California, once aroused, continued through the rest of his political career, both in Springfield and Washington.

CALIFORNIA AND SLAVERY

With so many of California's immigrants single men, each intent on making his own fortune panning for gold, there was little need for the large-scale organization of labor. The spirit of individual enterprise was hostile to it. Prospects, therefore, for its most distinctive form, that of negro slavery as developed in the plantations—mainly of cotton—in the southern states, were not promising in California. At the same time, with its vast increase in population following the discovery of gold, California's claims to admission as a new state of the Union could not be denied. Critically, in 1849, there was an exact balance, fifteen to fifteen, between "free" and "slave" states.[13] The place of California, on one side of the other, was bound to be contested. On which side would California, as the thirty-first state, come down?

On the face of it, there was little doubt as to how this question would be answered: California was not destined for slavery.[14] For one thing, far more immigrants came from northern than from southern states. At the same time Mexican law, which had abolished slavery in 1829,[15] could still be claimed to rule in the land ceded by the treaty of Guadalupe Hidalgo. This, however, was not how southern politicians regarded the question.

In ensuring that a way was left open to slavery, southern senators had scored a decisive victory in the US Congress in 1847, when, with the essential support of

1. Andrew Jackson: LC-USZ62-50467 *Library of Congress, Prints & Photographs Division*

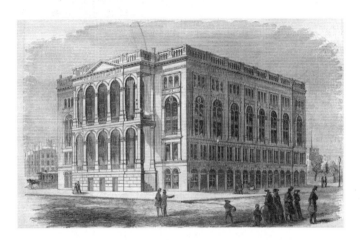

2. Cooper Union New York: LC-USZ62-132139 *Library of Congress, Prints & Photographs Division, NYWT&S Collection*

3. Daniel Webster: LC-USZ62-5128 *Library of Congress, Prints & Photographs Division*

4. David Broderick: LC-DIG-cwpbh-02515 *Library of Congress, Prints & Photographs Division*

5. Henry Clay: LC-DIG-pga-03227 *Library of Congress, Prints & Photographs Division*

6. James Buchanan: LC-USZ62-96357 *Library of Congress, Prints & Photographs Division*

7. James Polk: LC-pga-DIG-02631 *Library of Congress, Prints & Photographs Division*

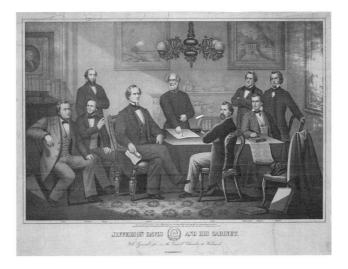

8. Jefferson Davis and his cabinet: LC-USZ62-5263 *Library of Congress, Prints & Photographs Division*

9. Lecompton Constitution Hall: HABS KANS,23-LECOM,1 Select B&W PHOTOGRAPHS and then Photo No. 1. *Library of Congress, Prints & Photographs Division*

10. Lincoln at Antietam: LC-DIG-cwpb-04339 *Library of Congress, Prints & Photographs Division*

CHIEF JUSTICE ROGER B. TANEY

11. Roger Taney: LC-USZ62-107588 *Library of Congress, Prints & Photographs Division*

12. Thomas Hart Benton: LC-USZ62-71877 *Library of Congress, Prints & Photographs Division*

13. Samuel Houston: LC-USZ62-75930 *Library of Congress, Prints & Photographs Division*

14. Zachary Taylor: LC-DIG-pga-02632 *Library of Congress, Prints & Photographs Division*

a majority in the House of Representatives, they finally blocked an amendment to outlaw slavery in former Mexican territories. As already related in chapter 5, this had been attached by David Wilmot, a Democratic representative from Pennsylvania, to a bill appropriating $3 million as compensation to Mexico for the loss of California and New Mexico. The bill was regarded by President Polk—who had sent it to Congress and helped rally support for it in the House of Representatives—as essential for agreeing with Mexico the terms for ending the Mexican War. Significantly Robert Rhett, representing South Carolina, argued that the amendment would in any case have been unconstitutional, on the ground that it disregarded the basic principle that land—even if originally acquired by the federal government—fell under the jurisdiction of the separate states. While southern Democrats strongly supported the so-called "common property doctrine," those from the north saw it as no more than a "lawyer's argument,"[16] which, if valid, would allow immigrants from southern states to bring their slaves with them to California. With the support of the prominent Illinois Democrat Stephen Douglas, the Senate adopted this doctrine, but in December 1848 the report of the House Committee on Territories advised that California be organized according to the Northwest Ordinance of 1787, with the inevitable result that slavery would be outlawed. The contest relating to slavery in California thus reached the point of stalemate to be resolved, in 1849, under the new Whig President, Zachary Taylor.

In spite of the stalemate, some southerners, such as Thomas Jefferson Green of Texas, not only succeeded in bringing slaves to California, but staked gold claims in their names.[17] He did so along the Yuba River—like the American River, a tributary of the Sacramento—which had proved to be rich in gold. (Another Texan, David Terry, having lost his slaves on the way to California, rather than mine gold opened a successful law office in Stockton.) The Yuba River miners, furious at the strategy adopted by Green, having assembled, on Sunday, July 29, 1849, at a local bar, voted that "no slave or negro should own claims or ever work at the mines."[18] A delegation brought the news to Green the same day, and overnight Green, his fellow Texans, and all their slaves fled. They were wise to do so. Three months later the miners hanged a prospector who, having come from Chile with a labor force of peons, ignored their vote. This was frontier justice, and back in Washington President Zachary Taylor had already realized that action was needed to bring some order to California. The only way forward was for it to become a state of the union governing its own affairs. On June 3, 1849, General Bennet Riley (who had succeeded Mason as military governor) summoned for this purpose a convention to meet at Monterey—then the administrative center of California—in September. The following day, June 4, T. Butler King, a slave owner who represented Georgia in Congress, arrived by ship at San Francisco with a commission from

President Taylor to support the movement toward statehood. Another passenger on the same ship was William Gwin, a wealthy Mississippi slave owner, whose political ambitions had been thwarted in his home state—where, following the election of a Whig president, Zachary Taylor, he had little immediate prospect of retrieving his fortunes. California offered the chance to do so.

By the summer of 1849, the first full year of the Gold Rush, those already resident in California from Mexican days were already outnumbered by about six to one by new arrivals. Except for a minority who had come from outside the United States, these identified politically with their home states, and it was on this basis that the delegates to the convention were chosen. The result was that the convention opened on September 3, 1849, with twenty-two delegates from "free" and fifteen from "slave" states, joining seven from California and four from overseas—making a total of forty-eight in all. Of these the eight who represented San Francisco outnumbered the entire delegation from southern California; this did no more than reflect the demographic balance.

Gwin had conducted his campaign—with a platform based upon the immediate grant of statehood—almost from the day of his arrival, and on August 1, in San Francisco, was elected one of the city's eight delegates to the convention. He failed, however, to be elected its president. His campaign trail had also brought him to the gold fields, where he was able to judge for himself the implacable opposition of the miners to the introduction of slavery. This visit inevitably led him to confront William Shannon, a lawyer from New York state, who had been appointed by Colonel Mason as *alcalde*—or sheriff—of Coloma, the township that had grown up at the point where gold was first discovered in January 1848. Shannon, who in 1848 had arrived in California as a soldier, was one of ten New Yorkers chosen to attend the convention, and with their support he became leader of the "free" delegation at Monterey.

Somewhat confusingly almost all delegates, whether from "free" or "slave" states, were Democrats, but this did no more than reflect the existing division of the party, between north and south, in the eastern states of the Union. (The fact that the president, Zachary Taylor, was a Whig, meant little: for one thing he had been elected mainly because of his success as a general in the Mexican War, and for another there were very few Whigs who sought their fortune in California.)

For the convention at Monterey a number of delegates, including Gwin, had arrived with draft constitutions in their pockets. The model, in almost every case, was that of a state already admitted to the Union—with that of Iowa, recently admitted, in 1846, as the twenty-ninth state—being most widely approved. The first week of the convention was spent cobbling together a constitution with 136 sections (with sixty-six borrowed from Iowa), but then, at the beginning of the second week, on Monday, September 10, Shannon moved to include a new section: "Neither slavery nor involuntary servitude, unless for the punishment of crimes, shall ever be tolerated in the State."[19]

STATEHOOD

To the surprise of a number of fellow southerners, Gwin immediately seconded Shannon's motion. However paradoxical it might be to own 200 slaves in Mississippi and yet outlaw slavery in California, Gwin was a master of realpolitik. Merely counting numbers convinced him that any southern faction he might lead would be outnumbered by men from New England, New York, and Pennsylvania. With Gwin's support Shannon's motion was adopted unanimously—a matter of considerable importance seeing that for California to be admitted as the thirty-first state of the Union the US Congress would first have to approve its draft constitution. And as all the delegates realized, there were other hurdles to cross if this result was to be achieved.

For one thing, California, as any other new state, would be carved out of territory owned by the federal government—acquired in this case as a result of the treaty of Guadalupe Hidalgo. The problem was comparable to that relating to the admission of Texas as the twenty-seventh state in 1845. As related in chapter 4, the question then at issue was how far the new state should extend to the west. In the case of California, the question was how far it should extend to the east. In purely geographical terms the question was wide open, given that California, whatever its boundaries, would be the first state west of Missouri—which, significantly, was where the most important overland trails started. Given the convention's unanimous vote against slavery, those representing southern states in Congress had every reason to keep California as small as possible. In Monterey there was little doubt about the power of the "slave" states in Washington, or that of those, such as Gwin, who supported their interests at the conventions. The result was that the natural boundary constituted by the Sierra Nevadas was accepted as that of the state of California and on this basis it was ratified by the Monterey convention on November 13, 1849.

The battle was far from over, for the US Congress still had to persuaded to admit California as a "free" state. This in the end depended upon a compromise crafted by the veteran Kentucky senator, Henry Clay, once referred to by Abraham Lincoln as "my beau ideal of a statesman, the man for whom I fought all my humble life."[20] In exchange for admitting California, the so-called "Adjustment of 1850" also incorporated a ban of slave-trading[21] (while confirming the right to slave ownership) in Washington DC, a new Fugitive Slave Law, the final settlement of the Texas boundary—as related in chapter 4—and territorial bills for Utah and New Mexico. If Henry Clay had succeeded in persuading Congress he was almost certain to fail with the White House. President Zachary Taylor, who had always made clear his wish to have California admitted unconditionally as a "free" state, would veto any such compromise as Clay proposed. Zachary Taylor, however, died of cholera on July 9, 1850, leaving his vice president, Millard Fillmore—a peacemaker rather than a soldier—to succeed him. This opened the way for the compromise bill incorporating the *adjustment* to be passed by Congress at the beginning of September 8, to be signed by the new president on the following day.

Outside California the grant of statehood still left open the future of the vast territory east of the new state—of which some had been acquired by the United States as part of the Louisiana Purchase in 1803, while the rest had been lost to Mexico in 1848 following the treaty of Guadalupe Hidalgo. As to all this land—as already related—claims to statehood, notably by settlers in the Kansas Territory, were becoming every day more insistent, and at the same time divisive in the nation as a whole. The territorial bills for Utah and New Mexico, while leaving open the question of slavery, were—as Lincoln noted at the time—concessions to the south which in intent repudiated the Missouri Compromise. Between Kansas and California the only community of settlers sufficiently well organized to constitute a new state was that of the Mormons in the Utah territory—but in contrast to the settlers in Kansas, these were people who were content to be left, almost indefinitely, to their own devices; they were certainly not clamoring for statehood in 1850.

On the other hand that part of the Oregon Territory along the Pacific coast north of California, south of the Columbia River, and stretching inland beyond the Cascade Mountains, had also attracted settlers—almost all coming over-land—in sufficient numbers for them to organize a new state. The admission of Oregon to the Union in 1859 was, at national level, far less divisive than that of Kansas. With California already admitted as a free state, those representing "slave" states in Congress had to accept that Oregon was a lost cause. Even so, with its admission to the Union in 1859, following that of Minnesota in 1858, there were eighteen "free" to fifteen "slave" states; and as those representing the latter well knew, restoring the balance was extremely problematical. After the admission of California in 1850 the south had to be content with the uncertain prospect of the admission of new "slave" states constituted out of the US territories inland from California and west of the Mississippi River. During the 1850s this was also a major preoccupation of politics in California, and one which colored not only the political lineup at state, city, and county levels, but also the way the state was represented in the US Congress. Given the divisiveness of politics during the 1850s the question of representation, at every level, was bitterly—and often violently—contested.

THE POLITICS OF CONFLICT AND VIOLENCE

When, on October 18, 1849, parades celebrated the arrival of the news in San Francisco that California had been admitted to the Union, not only was the apparatus of state government already operating, but the definitive political lineup was also taking shape. This had two aspects. The first was California's representation in the US Congress and the second, the division of power within the state government. On December 20, 1849, the legislature, as constituted by the Monterey convention, voted on California's representation in Washington. What counted, both at state and national level, was the choice of the first two US senators.

With twenty-nine out of forty-one possible votes, John C. Frémont won easily on the first ballot. Frémont had a high profile in California throughout the 1840s. After first becoming famous for exploring the Oregon Trail, he found in the Mexican War another opportunity for involvement in the future of the far west. In California he became a local hero in 1846 following his success in freelance actions carried out against the Mexican settlements. Although claiming to be carrying out orders from Washington, Frémont—ranking no higher than lieutenant colonel—clashed with General Stephen Kearny who, after defeating the opposing army in New Mexico, was appointed commander of US forces in California. Frémont's refusal to recognize Kearny's command led to his conviction, by court-martial, for insubordination, followed by dismissal from the army—both verdict and sentence winning him immense popular support, not least in California. After refusing first the offer of reinstatement offered by President Polk, and then other tempting offers of employment in the east, Frémont was finally persuaded by Thomas Hart Benton—his father-in-law—to pioneer a new all-season route to California starting at St. Louis. Financed by local Missouri businessmen intent on constructing the first transcontinental railroad to California, Frémont, in the winter of 1848–1849, led a small company of adventurers into the mountains of southern Colorado. Although the expedition was a disaster, with a third of its members left dead in the deep winter snow of the Sierra, Frémont's own achievement confirmed his status as a popular hero. By this time, however, the Gold Rush was already well under way, and the fact that Frémont had survived his appalling journey only reassured the many who were eager to reach California overland. Not only Frémont himself, but others also, learned from his mistakes. Conveniently, having survived the horrendous winter in the mountains, he arrived in California with sufficient time in hand to establish himself as a popular politician—particularly among the gold miners.

In his campaign Frémont was helped by his wife, who had arrived in San Francisco on the same ship as William Gwin and T. Butler King. These two men, both southerners, were the principal contestants for the second seat in the US Senate. In contrast to Frémont they were both southern Democrats, but only Gwin succeeded in turning this to his advantage in California. Based in San Francisco, he organized the "Chivalry" faction in the state Democratic Party. Its members were all, like Gwin himself, slave-owners in the east, whom Gwin had persuaded, nonetheless, to support the vote against slavery in California. In the US Senate, on the other hand, Gwin could assure the so-called "Chivs" that he would be an unswerving ally of the "slave" states. This was sufficient to bring Gwin victory over King in the third round of voting, so that he and Frémont would be California's first two senators. The two then agreed to draw straws for which of them would serve the longer, six-year terms; that Frémont—drawing the shorter straw—was left with only one year to serve in Washington was to have far-reaching consequences both for California and the nation at large. Gwin, with a full six-year term, was able to ensure that California would bring few problems to the south in the US Congress, although it hardly helped that at Monterey he had voted for its admission as a free state. Nonetheless Gwin's long-established friendship with fellow southerners and slave owners certainly helped California in the tumultuous early months of 1850 when Congress was deciding the terms upon which it would be admitted as a state.

On the other side, Frémont, who came originally from South Carolina, was greatly mistrusted by the south, not least because of his close relationship with Thomas Hart Benton, the renegade senator from Missouri. The critical question was then whether he would be reelected, in 1852, for a full six-year term in the US Senate. This was still a matter for the state legislature—not for the voters at large—and there the one concern of the sixteen members of the "Chiv" faction was to not to let the south down in the US Senate. Frémont, confronted by the "Chivs," had little choice but to return to California to fight his own corner. After serving only twenty-one days as a Senator in the Thirty-first Congress' short first session—which ended in March 1851—he left Washington to campaign back home. In spite of his success in 1850, Frémont was never able to overcome his Chiv opponents, but they, in turn, were not strong enough to get their own man, Solomon Heydenfeldt, in. After 142 ballots the legislature gave up, postponing the election until January 1852. With Frémont in California, only Gwin was left in Washington to represent the state in the US Senate.

By this time Frémont had given hope of being reelected to the US Senate, and by doing so had greatly strengthened the hand of the Chivs—so much so that on the eighth ballot one of their men, John B. Weller, was elected. Weller, coming originally from Ohio, was a doughface, a northerner with southern sympathies—and far from being the only one in California, or elsewhere. In the critical mid-1850s, the California representation in the US Senate could be relied upon to support the south. The same was true in the House of Representatives, where California's two members had also got in on the Chiv bandwagon.

One result of all this was that Gwin and the Chivs had a completely free hand in dispensing federal patronage. Top jobs, such as that of San Francisco collector of customs or US marshal for northern California, went to southerners, and all those appointed had in turn offered jobs to hundreds of subordinates. By this time also, the days of the "placer" miner, working alone panning and sifting icy river water for gold, were past, and open-cast and hard-rock mining operations by large-scale corporate enterprises were the order of the day. Although hundreds of wage laborers were still required, many who had failed as placer miners preferred to earn their keep elsewhere in California—not least in the rapidly growing city of San Francisco, where more recent immigrants from the east added to their number. With few of these men coming from the south, it was inevitable that they resented the way Chivs abused federal patronage; it was not for nothing that the San Francisco Custom House became known as the "Virginia Poorhouse." All that the men opposed to the Chivs needed was a champion to lead them.

DAVID BRODERICK AND THE PEOPLE OF CALIFORNIA

In June 1849, David Broderick, who had been a stonecutter and volunteer fireman in New York, arrived in San Francisco by sea. In the New York Democratic Party he had been a Tammany ward boss, finding his political base among his fellow firemen. In California he never made it to the goldfields, for once in San Francisco he met Colonel Jonathan Stevenson, a former head of the New York "volunteers," who had heard from local businessmen how they resented having to trade in gold dust. With Frederick Kohler—a New York jeweler who had been on the same boat—as his business partner, and financed by a $3,500 loan from Stevenson, he set up a mint, striking coins with face values of $5 and $10, but containing only $4 and $8 worth of gold. While still ahead of the game—in which others were beginning to compete—Kohler and Broderick were able to sell out within a year at a vast profit to themselves. Kohler became state assayer and chief engineer of the San Francisco Fire Department, while Broderick went on to make a fortune by speculating in waterfront properties.

At the same time, with his Tammany background, Broderick inevitably turned his hand to politics. Once again the volunteer firemen constituted his base, but it was much stronger than in New York, if only because in a city where almost all buildings were constructed with wood, fires were far more frequent. Broderick, who often led the team combating a fire, became a high-profile popular hero, and his fellow firemen were willing accomplices in his political career. In this way Broderick ensured that no one became an elected office-holder without his support, and in San Francisco, where remuneration was a prescribed proportion of the fees collected, many offices, such as sheriff and tax collector, were extremely lucrative. Those elected with the support of Broderick were committed to give half their fees to his Democratic Party. It was the typical Tammany model of "money from the rich and votes from the poor." All this Broderick achieved in his first year in California, in which he had also succeeded in becoming a state senator from San Francisco. If ever a man was cut out to oppose Gwin it was Broderick. Where the former rewarded his supporters with federal patronage, the latter used state elective offices for the same purpose. These were two political strategies with essentially the same purpose, which was to divert public money appropriated for the remuneration of government servants into the hands of politicians. No one in California in the 1850s expected otherwise.

When the battle opened there, Gwin was ahead; the challenge to Broderick was to turn the tables. Both in California and in Washington they confronted each other in the one contest that counted in the 1850s, that between south and north, "slave" and "free." The problem facing Broderick, at least in the early stages of his battle with Gwin, was that in California, as in other free states, Democrats were inclined to be soft on slavery. In 1852 Broderick failed—and not for want of trying—to block a retroactive fugitive slave law in the California assembly. At the end of the day, out of thirty-three Democrats only three voted against it,[22] whereas in the much smaller Whig Party seven out of eighteen assemblymen did so. Even in 1854, when the assembly was presented with a resolution in support of the Kansas-Nebraska Act of the US Congress—which, as related in chapter 11, defined the point of no return on the way to a decisive split between north and south—sixteen Democrats supported it, while not a single Whig did so.

By this time, however, Gwin was overplaying his hand, particularly in the way he overlooked northern, non-Chiv Democrats when dispensing federal patronage. The challenge to Broderick was to organize this faction so that it was strong enough to thwart Gwin. His own political power base was too narrow, but outside it his Tammany Hall background counted against him. But then, in 1851, as presiding officer in the state senate, he formed a key alliance with John Bigler, the speaker of the assembly. Broderick then went one better, and secured Bigler's appointment as California's third governor later in the year.[23] Bigler—a Democrat from Pennsylvania, where his brother, William, was governor—although hardly a natural ally of someone like Broderick, was equally convinced of the need to end Chiv dominance in California. The first step was to gain control of the state Democratic convention—a result Broderick and Bigler achieved by establishing a rule that representation would be on the basis of one delegate for every 200 Democratic votes. The result was that San Francisco, where Broderick's political machine was in complete control, had much the largest delegation. When the convention met at Benicia in May 1853, Broderick and Bigler's new Free Soil Democratic faction split the Democratic Party in two: the Chivs contested the choice of Bigler as the party's candidate for governor, so that the Free Soil victory which then followed was for them a very serious setback. The defeated Chivs, who included many federal office-holders, did little to help Bigler get reelected, with some even campaigning actively against him. Nonetheless Bigler won the election, but only with the support of San Francisco. As governor for an unprecedented second term he had little choice but to share the lucrative state patronage with Broderick, who had become lieutenant governor. Together, in a process that infuriated the Chivs, they assigned both the most prestigious and the most lucrative jobs to their cronies.

As always in the roller-coaster politics of California, Bigler and Broderick overplayed their hand, just as Gwin had in 1852. The issue that nearly broke them was that of the state's representation in the US Senate. The position was simple enough. Gwin, with his first term as senator due to end in March, 1955,[24] was up for reelection at the end of 1854; for Weller all this would happen two years later. In January 1854, Broderick and Bigler set in train an election bill, which once passed would allow an immediate election. In California they had a majority in both the state assembly and the senate. Forty assemblymen and fifteen senators signed an address denouncing those Democrats who "betraying the party on the field of battle"[25] had failed to support Bigler's campaign for governor. Finally, on March 6, 1854, the bill passed the assembly. In the Senate the vote ended in a tie, but the bill was carried with the casting vote of the presiding officer—needless to say a firm supporter of Bigler and Broderick. The party, however, was not over: one senator, Jacob Grewell, had second thoughts, and moved successfully for a reconsideration. With Grewell switching sides the assembly bill was defeated in the senate, seventeen to fourteen.

This led to a very heated summer in Democratic California, and when the Democratic convention opened in Sacramento—which had become the state capital in March—the two factions flew apart, with both going on to hold separate meetings. On one side the Chivs nominated two southerners for the House of Representatives in Washington, while on the other the Broderick faction nominated the party's two sitting representatives. Neither could be consulted, since both of them, returning over land to California, were quite out of reach. Once back home, one of the two, Milton S. Latham, originally from Ohio, withdrew from the race, leaving the way open to an overwhelming victory for the Gwin faction. Although this was sufficient for the assembly to vote for the two Gwin nominees for the House of Representatives, Gwin himself failed to be reelected to the senate. This was the result of effective campaigning by the small Know Nothing Party, which, with support from Broderick Democrats, came only one vote short of sending their own candidate, Henry Foote, to Washington. There was then no possibility of any candidate gaining a majority in the assembly, with the result that Weller, during the Thirty-second Congress, was the only California senator in Washington. After the prospective end of his term at the beginning of 1857, California faced the loss of its entire representation in the US Senate. Plainly some accommodation was needed before the state convened in January 1857.

Until nearly the end of 1856 Gwin had every reason to be upbeat about his prospects. In the early months of the year law and order had almost broken down in San Francisco as the result of the actions directed against Broderick and his supporters by the Know Nothing Party and the San Francisco Vigilance Committee of 1856. The Vigilantes had come into their own as a result of two high-profile assassinations, one of the US marshal, General William H. Richardson—who owed his federal appointment to Gwin—and the other of James King, editor of the San Francisco *Evening Bulletin*. The assassin in the former case was Charles Cora, a notorious gambler, with his wife a brothel-keeper, and in the latter, James P. Casey, a major beneficiary of Broderick's local patronage.

With the death of King, an active vigilante in 1851, a new Vigilance Committee came into action and, backed by over 2,000 men, seized Casey and Cora from the sheriff's custody and after a hasty trial hanged them in public four days later. Intent on cleaning the city of corruption, they listed twenty-nine men—almost all Broderick Democrats, for elimination by hanging, prison, or exile. Broderick, with a new Law and Order Party set up for this purpose, led the opposition to the Second Vigilance Committee. When the committee in turn ordered the arrest of Broderick, this was going too far. One of San Francisco's most powerful men, Gerritt W. Ryckman, himself a prominent vigilante in 1851, stormed into the 1856 committee rooms and threatened the direst consequences if the order to arrest Broderick, was not rescinded. The committee yielded, and Broderick persuaded it to disband. All these events, while at first reflecting Broderick's inability to keep law and order in his own city, in the end enhanced his power after he proved that he was still on top. By the end of 1856 Gwin realized that his power was waning; if he was to return to the Senate he would have to make a deal with Broderick.

One problem facing Gwin was that John B. Weller and Milton S. Latham were also in the field to represent California in the US Senate. At this critical time the fact that Weller was the only US Senator from California—following

Gwin's failure to gain a majority in the state legislature in 1854—meant that he had a very strong hand. Latham, for his part, had demonstrated his political strength by the way he had orchestrated the election of two Chivs to the House of Representatives in that year. If Gwin, Weller, and Latham had between them agreed as to which of them would become the Democratic candidate for the US Senate, the problem would have been solved, but there was little prospect of this happening. The only alternative was to seek the support of Broderick. Although, in principle, this should have been anathema to all three, California politics had little regard for principle.

While the legislature convened in January 1857 the Democratic caucus met to decide on the party's candidates for the US Senate. According to normal procedure the candidate for the shorter four-year term should have been chosen first, but Broderick, helped critically by Latham, moved successfully to reverse the order. This was a signal defeat for Gwin and Weller who used every possible tactic to prevent the motion from being carried. Their failure to so do left the way open for Broderick to become the caucus' nominee for the long six-year term with a majority of forty-two to thirty-two votes which then—following the established convention—led to unanimous endorsement.

Latham, by supporting Broderick, was in a strong position to claim his support for the second seat in the US Senate. Broderick's price, however, was that the second senator should surrender his share of federal patronage, and this Latham refused to pay. Gwin was less principled, and at a clandestine midnight meeting on January 11, 1857, in the Magnolia Hotel, agreed to give Broderick what he wanted. Gwin then had to put it all in writing, so when he finally left the hotel, Broderick had a letter ending with these words: "while in the senate I will not recommend a single individual to appointment to office in this state. Provided I am elected you shall have the exclusive control of this patronage, so far as I am concerned; and in its distribution I shall only ask that it may be used with magnanimity and not for the advantage of those who have been our mutual enemies and unwearied in their efforts to destroy us."[26] He also wrote a letter, dated January 13 and addressed to the "People of California," acknowledging Broderick's "timely assistance," and praising him for his magnanimity.

Gwin's abject climb-down and betrayal of his friends got him where he wanted to be—in Washington as senator for California. What is more, with Broderick there as well, life would be much easier for the Chivs back home. Gwin and Broderick traveled to Washington together, taking the route across Panama—made much easier in 1855 by the opening of the railroad across the isthmus. Their steamer, as it entered New York harbor on February 13, 1857, was welcomed with a hundred-gun salute, while a crowd of several hundred waited on the dockside. All this—as Gwin well knew—was intended solely for

Broderick, the native son returning home. For Gwin it was important to get to Washington as soon as possible, and once there he was able to take his seat in the Senate immediately—he was, after all, already two years into his term. Broderick, who arrived later to begin a full six-year term, had to wait until March to be sworn in as a new senator.

Gwin, with a month in hand before Broderick could join him in the Senate, made good use of his time. In this he was helped by his friends from the days when he lived in Mississippi (where he still had a plantation and several hundred slaves), and even more by his popular wife who used his wealth to become one of the sought-after Washington hostesses. In particular she charmed the bachelor president, James Buchanan, a man once described as having a southern heart and a Pennsylvania accent. In the offices he held before becoming president—secretary of state under President James Polk (1845–1849) and minister to Great Britain under Franklin Pierce (1853–1857)—he was zealous in forwarding southern interests such as Pierce's Ostend Manifesto under which Cuba would be seized, and eventually incorporated in the Union as a slave state.[27] All this was reflected in the votes in the electoral college that brought him to the White House. His election depended upon the fifteen slave states—all except Maryland—that provided him with two-thirds of his electoral votes, while eleven of sixteen free states had voted for the Republican John C. Frémont. Southern Democrats made sure that Buchanan never forgot what he owed them—not that he was ever inclined to do so. As to slavery he abominated abolitionists and "black Republicans," much preferring the company of slave-owners who, in his judgment, were humanitarians at heart. He unhesitatingly sided with the south on such critical issues as the future of Kansas as a slave state—as related in chapter 11—and the decision of the US Supreme Court in the Dred Scott case.

With such a man as president, Broderick was unlikely to have much influence. As for Gwin, the promises he had made in the secret letter written in the Magnolia Hotel were easily forgotten. For Broderick, access to the president was next to impossible, and he even failed to get his own man, former governor John Bigler, appointed to the lucrative office of collector of customs in the port of San Francisco. Instead the job went to a Chiv, Benjamin Franklin Washington, while Bigler was sent off as ambassador to Chile.

After barely a month in Washington, Broderick realized that it was time to return to California to mend some fences. The situation was dire. The divisions among the Chivs that Broderick had exploited to gain the Senate nomination in January were healed. Even worse, the collapse of the strongly anti-Catholic Know Nothing Party had led to many of its members joining the Democratic Party, where inevitably they supported the Chiv faction rather than one led by a New York Irishman with a Tammany Hall background.

Broderick—furious after seeing how weak his position had become in California—returned to Washington in time for the opening of the Thirty-fifth Congress on December 7. He was at the same time determined to see how he could use the rules of "senatorial courtesy" to block the confirmation by the Senate of federal government appointments in California. John B. Weller, who after losing his senate seat to Broderick had become state governor, wrote to Senator Stephen Douglas of Illinois—one of the most respected northern Democrats in the Senate but none the less no abolitionist—to ask him to help frustrate Broderick's plans.

Douglas, whom Weller saw as a friend from his days as senator, was unable to help, for—as related in chapter 11—he was set on persuading the Congress to reject the fraudulent Lecompton Constitution, adopted by a convention rigged by southern democrats in the Kansas Territory so as to secure its admission to the Union as a slave state. Although Robert Walker, whom James Buchanan had himself appointed as territorial governor, had done his best to persuade the president not to support the Lecompton Constitution, he failed to do so—although none knew better than he its whole sordid history. The president preferred to side with his southern friends, and gave them his full support. The only support Douglas could count upon in his own party was that of Michigan Senator Charles Stuart and California Senator David Broderick; otherwise he would have to rely on the twenty Republican senators, all from northern states. Stuart, in condemning the Lecompton Constitution, took care not to involve the president. Broderick, speaking in the Senate on December 23, did not hesitate to do so:

> If I understand this subject, and I hope I do, I think that the President of the United States is alone responsible for the present state of affairs in Kansas. It is the first time, I believe, in the history of this country, that a President of the United States ever stepped down from the exalted position he held, to attempt to coerce the people into a base submission to the will of an illegalized body of men.

This was only the half of what he said that December day, but when the new year opened he kept silent.

Then, on March 21, 1858, Senator James H. Hammond of South Carolina, in a long speech close to the end of the debate on the Lecompton Constitution reported in chapter 11, specifically excluded California and Oregon from the list of northern states opposed to it—and by doing so was able to claim that the territory of the northern states was "one hundred thousand square miles less than ours." This same speech, containing the famous assertion "cotton is king," was also unequivocal about the virtue of slavery as an institution for providing the unskilled labor essential to a plantation economy.

The following day Broderick broke his silence in the Senate. He found the weakest point in Hammond's economic case for slavery by showing that, however much the south contributed to the nation's economy, numbers—in terms of population—would never be on its side in any contest with the north:

> How foolish of the South to hope to contend with success in such an encounter. Slavery is old, decrepit and consumptive; freedom is young, strong and vigorous. The one is naturally stationary and loves ease; the other is migratory and enterprising. There are six millions of people interested in the extension of slavery; there are twenty millions of free men to contend for these territories, out of which to carve themselves homes were labor is honorable.[28]

Broderick then pitted California against the south by ridiculing Hammond's "King Cotton" claim:

> the single free State of California exports the product for which cotton is raised, to an amount of more than one half in value of the whole exports of cotton of the slave States. Cotton king! No, sir. Gold is king. I represent a State . . . where labor is honorable; where the judge has left his bench, the lawyer and doctor their offices, and the clergyman his pulpit, for the purpose of delving in the earth; where no station is so high, and no position so great, that its occupant is not proud to boast that he has labored with his hands.

At the end of the speech Broderick focused his attack on President Buchanan: "I hope . . . that the historian, when writing the history of these times, will ascribe the attempt of the executive to force this [Lecompton] constitution on an unwilling people to the fading intellect, the petulant passion, and trembling dotage of an old man on the verge of the grave."

Broderick gained little in Washington by attacking men much more strongly entrenched in the established power structure than himself. If anything he strengthened the resolve of men such as Gwin and Hammond in the Senate and Buchanan in the White House to pursue their chosen policies to the bitter end. Gwin was able to remove Broderick from the Senate Committee on Public Lands and Douglas—one of the most respected men in Congress and the likely Democratic candidate for president in 1860—from the Chair of the Committee on Territories. President Buchanan, shameless in his abuse of federal patronage in northern states, even won sufficient support in the House of Representatives for the Lecompton Constitution to be adopted on a majority—which had never been a problem in the Senate. While all this was going on, Gwin used both his wealth and his connections to dominate the Washington social scene in a process that came to a climax when, on April 9, 1858, his wife was escorted by President Buchanan onto the dance floor at a fancy-dress ball that had cost her husband $12,000.

Broderick, after spending the summer in California, returned to Washington for the final session of the Thirty-fifth Congress; this meant that he was out of state for the November elections. These were disastrous for Broderick. His strongest candidate, John Currey, failed to win a place on the state supreme court in spite of strong support in both San Francisco and Sacramento, and endorsement by the Republicans, who had greatly increased their strength after John C. Frémont's defeat in the 1856 presidential race. At the grassroots level outside the two cities, the Chivs had simply organized far more people to round up voters.

Setbacks in both Washington and California left Broderick deeply distressed. In the summer of 1859, after attending the first session of the Thirty-sixth Congress, it was clear that he had to be back in California for the state elections coming up later in the year. By this time an old issue had been revived: Andrés Pico—born, as a Mexican citizen, into a wealthy, land-owning family—represented Los Angeles in the state legislature, and although first elected as a Whig, had become an ardent Chiv. As a state assemblyman, he introduced legislation to divide California in half, with the southern part to become a new "Territory of Colorado." Pico, with considerable local support, saw this becoming a new state of which he would become governor. He would get nowhere, however, without support from northern California, whose legislators not only outnumbered those from the south by ten to one, but also had little interest in seeing the state dismembered. Nor did the Chivs in northern California, unless it was for one reason: Pico would allow slavery. On this basis—which was never quite explicit—Pico's legislation passed both the assembly (with thirty-four votes to twenty-six) and the state senate (with fifteen to twelve) in the spring of 1859, and of all these votes only four came from the south.

The election for state governor on September 7 was bitterly contested. In July Broderick took his case to the people. With his first stump speech at Placerville, in the heart of the gold country, he went to Forest Hill, Marysville, and Nevada City, challenging Gwin at every stage. Gwin at first ignored these challenges, but in the end he had little choice but to debate with Broderick at one small town after another. By this time Broderick, who had retrieved the midnight letter written by Gwin in the Magnolia Hotel in January 1857, used it to justify his assertion that Gwin was a liar, cheat, and traitor—to cite only a few of his chosen epithets—but above all he used Pico's plan to divide the state to discredit the Chivs. One question was continually asked of his audiences: "Can you support an administration that would bring slave labor into the West to compete with free labor?"

Slavery, as Broderick saw it, was the real issue, and although he eventually spoke to nearly ten times as many people as Gwin, it was the Chiv candidate,

Milton S. Latham, who was elected governor. Partly this was the result of better Chiv organization at the grassroots level, but Broderick's faction also lost critical votes to the Republicans, who no longer endorsed its candidates. Critically Broderick was let down by Stephen Douglas, who in spite of promises made in Washington, held back his support knowing that the California Chiv vote would be decisive if he was to be the Democratic candidate for president in 1860.

Once again the Gwin faction overplayed its hand, with one Chiv after another denouncing Broderick at the Democratic nominating convention. One in particular, Chief Justice David S. Terry, described Broderick's supporters as "a miserable remnant of a faction sailing under false colors ... they belong, heart and soul, body and breeches, to David C. Broderick." Broderick did not hesitate to conceal his contempt for Terry as a "damned miserable wretch" and did not care when these words and others like them reached the chief justice. Terry demanded a retraction, and when it was refused, challenged Broderick to a duel. This took place on September 13, 1859, and Broderick, after his first shot has misfired, was mortally wounded by Terry's return. Before he died, three days later, he stated, "I die because I was opposed to a corrupt administration and the extension of slavery."

One shot from Terry's pistol had made Broderick a political martyr. The Chivs were finally on the defensive, challenged with responsibility for a "murder most foul." Broderick's final accusation echoed from one end of California to another. The *Alta California*, a San Francisco newspaper that had long supported the Chivs, referred to them as "jackals [whose] lion hunt [had finally ended] after their feast of blood," advising Gwin, at the same time, to look at the empty seat in the Senate chamber and then consult his conscience "if he still had one." When Gwin, with California's two representatives in Congress, left by ship from San Francisco, the crowd on the dockside—which included none of their supporters—had a banner reading "The Will of the People—May the Murderers of David C Broderick Never Return to California."[29]

Once back in Washington, California's four congressmen—two in each house (of whom one, Henry P. Haun, had been nominated by the California Chiv governor, John B. Weller, to replace Broderick in the Senate)—did their best to have Pico's proposed measure to divide the state in two adopted by the Thirty-fifth Congress in its final session. By this time the political tide was moving against them, and the nationwide elections in November 1858 not only greatly increased the Republican strength in Congress, but also brought Milton S. Latham to replace Haun in the Senate. In the opening session of the Thirty-sixth Congress in 1859, Latham, in his maiden speech, conceded that "the measure must be deemed, for the present, at least impolitic," going on to add, "We in California would have reasons to induce us to become members neither of the southern confederacy nor of the northern confederacy, and would be able to sustain ourselves the relations of a free and independent state."[30]

In the late summer preceding the 1860 presidential election Colonel Edward D. Baker, a California friend of Abraham Lincoln, went up north to Oregon to become the Republican candidate for the US Senate, to be elected on October 10[31] by the state legislature—on a joint Republican/Douglas-Democrat ticket—to replace Joseph E. Lane, the Chiv senator elected when Oregon became the thirty-third state in 1859. There could hardly have been better news for Republicans on the west coast. On October 26, Baker, on his way to Washington made a powerful and widely reported speech in San Francisco in favor of Lincoln, who, in November went on to win both Oregon and California. When the news reached the east coast, it greatly strengthened the resolve of the southern states to leave the union if Lincoln was elected president—as was, by this time, almost certain to happen.

While even after the election of Lincoln as president in 1860 Chivs still talked about secession, in the US Senate Latham supported the Union, and after the Civil War broke out in April 1861, the state legislature, following his example, resolved on May 17 "that the people of California are devoted to the Constitution now in the hour of trial and peril."[32] The state also pledged two cavalry and five infantry regiments to the Union army. Californians were, however, exempted from conscription (which in the summer of 1864 led to large-scale immigration, overland, from the east).[33] The state's most important contribution to the Union cause was gold, for as General Ulysses S. Grant said, "I do not know what we would do in this great national emergency were it not for the gold sent from California."[34] Latham, although supporting the Union, still defended slavery and attacked the Lincoln administration. The strength of the Union cause in California was made clear by his defeat for reelection to the Senate in 1862. The tactical successes of the Chivs during the 1850s had in the end achieved nothing for them: their legacy was a bitterly divided state, in which it was generally accepted that violence and corruption were part and parcel of politics.

Washington: 1847–1849

LIFE IN THE NATION'S CAPITAL

Before going to Washington in 1861 as president, Abraham Lincoln had been active in Illinois politics for nearly thirty years. In the middle of this period he was a one–term congressman, representing, as a Whig, Illinois' Seventh District in the US House of Representatives during the two sessions of the Thirtieth Congress. Although the elections had taken place at the end of 1846, the first session of this Congress only opened on December 6, 1847, to continue until August 14, 1848. This was a long session during which Lincoln was in Washington for the first time in his life. He arrived there, with his wife, Mary, and his two young sons, Robert and Eddy, on December 2, 1847. After a short stay in a hotel the family moved into Mrs. Ann G. Spriggs' boarding house, where eight other Whig congressmen also boarded. Life in a single large room proved to be so burdensome for Mary Lincoln that in the spring of 1847 she moved, together with the two children, to her father's house in Lexington, Kentucky—a town roughly halfway between Washington and Springfield. What sort of city was it then that she had left behind, leaving her husband to look after himself until the end of his first session as a congressman?

There had always been doubts about the location, on both sides of the Potomac River, chosen for the nation's capital. When the prospect was first considered at the end of the eighteenth century, Benjamin Rush of Pennsylvania warned of a city on the banks of the Potomac "where negro slaves will be your servants by day, mosquitoes your sentinels by night, and bilious fevers your companions every summer and fall, and pleurisies every spring." Some 200 years later the historian Morton Keller[1] wrote, "before the Civil War, Washington was a slovenly, indolent, half–finished city . . . the physical embodiment of American distaste for centralized government." To the Lincolns, however, when they first settled in Washington during the winter of 1847–1848

the city, with its 40,000 inhabitants—including 2,000 slaves and 8,000 free blacks—was the largest and most cosmopolitan place either of them had ever known. The Capitol building . . . was an imposing though still unfinished, structure, its temporary wooden dome suggesting the fragility of the Federal Union. At the opposite end of Pennsylvania Avenue loomed the White House, certainly the grandest residence either Lincoln had ever seen. . . . Most of the streets . . . were still unpaved, but a cobblestoned stretch of Pennsylvania offered a tempting array of specialty shops with luxury goods.[2]

On the other hand the city lacked all modern services—gas lighting on its streets, water-borne sewage disposal, and garbage collection—but here it was no worse than the hometowns of the 230 districts nationwide represented in the US Congress. If heating by wood–burning stoves made life indoors more or less comfortable during the winter, there was no way of mitigating the heat and humidity of the Washington summer. The city—much of it low–lying and poorly drained—was notoriously unhealthy, which is one reason why Mary Todd Lincoln left it, with her two sons, after only a few months residence. Two years after her departure, cholera, a constant threat, claimed the life of President Zachary Taylor in 1850, but he was far from being the only victim of this dread disease—of which epidemics, as in 1832 and 1848–1849, could ravage the whole country.

Washington—in the antebellum era always somewhat provisional in character—was also a city of transients, of which the eighty five one-term members of the House of Representatives in the Thirtieth Congress were exemplary. This meant, for one thing, that they had little of the influence and status of the long-term residents who dominated a conspicuously exclusive society. Congressmen, it is true, could attend levees at the White House,[3] but with President James Polk forbidding dancing and offering neither food nor drink, few were inclined to do so. The biweekly concerts given by the band of the Marine Corps in the grounds of the White House were much more enjoyable. None of this mattered much to Abraham Lincoln, who was a notorious workaholic—the more so during the summer months of 1848 after his family had left him for Lexington.

Inevitably, given the way they were chosen, the members of the House of Representatives were "mostly men of mediocre ability and only local reputation."[4] When Lincoln first entered the House, one member, John Quincy Adams of Massachusetts—who some twenty years earlier had been the sixth president of the United States—shone above all the others, but he died, eighty years old, early in the session. Another key congressman was David Wilmot of Pennsylvania, whose attempt to frustrate the extension of slavery is described in chapters 5 and 9. For the most part the men who counted were not in the House, but in the Senate. This was almost inevitable, given that they were both much fewer in number, with a third being elected every two years on a rotating system for six-year terms. The position obtaining in the House of Representatives, where over half the members were either freshmen, or destined not to belong to the next Congress, was impossible in the Senate. Men such as Stephen Douglas (1847)—Lincoln's powerful adversary in Illinois—Daniel Webster of Massachusetts, Thomas H. Benton of Missouri, John C. Calhoun of South Carolina, and Sam Houston of Texas, who between them served more than a hundred years in the Senate, are still remembered—as can be seen from the way I recount their achievements in other chapters of this book. At this time such giants—all of whom were senators for at least ten years—could hardly have given much attention to a freshman congressman such as Lincoln, however hard he tried to gain it. What is more, the public figure he most admired, Henry Clay of Kentucky, was not a member of either house in the Thirtieth Congress—although he did return as senator in the Thirty-first Congress.

The Thirtieth Congress was somewhat exceptional for having a small Whig majority in the House of Representatives. In the Senate, on the other hand, there was a substantial Democratic majority, which was, until Lincoln became president in 1861, never threatened during all the years he was politically active. The fact that for most of this time he was in Illinois meant that he was already experienced in confronting a powerful Democratic Party. Nonetheless, in Washington he had to come to terms with national issues that counted for much less back home.

In weighing Democrats against Whigs in the political scales, the two parties were ill-balanced. From the turn of the century the Democrats, as they came to be known during the presidency of Andrew Jackson (1829–1837), had been a party with a nationwide political base, which was particularly strong in the southern states. This, as already shown in chapter 6, was critical in relation to issues, such as notably slavery, on which the south consistently refused to yield any ground. The "solid south" had been a fact of life in American politics at least since the days of the Sixteenth Congress and the Missouri Compromise—nearly twenty years before Lincoln entered Congress. The Democrats were also a party very strongly in favor of expansion, and in the mid-1840s their attachment to the principle of "manifest destiny" led first to the admission of Texas as the twenty-seventh state of the Union, and then to war with Mexico. All this is a story told in chapter 4.

The Whigs were a much more recent party than the Democrats. They emerged as a reaction to the high-handed policies of Andrew Jackson during his second term (1833–1837) in the White House. At the beginning of this term these focused on the excessive power, as Jackson saw it, of the Bank of the United States (BUS). This, in spite of its name, was legally quite independent of Jackson's administration. The president nonetheless resented the dependence of his—and, for that matter, preceding—administrations on the BUS, where the US Treasury kept its own deposits. What is more, he believed that the BUS was using its considerable resources to support his political opponents, notably John Quincy Adams—his predecessor in the White House. The president chose the US Treasury Department as the vehicle for reducing the power of the BUS. This inevitably brought him into conflict with Nicholas Biddle, who today would be called its CEO.

Although in the end Jackson won the so-called "Battle of the Banks," it was something of a Pyrrhic victory. Where, in his first term of office, he was riding on the crest of a wave, with congressional opposition weak and divided, in his second, not only did his opponents increase in number, but they also acquired a very formidable leader, the Kentucky senator, Henry Clay—who had already made his name at the time of the Missouri Compromise. By 1834, following its unexpected success in New York City local elections, this new coalition acquired a name—the Whig Party, chosen to recall the opponents of King George III in the British Parliament at the time of the American War of Independence.[5] This was the party that Lincoln joined when he became active in state politics in Illinois, and under whose banner he was elected to the US Congress in 1846. What then did the Whigs stand for?

Broadly speaking the Whigs were in favor of consolidating the United States at the stage reached by the beginning of the 1840s; in other words, the nation had plenty to get on with without further expansion. This meant promoting three policies which went back to the early days of the nineteenth century when the Federalists still counted in American politics—a position they had forfeited during the battle over the Missouri Compromise (as related in chapter 7). The first policy, which was to establish a national bank, had run aground with Andrew Jackson's final success against the BUS. The second policy was to protect local industrial enterprise, which was already making considerable gains by the 1840s, by imposing customs duties on imported manufactures. Although this would have made American industry more competitive in the home market, the benefits would have gone mainly to the north, where there was much more investment both in manufacturing and in supporting services such as railroads and canals. For the south, whose economy depended mainly on the export of cotton, import duties would have meant higher prices at a time when manufactured goods were still largely imported from England. The third essential Whig policy was federal support for improvements. In the years leading up to 1825 this had become a key issue with New York Governor DeWitt Clinton's program for constructing the Erie canal, which, without such support, had to depend on his home state for all public finance—a key factor in Clinton's maintaining his own faction within the Democratic Party at the time of the Missouri Compromise.

THE MEXICAN WAR

One problem facing Lincoln and the other Whig members of the Thirtieth Congress was that in the circumstances of the day none of the three traditional policies resonated with the American public. The reason for this was the nation's involvement in the Mexican War, into which it had been led by President James Polk, a Tennessee Democrat with wide popular support. Whig congressmen were certainly able to question Polk's reasons for pursuing the war so ardently, but it was difficult to get around the fact that the actual declaration of war, on April 23, 1846, was made by Mexico. Moreover, by the time Lincoln sat in Congress for the first time, in December 1847, American soldiers had won one victory after another, and the war was generally popular with the public. Indeed it ended—with the vast gains to the United States related in chapter 4—on February 2, 1848, with the signing of the Treaty of Guadalupe Hidalgo.

To Whigs such as Lincoln, the chance to question President Polk's conduct of the war came with his annual message to Congress in December 1847. The fact that he asked for additional funds to bring the war to a successful conclusion justified some critical scrutiny of the historical background. The opportunity was provided by the president himself, when he claimed that Mexico had initiated the war by "invading the state of Texas, striking the first blow, and shedding the blood of citizens on our own soil."[6] The statement—plainly drafted with an eye to its popular appeal—was tendentious, because the events referred to had taken place in disputed territory.

The question was whether the Rio Grande, as Texas claimed, was the southern boundary of the state—and derivatively of the United States also—or the Nueces River, which was some distance to the north. It was natural for Lincoln, who had once worked as a surveyor, to introduce a resolution asking the president to provide the House of Representatives with "all the facts which go to establish whether the particular spot of soil on which blood of our citizens was so shed, was, or was not, our own soil." Another even stronger resolution, introduced by the Massachusetts Representative George Ashmun on January 3, 1848, declared that the war had been "unnecessarily and unconstitutionally begun by the President of the United States."

This was not the end to the display of a talent for rhetoric acquired in Illinois courtrooms, but in Washington Lincoln got nowhere. President Polk prudently refused to react in any way, and the same was true of almost all of Lincoln's fellow congressmen. One of them, however—Missouri Representative John Jameson—was astonished that a fellow congressman could follow the line chosen by Lincoln, when one of those who had represented the same Illinois district in the two preceding congresses, John Hardin, had lost his life in the Mexican War, while the other, E. D. Baker proved himself a hero at the battle of

Buena Vista.[7] While the St. Louis *Missouri Republican* praised his "spot of soil" speech as being "one of great power . . . replete with the strongest and most conclusive arguments," outside Illinois no other newspaper paid it any attention. Even in his home state he was roundly condemned, and although some Whig newspapers placed him in the "front rank of the best speakers in the House,"[8] most were much more muted in their praise. Prominent Whigs who knew Lincoln well—including William Herndon, his law partner—made it plain to him that opposition to the territorial annexations that would follow victory in the war would ensure that the Whigs would long be the minority party. In all this Lincoln was following Henry Clay, the Whig candidate for president whom the Democratic "dark horse" candidate, James Polk, had unexpectedly defeated in 1844. The lesson from that result was that the American public, as a whole, was strongly in favor of territorial expansion. By the summer of 1848, it was clear to Lincoln and other Whigs that if they were to find a candidate who could win the presidential election due at the end of the year, they should take this into account.

Before looking at what this involved, it is as well to consider another issue that was a constant theme of American politics. This, needless to say, was slavery, coupled with the status of negroes in the different states of the Union. The recent background to this issue in national politics was critical to what happened in the mid-1840s. In the course of Andrew Jackson's second term in office (1833–1837) the flood of petitions against slavery reaching the US Congress as a result of fanatical abolitionist agitation in the northern states led the prominent South Carolina Democrat, Senator John C. Calhoun, to introduce legislation requiring that "offending appeals be laid on the table unread, unrecorded and not open to discussion."[9] Congress, eager to silence the fanatics—who represented only a very small part of the US population— accepted Calhoun's proposed legislation, and by doing so instituted the "gag rule." That it would restrict free speech at the heart of government was accepted by the majority in Congress as a price worth paying for preserving a "broad middle ground of moderation and common interest."[10] This was too much for the Massachusetts Representative (and former US president) John Quincy Adams, whose dedicated opposition to slavery was only exceeded by his belief in free speech, and in December 1844 the rule was formally voted down.[11] Underlying this event was the way in which James Polk—in the Democratic convention held in the summer of 1844—was nominated by the party to be its candidate in the forthcoming presidential election.

Up until the convention it was generally expected that Martin Van Buren—who had been Democratic president of the United States in the years 1837–1841—would be nominated to oppose the Whig Henry Clay. Van Buren and Clay—acting in the spirit of the gag rule—agreed not to advocate war against Mexico in the course of their campaigns, realizing how radically it would affect the whole future of slavery in the United States—a view shared incidentally by that powerful southern Democrat, John C. Calhoun. James Polk, making clear that he had no inhibitions about such a war—and indeed was ready for it to be pursued during his administration—effectively nullified the gag rule. At the same time, the convention, realizing the popularity of "Mr. Polk's war" with voters, went on to nominate him for president, disregarding what his policies might import for the future of slavery. Politically the convention took the right decision. While Clay would most probably have defeated Van Buren, he was, in the presidential election of 1844, convincingly defeated by Polk. In short, the Democratic convention had picked a winner. Abraham Lincoln, with his devotion to Henry Clay, had every reason to discomfort President James Polk, when, during the first session of the Thirtieth Congress, he had the means to do so. His problem was that Mr. Polk's war had gone only too well. After a series of victories on three different fronts, the president was—as already noted—in sight of victory when Representative Abraham Lincoln started sniping at him. Politically the war had, on the question of slavery, the very consequences feared by Clay, Van Buren, and many others. When, as recounted in chapter 5, the Pennsylvania Democrat David Wilmot proposed to the House of Representatives—as a legislative proviso—a restriction upon the extension of slavery to new territories acquired by the United States, the gag rule was no longer in force. The proposal was defeated but it brought the day of reckoning much closer.

THE PRESIDENTIAL ELECTION OF 1848

The fact that Whigs were getting nowhere in Congress did not necessarily mean that they had no chance of success in the presidential election due at the end of 1848. In the spring of that year Lincoln and a small number of fellow Whig congressmen who chose to call themselves the "Young Indians" came together to plan a winning strategy. If there was little future in attacking the Democrats for starting a war that had already been won, it might still be possible to turn the tables by nominating—as the Whig candidate for president—one of the popular generals who had led American soldiers through a succession of victories.

The obvious choice was Zachary Taylor, who in November 1847 had returned home a national hero after he had defeated the Mexican commander, Santa Anna—whose forces outnumbered the Americans four to one—at the battle of Buena Vista earlier in the year. For the Young Indians the issue, during the summer of 1848, was entirely political, for as Lincoln explained, "our only chance is with Taylor. I go for him not because I think he would make a better president than Clay, but because I think he would be a better one than Polk, or Cass, or Buchanan, or any such creatures, one of whom is sure to be elected, if he is not." If Taylor—who besides being a general was the owner of a Louisiana plantation which employed more than 200 slaves[12]—was hardly a standard Whig, he was available, and that was what counted.[13]

Having chosen Taylor as their candidate, the Young Indians worked hard to secure his nomination at the Whig National Convention held at Philadelphia in early June. Lincoln attended, making Philadelphia the first of the cities in the Atlantic states which he would discover in the course of the summer while campaigning for Taylor, whom the convention nominated on the fourth ballot. After this success, Lincoln returned to Washington, stopping to address a ratification meeting at Wilmington, Delaware, on the way. Billed as the "Lone Star of Illinois," three hearty cheers greeted his prediction that the Whigs would win the presidential election.

Once back in Washington the Young Indians worked hard to put together a platform on which Taylor could fight the election. From the beginning they were resolute in excluding appeals to sectional interests, which—among other issues—in the south meant the defense of slavery and in the north the restriction of new immigration. Lincoln therefore urged Taylor not to become involved in regional issues, and persuaded him also to make this pledge: "Were I president, I should desire the legislation of this country to rest with Congress, uninfluenced by the executive in its origin or progress, and undisturbed by the veto unless in very special and clear cases."[14] For Lincoln this meant that Taylor would not even veto the Wilmot proviso. This, however, would never be a real issue[15] given the strength of southern Democrats in the Senate. With the virtue of hindsight it would seem that Lincoln's strong preference for a weak chief executive—which in 1848 usefully concealed the fact that the Whig candidate stood for nothing—would tie his hands when some thirteen years later he himself came to occupy the White House. During the Civil War years, however, the absence of any representation in Congress of the eleven states that seceded from the Union in 1861 meant that Lincoln had relatively few problems with either house, so that he seldom needed to use the presidential power of veto. It was always Lincoln's nature to give those he worked with a free hand. Moreover in the summer of 1848 he knew—with his promise only to serve one term in Congress—that he would not be directly involved by the actions of whoever occupied the White House after 1849.

Whatever his own future in Washington, Lincoln still spent the summer of 1848 working hard on behalf of Taylor. He was in his element in the House of Representatives, which instead of getting on with its legislative program preferred to be a forum for campaign speeches in favor of the three presidential candidates. With Polk content to serve only one term in the White House, the Democrats had also chosen a general from the distant past as their candidate: this was Michigan Senator Lewis Cass whose military honors were acquired fighting against the British in the War of 1812. In spite of the fact that Michigan (only admitted as a state in 1838) had been part of the Northwest Territory where slavery was banned by the Ordinance of 1787, Cass was a leading supporter of the doctrine of popular sovereignty, according to which it was up to the people who lived in a territory to decide whether slavery should be permitted. This, as everyone realized in 1848, was in direct conflict with what had been agreed nearly thirty years earlier in the Missouri Compromise. As a result Cass' nomination led to a split in the Democratic Party, with antislavery members joining the Free Soil Party. One of these, Martin Van Buren—the last (1837–1841) Democratic president before Polk—was nominated as the Free Soil candidate in 1848. This explains why the House of Representatives, during the summer of that year, had to listen to speeches in favor of three candidates.

Lincoln finally gained the floor on July 27 and after briefly praising Zachary Taylor turned on the Democrats. Cass' long career came in for ridicule, with Lincoln able to show how the general's greatest achievements were to be found in the way he looked after his own interests. With Lincoln as the eighth speaker in the debate, the House was particularly captivated by his humor—a welcome relief in a summer afternoon in Washington. His manner, according to the *Baltimore American*, "was so good-natured, and his style so peculiar, that he kept the House in a continuous roar of merriment for the last half hour."[16]

Lincoln continued working in Washington after Congress adjourned on August 13, but in September he was on the campaign trail in New England, where, to his great joy, Mary and his two sons joined him. This continued the process of discovering the Atlantic states, with particular attention paid to Massachusetts, where audiences in such places as Boston, New Bedford, Lowell, Dedham, Worcester, and Taunton heard much the same speech as Lincoln had made in Congress. Because in a strongly Whig state the threat to Taylor came not so much from Cass as from Van Buren. Lincoln worked hard to establish his own credentials on the slavery issue. He reminded one audience "that the people of Illinois agreed entirely with the people of Massachusetts on this subject, except perhaps that they did not keep so constantly thinking about it." Given that Lincoln was the only Whig representing Illinois in Washington, with six Democrats on the other side, he was perhaps claiming too much for his own state when all of Massachusetts' ten representatives in the House and both its senators—one of whom was the illustrious Daniel Webster—were Whigs. Massachusetts was hardly more interested in Lincoln than Washington had been. Such press comment as there was followed party lines, with the *Boston*

Herald calling Lincoln "a tremendous voice for Taylor and Fillmore"[17] while the *Norfolk Democrat* found his words "absolutely nauseous."[18]

While on the campaign trail for Zachary Taylor, Lincoln had learned a great deal in states that would be critical for his own future; in Illinois—where he finally returned home in October after a long journey from New York which included a visit to Niagara Falls that left him wondering "where all the water came from"[19]—the Whigs were fighting a losing battle. The election for the Seventh Congressional District had already been lost by the Whig Stephen Logan—whom voters thought "mean-spirited and avaricious." It had not helped him either that he had endorsed Lincoln's "spot of soil" resolutions in Congress, when his Democratic opponent, Thomas Harris, was a veteran of the Mexican War who had been wounded at the battle of Cerro Gordo. Worse was to come after the defeat of Logan: in the presidential election in October, Cass won Illinois.

LINCOLN AND SLAVERY

Lincoln, however, was able to return to Washington for the second "lame duck" session of the Thirtieth Congress, satisfied with the part he had played on securing the election of Zachary Taylor in November 1848. His final three months in Congress were taken up with issues which had not much occupied his thoughts during the first session: these related to slavery and its expansion.

Although Abraham Lincoln was born in Kentucky, a slave state, from the age of seven he lived in two states, first Indiana and then Illinois, both former US territories in which slavery was ruled out by the Northwest Ordinance of 1787. In both states—and particularly in Illinois where Lincoln spent almost his entire adult life—the earliest American settlers came to the southern counties, having crossed the Ohio River. This meant that in the states they had left behind, slavery was permitted. For some, such as the Lincoln family—who, as described by Abraham, were "naturally anti-slavery"—migration across the river provided a way of escape. Some, however, attracted by the prospects north of the Ohio, persisted in bringing slaves with them. That this was in defiance of the law was no obstacle, as witness the fact that Illinois' first two senators both continued as slave owners after they settled there. Even so, in Illinois—as in all the other states created out of the Northwest Territory—the state Constitution prohibited slavery. In the course of time, as more and more immigrants to Illinois came from the north, to settle mainly in the northern parts of the state, the number of slaves steadily declined to the point that within the state slavery was no longer an issue. As chapter 11 shows, the expansion of slavery into new states admitted to the Union was a quite different question.

Although this stage had already been reached when Abraham Lincoln became active in Illinois state politics in the 1830s, the abolitionist cause—whose main support was in New England—had little appeal. At the national level Illinois Democrats—who in the Thirtieth Congress represented every one of the state's seven districts except that won by Lincoln in 1846—could be relied upon to support the rock-solid group of forty-seven southern Democrats in the House of Representatives on almost any issue relating to slavery. This was not true of the seven original northern states: the Pennsylvania Democrat David Wilmot was by no means alone in the party in the stand on slavery incorporated in the proviso bearing his name. Living and working in Illinois, Lincoln inevitably saw much more of slavery at first hand than he would have had Pennsylvania been his home-state. Although the population of northern Illinois, and particularly that of Chicago—a city only founded in the 1830s—steadily gained ground at the cost of the southern counties, Springfield was not only still closer to St. Louis but also largely dependant upon it for commerce with the outside world. The fact that Missouri was a slave state would have made an immediate impact upon any visitor such as Lincoln—who would have seen even more of the "peculiar institution" on his steamboat trips to New Orleans, or during visits to the family of his wife, Mary Todd Lincoln, in Lexington, Kentucky. All this left Lincoln convinced that slavery, where it was permitted, was too well entrenched to be eradicated. Here he had the law on his side, for "the Congress of the United States has no power, under the constitution, to interfere with the institution of slavery on the different states."[20]

The position was quite different when it came to two key issues of the day; one was the extension of slavery beyond the states where it was already established, and the other, its status within the District of Columbia. Congress had the constitutional power to decide upon both these issues. Although—as already made clear above—the first of them had become critical as a result of the Mexican War—on which Lincoln took issue with President Polk—he was never much concerned by the fact that without the admission of Texas as the twenty-seventh state of the Union the war would never have taken place. As for slavery in Texas he said:

> I never could see much good to come from annexation . . .; on the other hand I never could very clearly see how the annexation would augment the evil of slavery. It always seemed to me that slaves would be taken there in about equal numbers, with or without annexation. And if *more* were taken because of annexation, still there would be just so many of the fewer left, where they taken from . . . I hold it to be a paramount duty of us in the free states, due to the Union of the states, and perhaps to liberty itself (paradox though it may seem) to let slavery of the other states alone; while, on the other hand, I hold it to be equally clear, that we should never directly lend ourselves directly or indirectly, to prevent that slavery dying a natural death.[21]

He went even further in his statement of principle by adding that the duty of free states included opposition to schemes "for it to find new places for it to live in, when it can no longer exist in the old."

From such a position Lincoln knew that he should remain silent during the acrimonious debates in Congress over the Wilmot proviso, although on the occasions that it actually came to a roll call he voted in favor of it. As to slavery in the District of Columbia, the issue was much more immediate, and no one working there could turn a blind eye to it. The problem, from the beginning, was that the District was formed out of some hundred square miles of land ceded by Maryland and Virginia, and the two states—with the Potomac River as their common frontier—both permitted slavery. Nonetheless, the fact that article 1, section 8, paragraph 17 of the Constitution gave Congress the right to "exercise exclusive legislation in all cases whatsoever" over the district that was to be created as "the seat of the Government of the United States" meant that Maryland and Virginia gave up all right to land within the District; congressional control was absolute. When, however, Congress first moved to the District of Columbia in 1801, it ruled that the laws of Maryland should continue to apply to that portion of it ceded by Maryland, and with the same provision governing the portion ceded by Virginia[23]—so ensuring that slavery would continue indefinitely in the new capital of the United States.

In Washington's early days there were relatively few slaves, but long before the 1840s the demand for labor both in construction and in the part of the district which still belonged to farms had ensured that a quarter of its population consisted of negroes—although, significantly, only about a fifth of these were slaves. But of this slave contingent a large number were in transit as part of an organized trade that operated on a considerable scale. The reason for this was to be found in the changing plantation economies of the southern states. While in Maryland and Virginia the declining demand for tobacco meant that plantations switched to the much less labor-intensive cultivation of wheat,[23] the steadily increasing demand for cotton cultivated in the deep south inevitably meant an increased demand for slave labor. Washington—with its location at the head of the Potomac's tidal reach making it accessible to ocean-going shipping—was an ideal center for trading slaves, and the largest of the trading companies, Franklin and Armfield, was located there. Ships carrying slaves constantly sailed down the Potomac to Chesapeake Bay, and out into the Atlantic, to proceed round Florida into the Gulf of Mexico, with, as their final destination, the great harbor city of New Orleans. There, in the heart of the cotton belt, the slaves were sold to plantations. Within the district most of them were held in the notorious Georgia Pen—described by Abraham Lincoln as "a sort of negro livery-stable"—only seven blocks away from the Capitol.

The slave trade within the District of Columbia, an obvious target for abolitionists, was the subject of numerous petitions sent to Congress, which in turn voted any number of times on motions to impose a ban. Most failed in both Houses, but on one occasion, Daniel Gott, a Whig from New York in the House of Representatives, succeeded in carrying a vote that the slave trade in the District of Columbia was "contrary to natural justice and the fundamental principles of our political system—notoriously a reproach to our country throughout Christendom, and a serious hinderance [sic] to the progress of republican liberty among the nations of the earth."

Abraham Lincoln, although consistently upholding the constitutional right of citizens to petition Congress—whether on the subject of slavery or any other matter—kept a low profile, acting in accordance with his belief, stated in 1837, "that the Congress of the United States has the power ... to abolish slavery in the District of Columbia; but that power ought not to be exercised unless at the request of the people of the said District."[24] Finally, on January 10, 1849, he was ready to introduce a compromise resolution calling for a referendum on slavery in which "every free white male citizen" could participate, while including, as a concession to the slaveholding states, a requirement for the municipal authorities "to provide active and efficient means to arrest, and deliver up to their owners, all fugitive slaves escaping into the said District." Lincoln's initiative failed. Once the resolution was made public, the backing he relied upon melted away and he never introduced his resolution. It was, however, noted by its most powerful southern opponent, South Carolina Senator John C. Calhoun, who referred to the proposal of "a member from Illinois" as a reason for southerners to band together to protect their rights, and cause the north to be "brought to a pause, and to a calculation of consequences."[25] Lincoln, humiliated just at the end of his one term in Congress, accepted that "it was useless to prosecute the business at that time."

THE SUPREME COURT

A final question to be asked about Lincoln's time as a congressman is what did the US Supreme Court then add up to? Surprisingly it only acquired a building of its own during the 1930s. Until then it had, since the day Washington became the nation's capital in 1800, the use of different chambers in the Capitol—the only exception being a short period in a private house after the British had set fire to the building in the War of 1812. Although without a home of its own, the Court, presided over—during almost the whole of Abraham Lincoln's lifetime—by two strong and very long-serving chief justices, John Marshall (1800–1835) and Martin Taney (1835–1864), still produced a long list of important decisions, mostly the work of remarkably undistinguished associate justices.

Although in the years 1847–1848 no decision of the court directly affected issues—notably slavery—of concern to Lincoln, its character, as defined both by its members and their recent decisions, was crucial to the historical process. The first point to make is that—in contrast to the House of Representatives—membership of the court was extremely stable. At the beginning of the Thirtieth Congress' first session in December, 1847, the senior justice, John McLean of Ohio, had been a member of the court for eighteen years, while four others, James Wayne of Georgia, Martin Taney of Maryland, John Catron of Tennessee, and John McKinley of Alabama, had all served for more than ten years. Of these Taney counted for most, since President Andrew Jackson had appointed him chief justice—in succession to the renowned John Marshall—in 1835.

Besides Taney, three of the justices had also been appointed by Jackson, while McKinley had been appointed by President Martin Van Buren (1837–1841), who also appointed Peter Daniel of Virginia in 1841. Samuel Nelson, who was appointed a justice in 1845, by James Tyler, was the only member of the court not to have been appointed by a Democratic president. Finally, in 1846, President James Polk appointed two new justices, Levi Woodbury of New Hampshire and Robert Grier of Pennsylvania. This led to a court in which five justices (including Taney himself) came from the south, and only four (including the two most recent appointments) from the north.

For all its accumulated experience on the bench this was not a distinguished court. One historical verdict on its senior member, John McLean, that "few justices have worked so hard, for so long, with such little impact"[26] is more favorable than most of his fellow justices deserved. When a vacancy occurred in the Supreme Court, two considerations more than any others influenced a US president in making his choice. The first was to reward loyal support given by possible candidates before appointment; the second was the need to find a justice who could be relied upon to support his policies when they came to be considered by the Court. President Jackson's appointment of Roger Taney as an associate justice in 1834 met both conditions.

Taney, after campaigning for Jackson in 1828, was first rewarded by being appointed US attorney general in 1831; while occupying this post he proved sound on the key question of the right of southern states to prohibit free negroes—whether from other states or British possessions offshore—from entering their borders. Taney made his position on presidential policy clear in a written opinion: "The African race in the United States even when free, are everywhere a degraded class, and exercise no political influence. The privileges they are allowed to enjoy, are accorded to them as a matter of kindness and benevolence rather than right ... They are not looked upon as citizens by the contracting parties who formed the Constitution."[27] Jackson was also indebted to Taney for the advice he had given on the question of rechartering the Bank of the United States, which had led to Congress blocking his appointment as treasury secretary in 1834. This led him return to private law practice in Maryland, where Jackson, in a letter, acknowledged a "debt of gratitude and regard which I have not the power to discharge," a questionable apology seeing that he appointed Taney chief justice only a year later.

On the question of African slavery, the Supreme Court counted above all for the line it took on fugitive slaves who had found sanctuary in one or other of the northern states—an issue on which, as a result of the Dred Scott decision in 1857, Taney's opinion is remembered more than on any other question. That, however, was given some ten years after the end of the Thirtieth Congress. In 1847, the relevant recent judgment of the Supreme Court—which foreshadowed Dred Scott—was that in *Prigg v. Pennsylvania*,[28] a case that turned on the right of a professional slave catcher from Maryland, Edward Prigg, forcibly to remove from the neighboring free state of Pennsylvania a female slave, and her children, who had found sanctuary there. As often in the history of the Supreme Court the narrow legal question at issue turned on the rights of a state in relation to federal legislation, in this case the Fugitive Slave Act of 1793.

The judgment of the Court was written by its senior justice, Joseph Story, who had been appointed by President James Madison in 1811—when Abraham Lincoln was only two years old—to die, after thirty-four years service, just before Lincoln came to Washington as a congressman. Story, appointed to serve under John Marshall, became the hidden brain behind the chief justice's judgments: his three-volume *Commentaries on the Constitution*, published in 1833, alone justifies his reputation as the Court's leading nineteenth-century scholar.

Being handed down by the "Massachusetts" justice, Story's ruling that "all state laws relating to fugitive slaves violated the Constitution," was interpreted in many northern states as ruling out any legislation giving state officials authority to aid slave catchers, while at the same time causing distress to Chief Justice Taney, in whose opinion this restriction only governed legislation hindering the return of "property"—for which read "slaves"—to its owners. However much Story's judgment encouraged abolitionists, it made little difference when it came to the fate of runaway slaves. In practice, if apprehended in a state bordering on the south, such as Pennsylvania, their chances of remaining free were relatively poor—as *Prigg v. Pennsylvania* illustrates—while they were very much better off if they made it to a state further afield such as Massachusetts. If, at the end of the 1840s the strict legal position was stable, and generally unhelpful to fugitive slaves, their numbers steadily increased as did the support they received from dedicated abolitionists—the 1850s were to show what all this would lead to.

While the law prescribed, and was committed to defend, an ideal state, the reality was quite different. Owners had sleepless nights worrying about the possibility of their slaves absconding, and the slaves knew it. According to one fugitive from Maryland, "no power in this world will arrest the exodus of the slaves from the South" which he saw as "the divinely ordered method for the effectual destruction of American slavery."[29]

In the spring of 1848, while Lincoln was still in Washington, there was a dramatic instance of an attempted large-scale escape to freedom. This was orchestrated by Daniel Drayton a Philadelphia sea captain who sailed up to Washington with the *Pearl*, a schooner carrying a cargo of wood, intending to return home with a family of nine runaway slaves. News of the plan spread among Washington's slaves, so that on the night of the planned departure some seventy-six turned up to board the *Pearl*, and Drayton took them all. Soon after setting sail the schooner was forced to seek a safe anchorage to wait out a storm. There they were arrested after a steamer manned by some of the slave owners caught up with them. While the slaves were either returned to their owners or were sent to dealers in the Georgia Pen, Drayton was put on trial in a federal court in the District of Columbia. Following the established practice he was charged under a Maryland statute of 1737 which provided for a maximum jail sentence of twenty years for stealing slaves. The indictment had forty-one separate counts—one for each of the owners—and a further seventy-four (each carrying a fine of $200) for helping slaves to escape.

There were two separate trials which led to the maximum sentence of twenty years for larceny, but on appeal the convictions were reversed on the ground that the prosecution had failed to prove that Drayton had taken the slaves either for his own enjoyment or for pecuniary gain. The district attorney continued to pursue the case, but was finally ready to accept a plea of guilty to the charge of helping slaves escape. The owner of the *Pearl*, Edwards Sayres—who had been on board at the time of the escape—had been tried separately, and having accepted similar terms, was fined $150 for each one of the slaves caught on board the schooner.

THE FEDERAL GOVERNMENT

By present-day standards, Washington during the 1840s was home to a very small number of government departments—state, army, navy, treasury and from the very end of President Polk's term of office, interior, comprised the list, together with the post office. There was an attorney general but no Justice Department to support him. Partly because such matters as health, agriculture, commerce, and education were seen as the responsibility of individual states, for some of them it would only be in the twentieth century that they were looked after by their own departments in Washington, with employees counted in thousands.

In the 1840s the federal government, nationwide, had some 20,000 employees, of whom only a thousand worked in Washington. Although the lion's share of the federal budget went to the army and navy, the majority of federal employees, some 14,000 in all, worked for the post office,[30] scattered across the country in local post offices, with the appointment of the postmasters being an important component of federal patronage. A similar distribution of government servants was to be found in the General Land Office, which, belonging first to the treasury and then after 1849 to interior, had expanded greatly during the 1830s in step with the increase in public land, mainly in the newer states, subject to its jurisdiction. The office offered employment to a wide range of surveyors (as Abraham Lincoln once was for a short time), receivers, and bookkeepers—and given its power to control the allocation of public land during a period of rapid development of industry, agriculture, and transport (particularly by railroad)—was subject to continual political pressure.

The post office and the General Land Office were the two federal agencies with most impact on people at the grassroots level, although in the case of the latter the impact varied considerably from one part of the nation to another. The post office, on the other hand, reached every small town with little regional differentiation. During the 1840s the amount of mail increased rapidly with cheap prepaid carriage introduced by Congress in 1845[31] and facilitated by the use (adopted from Britain) of postage stamps—which after 1857 became obligatory.[32] With no free home delivery the local post office became an important meeting point, and because a great part of all mail consisted of newspapers—which had enjoyed cheap preferential rates ever since the US Post Office was first set up by the Post Office Act of 1792[33]—there was an immediate opportunity for political controversy at a time when the American press almost never pulled its punches.

The interest that a congressman such as Abraham Lincoln had in the executive branch owed everything to presidential patronage. Offices coveted by Illinois voters included that of a local land registrar, a US attorney, secretary to the governor of the Minnesota territory, US marshal in the state, purser in the US Navy[34]—the list seemed almost endless, as it did in almost any congressional district. While Lincoln was actually in Washington he could achieve little with James Polk as president beyond promising to do more for Illinois office seekers if Polk were to be succeeded by a Whig. They were disappointed. Zachary Taylor, although a Whig, confirmed the office of any number of Democrats appointed by Polk's administration. When Lincoln became president twelve years later he would find out for himself how much of his time would be taken up with matters of patronage—and doubtless have a better understanding of the line taken by Taylor.

THE CHANGING FACE OF THE NATION'S CAPITAL

Where the post office defined that part of the communications infrastructure in government hands, railroads, from the 1830s onward, were beginning to add an entirely new dimension to it. James Polk was the first president to arrive in Washington by train, although he in fact only traveled a short distance from a nearby station in Maryland. The station where he arrived was an extremely modest building compared to today's imposing Union Station, which was only completed in 1908. Although Abraham Lincoln was from the beginning an ardent supporter of railroad expansion, this had to wait until his return to Illinois before he played an effective role. The same is true of the electric telegraph—unlike railroads, an American invention—which was also introduced in the 1840s. This time, however, was still the heyday of steamboats, as could be seen in Washington from the busy traffic on the Potomac—which on a spring day in 1848 included the steamer that sealed the fate of the *Pearl*.

Next to the Capitol and the White House, the most imposing buildings in Washington were its churches, such as St. John's Episcopalian Church opposite the White House—where by tradition Pew 54 is set aside for US presidents— or, for negroes, the Ebenezer Methodist Church close to the Capitol—both of which are still part of the local scene. Another church known to Congressman Lincoln was the First Baptist Church, built in 1833. Abandoned as a place of worship in 1859, it was converted to a theater by the Baltimore entrepreneur John T. Ford in 1861, only to burn down two years later. Rebuilt, and reopened as Ford's Theater, it was the scene of Lincoln's assassination in April 1865. Reconstructed in the 1960s, it is now, together with the Petersen House on the opposite side of the road—where the president actually died—a historical monument.

The only government building to survive from the 1840s is the oldest, center part of the Treasury Building, which was built between 1836 and 1842. The building as it now is includes the south and west wings, constructed in the same style in the years following 1855. The Smithsonian Institution was chartered by the Twenty-ninth Congress in 1846, and members of the Thirtieth Congress, such as Representative Abraham Lincoln, could hardly have failed to miss the first stages of the construction of the famous "castle"—which was finally completed in 1855.

A number of town houses, many with important historic associations, also go back to the early nineteenth century. Among the best known are the

Octagon House, where President Madison in 1815 signed the Treaty of Ghent which ended the war of 1812, and close to the White House, Decatur House on Lafayette Square, and Blair House at 1651–1653 Pennsylvania Avenue. In the 1850s, its owners, the Blair family, noted opponents of the Kansas-Nebraska Act (see chapter 11), played an important part in forming the Republican Party. During Lincoln's years in the White House, next door, Montgomery Blair, who had played a key part in keeping Maryland out of the Confederacy, was postmaster general and a close adviser to the president.

The one substantial residential district dating back to Washington's earliest days is that to the east of Capitol Hill, where the street plan still follows that proposed by the French architect, Pierre L'Enfant, in 1791. The buildings were always heterogeneous, with both brick and frame houses, in various styles and sizes, as today's visitor can see from those that still survive. Of the rest little now survives of Washington to give an idea of how it was in the 1840s, which—to judge from the character of the city as described by contemporaries—is probably just as well. It is not so much the buildings as the institutions that still survive, operating on a massive scale that provides a livelihood for bureaucrats, lawyers, lobbyists, diplomats, and many others outside politics who, in the days of Congressman Abraham Lincoln, formed a very small community. In the 1840s Washington—apart from the uncertain status of its negro population—was a small, remarkably homogeneous city whose English-speaking citizens saw themselves as heirs to a common political culture. In the 1840s, however, this was beginning to fall apart, to lead to crisis in the 1850s and war in the early 1860s. These are the subjects of chapters 11 and 12.

Bleeding Kansas

THE END OF THE MISSOURI COMPROMISE

Chapter 9 relates how the admission of California as the thirty-first state of the union in 1850 made that year a historical watershed in the American politics of slavery. Although there was no immediate threat to the fifteen states in which slavery was not only permitted, but also regarded as essential to the established lifestyle of the white population—of which the last was Florida, admitted as the twenty-eighth state under President Polk in 1845—the prospects of extending it to such new states as would sooner or later join the Union were extremely uncertain. On the contrary the most immediate prospect, in the ten years up to 1860, was of both the Minnesota and Oregon territories becoming free states, as actually happened in 1858 and 1859. Although this was something leading southern politicians always accepted, they worked hard to maintain the balance between north and south established—as related in chapter 7—by the Missouri Compromise of 1821. In the 1850s there was a distant, if uncertain, prospect of creating new states out of the vast New Mexico Territory ceded to the United States under the Treaty of Guadalupe Hidalgo in 1848, but this was a very long-term possibility, only realized in 1912, when Arizona and New Mexico joined the Union. The critical east-west line laid down by the Missouri Compromise at latitude 36°30" north ruled out any new states in the rest of the land—such as the Utah territory—ceded by Mexico. The same was true of the vast and still "unorganized" lands—prairie, mountain, and desert—comprised in the Louisiana Territory. By the end of the 1850s, only the five states—Louisiana, Missouri, Arkansas, Iowa, and Minnesota—whose eastern boundary was the Mississippi river, had already joined the Union. The fact that of these the first three were admitted at a relatively early stage—in 1812, 1821, and 1836—while the last two joined only in 1846 and 1858, meant that during the years following the Mexican War (1846–1848) the scales were tipping in favor of the free states, a result anticipated, if not welcomed, by many of the southerners, who, led by a Tennessee president, James Polk, had ardently supported the war.

The history of the compromise of 1850, which—as related in chapter 9—left the door open for California to join the Union—foreshadowed the conflict in Kansas which is the subject matter of this chapter. Note first, however, the serious attempts—now no more than a footnote in history—made to acquire new territory beyond the reach of the Missouri Compromise. First President Polk, helped by his secretary of state, James Buchanan, tried unsuccessfully to buy Cuba from Spain in 1848;[1] then there was a failed attempt to split California in two, with the southern half destined to become a slave state; a third initiative was that of George Crabb, a Mississippian who had emigrated to California, to take over the unruly Mexican state of Sonora—an adventure which he paid for with his life ending in front of a Mexican firing squad;[2] and then, finally, another reckless adventurer, William Walker, originally from Tennessee, after several attempts to take over the Central American republic of Nicaragua, lost his life to a firing squad in neighboring Honduras in September 1860.[3] This ended a period of twelve years of frustration, in which no new territory was gained by the United States. Foreign adventures were plainly not a good way of extending slavery, but the lesson was very hard learned. It would be even harder in Kansas.

The adventures recounted in the previous paragraph were a diversion from the real challenge facing the United States in 1850, which was to organize the vast territories—mostly acquired as a result of the Louisiana Purchase in 1803—to the point that they were ready to become new states of the Union. The problem could not simply be shelved—say by leaving the land mainly to Indians, whose numbers beyond the Mississippi had increased as a result of the forced migration of eastern tribes initiated during the presidency of Andrew Jackson. For this there was one reason that could hardly be contested: sooner rather than later, California, with its vast economic potential—stretching far beyond its mineral resources—and growing population, would have to be linked to the eastern states by railroad. In 1850 this was extremely problematic, for even in the east the railroad network, operated by any number of different companies, was far from complete—as chapter 8 makes clear. The Baltimore and Ohio Railroad only reached the Ohio (at Wheeling, Virginia)[4] in 1852, and the Mississippi (at East Saint Louis, Illinois) in 1857. Later in this same year the Rock Island Railroad, running west from Chicago, became the first to successfully bridge the Mississippi, to continue on across Iowa on the far side of the river, with its final destination, Councils Bluffs, on the Missouri River, with the Nebraska territory on the other side. What, however, was achieved later in the 1850s, was already clearly in prospect at the beginning of the decade, and significantly two key cities, Chicago and East St. Louis, were in the state of Illinois.

On the other side of the Mississippi, the Missouri legislature, encouraged by Senator Thomas Hart Benton, had already approved in 1849 an ambitious plan for constructing railroads in the state: this included five main lines, with St. Louis as the main hub. One of these, the Missouri-Pacific, would cross the state through the counties on the south bank of the Missouri River to the point where the Kansas River joins it. This location was geographically extremely significant: along a straight line running due south, its longitude defined the western boundary of the state of Missouri. To the north, on the other hand, the Missouri River was the boundary up to the east-west line separating the state from Iowa. Along this stretch of river, therefore, the west side belonged not to Missouri but to the Kansas-Nebraska Territory. Critically, also, the confluence of the Kansas and Missouri rivers was also the location of Kansas City, the second city—after St. Louis—in the state of Missouri, which throughout the 1840s had been the point from which the wagon trails led to the far west.

In the south railroad construction was far less advanced. The Mississippi river system still dominated the transport infrastructure—based on steamships as related in chapter 2—with the railroad network playing a subsidiary role. In 1850 there was next to nothing west of the Mississippi river, and little was constructed during the next ten years beyond short local lines—mainly in Texas. This was a poor base for building a transcontinental railroad taking a southern route. What is more, such a route would have its Pacific terminus in southern California, when almost all the activity generated by the Gold Rush was in the north, making a location in the San Francisco bay area the obvious destination for any transcontinental railroad. When it came to the terrain, inland from California, that any line must follow, the hazards of a southern route—as recounted in chapter 8—were at least as great as those of any northern route.

None of these adverse factors discouraged southern railroad entrepreneurs, so that when, in 1850, Illinois Senator Stephen Douglas presented in Washington his plans for a railroad linking St. Louis to Northern California he found that they were extremely divisive.[5] Not only did they threaten southern economic interests all the way from the Atlantic coast to Texas, but much more critically—for the south as a whole—they would involve organizing the Nebraska territory subject to the restrictions on slavery contained in the Missouri Compromise. In face of considerable southern support in Congress for the southern railroad—with Jefferson Davis, President Franklin Pierce's secretary of war (and later president of the Confederacy), playing an important part offstage—Douglas introduced in the Senate a bill that would become the Kansas-Nebraska Act of 1854. This established in law the principle of "popular sovereignty" adopted by the California Compromise of 1850, effectively redefining slavery as a local territorial issue, at the same time banishing from Congress—even more effectively than the gag rule (as reported in chapter 10)   any further discussion of the issue.[6] This was not enough for the southern senators. Under duress Douglas agreed to include an explicit repeal of the Missouri Compromise in the act, knowing that "it would raise a hell of storm."[7] At the same time the act provided for the territory to be divided into the Kansas Territory, between 37° and 40° north, and the Nebraska Territory between 40° north and 49° north—which brought it right up to the Canadian frontier.[8] This was in its way a compromise—at least so long as it was accepted that Kansas, to the west of Missouri, would become a slave state, and Nebraska, to the west of Iowa, a free state.[9] The problem here was that Missouri, having been a state since 1821, was far stronger—in its economy, infrastructure, and population—than Iowa, which had only been admitted in 1846. It was clear to all that statehood for Kansas was a much more immediate issue than it was for Nebraska. What is more, the implicit assumption about Kansas' position on slavery was more wishful thinking on the part of the south than a self-evident truth.

Abraham Lincoln, speaking for many—and not only in his home state of Illinois—said that the act "took us by surprise—astounded us ... We were thunderstruck and stunned."[10] At this stage however he said little in support of two northern senators, Charles Sumner of Massachusetts and Salmon P. Chase of Ohio, who saw the repeal of the Missouri Compromise "as a gross violation of a sacred pledge; as a criminal betrayal of previous rights; as part and parcel of an atrocious plot to exclude from a vast unoccupied region immigrants from the Old World and free laborers from our own States, and convert it into a dreary region of despotism, inhabited by masters and slaves."[11]

The issue raised by the two senators was critical to the future of the Kansas Territory, particularly if, as expected, it were to become a state of the Union. How far, in reality, would the Act of 1854 exclude from it "immigrants ... and free laborers"?

THE KANSAS BATTLEFIELD

To answer this question one must look first at the geography of Kansas in the context of the demography of the United States, and particularly that of Missouri—the only neighboring state on Kansas' eastern frontier. Given that the natural lines of communication overland in both states run east-west, and that the natural flow of migrants was from east to west, then anyone who chose to settle in Kansas was almost certain to come there by way of Missouri, a slave state. What is more, the pattern of settlement in Missouri, in which the Missouri River—as it crossed the state from east to west, from St. Louis to Kansas City—always played a key role, had led to relatively large populations in the counties adjacent to the Kansas state line. In so far as any Missouri residents were inclined to resettle—following the well-established American practice—Kansas was in many ways an attractive destination, made the more so, for some, by the fact that they could take their slaves with them. On the other hand, Missouri itself was far from being densely populated, and there was enough land for resettlement within the state. Moreover Arkansas and Texas, both slave states, also welcomed new settlers.[12]

For those coming from further afield—including "immigrants and free laborers"—Kansas offered abundant and accessible new land; although cultivating it could involve years of hardship, this was the lot of new settlers almost everywhere west of the Mississippi River. That northern settlers, coming without slaves, would live side by side with southerners with slaves, was not necessarily a problem. There was room for everyone, and since the ownership of slaves provided little advantage in exploiting the potential of the land for farming, those without slaves would in no sense constitute a sort of underclass—as was often the case in the deep south.[13] What is more, population changes in the existing states of the union—partly the result of European immigration—meant that the demographic advantage lay with the north; sooner or later, if not in Kansas, then certainly in the still unorganized territories to the north and west, the southerners would simply be outnumbered. If then they were to establish slavery by applying the principle of popular sovereignty, as enabled by the Kansas-Nebraska Act, they had little time to lose. If the question were to come to a vote, they would have to be in the majority. This, then, was the state of the game in 1854. By securing the passage of the Kansas-Nebraska Act the southerners had won a key round; but they had not won the match and they knew it. As Lincoln said later in a speech,[14] Kansas was "the concrete embodiment of the choices facing the nation's future."

In principle all that was needed was for the Kansas Territory quietly to accept as settlers such residents of the already existing states of the Union—whether north or south—as should choose to establish a new life there. Some, but not all, of those who would then come from the south would bring slaves with them; almost none of those coming from the north would do so. Then at some future stage, when the settler community found that the time was ripe, a convention could be summoned to decide on the question of slavery, and petition the US Congress for admission to the Union according to the decision actually made. In other words, there would sooner or later be a head count of those for and against slavery, so that numbers would decide the question. This was more or less what happened in the course of the seven years between the Kansas-Nebraska Act of 1854 and the final admission of Kansas as the thirty-fourth state of the Union on January 29, 1861. The process was far from peaceful, and ended only after six southern states, South Carolina, Florida, Mississippi, Alabama, Georgia, and Louisiana, by seceding from the Union in the preceding six weeks, no longer had an effective voice in the US Congress—all part of the history related in the final chapter of this book.

On May 30, 1854—the day that President Franklin Pierce signed the Kansas-Nebraska bill—there were fewer than 800 settlers in the Kansas territory; within a year there were more than 8,000 white settlers (almost all farming families) together with 192 slaves.[15] Although nearly half had come from Missouri and an absolute majority from southern states as a whole, about a third had come from northern states. Only 4 percent, however, were from New England, where the abolitionist movement was most powerful. The relatively small number of slaves was significant, given that some 17,000 of Missouri's 87,000 slaves worked in the hemp- and tobacco-growing counties, known as Little Dixie, bordering Kansas.[16] Where families who left Missouri for Kansas had on average only two slaves, for those who stayed behind the number was six. Given the relative abundance of land in Missouri, there was little economic incentive to cross the state line into Kansas—to say nothing of the political risk that the territory might one day vote to exclude slavery. Indeed this possibility had attracted a number of free-soil settlers from Missouri, while others, who were pro-slavery, were stigmatized as "border ruffians,"[17] supported by organizations known as "Blue Lodges" or "Self-Defensives" acting as secret societies to extend slavery to Kansas.[18] One leading Self-Defensive, B. F. Stringfellow of Platte County went on record as defending slavery as "a blessing to the white race and to the negro."[19]

The problem, from the very earliest days, was the opposition between massive support—by dedicated abolitionists in the north—of free-soilers settled in Kansas, and equally strong support, from the south, of settlement by dedicated opponents of free soil, not all of whom were border ruffians. Although many settlers, from both north and south, went to Kansas with peaceable intent, few when they got there were able to forget their origins; neutrality was hardly a real option. Apart from peaceable settlers—who at least in early days might even have been in a majority—there were all too many, from both sides, who came ready to fight a battle.

Potential troublemakers from the north, as well as the south, were soon on the scene. Many were supported by companies such as the New England Emigrant Aid Company (NEEAC), chartered in Massachusetts in 1855, which by supporting settlement "offered both opportunity for economic advancement on the frontier and the satisfaction of participating in the holy cause of saving Kansas for freedom."[20] In addition to bringing new settlers the NEEAC provided resources for local development; this was focused on the new township of Lawrence, named after NEEAC's leading backer in Massachusetts, Amos A. Lawrence, whose dislike of slavery was somewhat tempered by the fact that he had become rich by selling cotton cloth. In Lawrence the NEEAC built hotels, sawmills, and gristmills, financed a newspaper, and controversially armed local settlers—prospective as well as actual. Inevitably the activities of the NEEAC in an area with many competing claims to land led to titles disputed between southerners and the northern settlers it supported. Although southerners were more often than not the first to take up arms, the fact that northern settlers, even before they arrived in the territory were armed with Sharps rifles purchased by the NEEAC, was certainly provocative. According to the recollection of one member of an Illinois party headed for Kansas, "it was a military company that could be changed to a colony or a colony ready for military service."[21] In any case Missourians in Kansas had reason to believe that free-soil settlers were the tools of abolitionists sent to the territory on account of their prospective voting power.

The south retaliated in kind. To cite one instance, Major Jefferson Buford, an Alabama lawyer and veteran of the second Creek War,[22] led a party of 400 to Kansas in the early summer of 1856, but when fighting broke out later in the year many chose to leave rather than engage free-soilers. With Mississippi, Arkansas, and eastern Texas all welcoming new immigrants, Kansas was an expensive choice to make on a matter of principle. Senator David Atchison of Missouri complained of the inadequate help received by his state from the rest of the south, even though "the prosperity or the ruin of the whole south depends on the Kansas struggle." A pro-slavery convention agreed with the senator that "large monied associations [intended] to abolitionize Kansas, and through Kansas to operate upon the contiguous states of Missouri, Arkansas and Texas."[23] Hostile sentiment in Missouri made it so hazardous for northern settlers traveling through the state on their way to Kansas that life promised to become notably safer once they reached their destination. More than in any other slave state, citizens of Missouri saw—rightly as events would prove—their own future tied to that of Kansas. This, as both pro-slavery and free-soil men recognized, could only be decided by the ballot box,[24] and Senator Atchison urged southerners "to go peaceably and inhabit the territory, and peaceable to vote and settle the question."[25]

Northerners also saw that everything would turn on the first elections. As Samuel Pomeroy, the NEEAC agent in Lawrence, reported, "A *terrible* struggle is before us at this very *first election*. They are determined to have a law recognizing slavery at the very *first meeting* of the *Legislature*. If they do not get it at the *first* legislature, they *never* will." There was a crucial difference between the two sides, which was noted by Abraham Lincoln: for Missourians it was beyond argument that "slavery already exists in the territory," while migrants—above all those from New England—expected "the question to be decided by voting."[26] This brought the conflict down to a more fundamental level; it was not just about slavery, but about liberty and political rights.

The Kansas-Nebraska Act required the organization of Kansas as a US territory, with a governor appointed by Washington and a popularly elected delegate to the House of Representatives. The question as to who would qualify as a voter was to be decided by the governor. In June 1854 President Franklin Pierce appointed to this office Andrew Reeder, a Pennsylvania Democrat known to be a champion of Stephen Douglas' principle of popular sovereignty as it was enshrined in the act—which had only become law on May 30. Reeder arrived in the territory in the early fall, and on October 7 set up his first executive office in Leavenworth, a township on the banks of the Missouri, with the state of Missouri on the opposite side of the river.[27] He lost little time in organizing the election of the congressional delegate, prescribing that only residents could vote, and defining "residence" as "the actual dwelling or inhabiting in the Territory to the exclusion of any other present domicil or home, coupled with the present *bona fide* intention of remaining permanently for the same purpose."[28]

When the election was held on November 29, hundreds of Missourians, who came nowhere near to meeting the residence qualification, crossed over into the territory to vote, intimidating and browbeating the judges appointed as supervisors. Their object was to ensure the election of the "southern rights" candidate, General J.W. Whitfield. As reported by one man in Leavenworth, "the whole country was . . . overrun by hordes or ruffians, who took entire possession of the polls in almost every district . . . forced their own votes into the ballot box for WHITFIELD, and crowded out and drove off all who were suspected in being in favor of any other candidate."[29] According to another observer the election "was the greatest outrage on the ballot box ever perpetrated on American soil."[30] The free-soiler candidate, John Wakefield, having asked a Missourian what would happen if he challenged the results, was told "you will be badly abused and probably killed."[31] Lawrence, which was firmly in the hands of free-soilers, was about the only place where it was safe to vote against Whitfield. The results, when declared in early December, gave Whitfield 2,258 votes, nearly 2,000 more than either of the two rival candidates. Later, according to the findings of a congressional investigation, some 1,700 votes were declared fraudulent. Governor Reeder, who could hardly have been blind to what was happening on his own doorstep, still confirmed the results of the election.

If this was not a good start to democratic government in Kansas, worse was to follow with the elections to the territorial legislature which Reeder had set for March 30, 1855. Already in January, Missouri senator David Atchison[32] had written, "The Abolitionists will make great efforts in the Spring to send into Kansas their Battalions and Regts. for the *holy* purpose of excluding Slaveholders. They should be met by corresponding efforts on our part. *We can and must defeat them.*"[33] Missourians did not disappoint Atchison. In the days leading up to the elections ferries brought hundreds across the river to Kansas, and others came in overland. Where a census ordered to be carried out by Governor Reeder in early March listed 2,905 qualified voters, over 6,000 voted on polling day, with 5,427 pro-slavery votes being counted.[34]

In the opinion of many throughout the southern states the Missourians had gone too far, discrediting rather than helping the cause of slavery. One southerner asked "how the Missourians can expect to be sustained by any persons who have the slightest pretentions to fairness, or even to civilization."[35] Even Atchison was at pains to declare that he had not voted, although he had been in the territory encouraging his fellow Missourians. Referring—in a letter to his friend, Colonel Osborn P. Anderson—to a Russian city then under siege by the French and British armies in the Crimean War, he wrote, "What a glorious thing it then was to carry the Sebastopol of Abolitionism in the gallant style in which it was done."[36]

Governor Reeder, finding it impossible to accept all the results of the March election, and realizing that they made it impossible for all parties to have a voice in the future of the territory, ordered a special election on May 22 in all the disputed seats. This was an unwise move. The result once again was an overwhelming vote in favor of a pro-slavery legislature, but this time round with the majority who had voted in favor antagonized by the governor's action.

This majority was soon able to frustrate the governor, who, simply because—as a Douglas Democrat—he wanted popular sovereignty to have a fair trial in Kansas, was identified as a free-soiler. Confronted with the results of the May election, Reeder designated the town site of Pawnee, some hundred miles west of Leavenworth, as the place for Kansas' first territorial legislature to meet on July 2. As almost everyone knew there was a conflict of interest involved in this choice, since Reeder had invested in local land claims—a matter which in other circumstances could easily have been overlooked. After all, few of the legislators had clean hands when it came to land claims. This did not deter them from adjourning—after only four days sitting in Pawnee—and in the face of a veto by the governor, to reconvene at Shawnee Mission, a few miles further on. There they adopted Missouri's harsh slave code and petitioned President Franklin Pierce for Reeder's removal. On August 15 Reeder received notification from Washington that a Democratic president too weak to withstand pressure from southerners within his own party had dismissed him for engaging in illegal land speculation. Although Reeder chose to remain in Kansas to be remembered by history as "the first in a long series of failed territorial governors,"[37] his stand against the legislature in Pawnee made him the natural leader of the free-soilers, one of whom—from Lawrence, the free-soil stronghold—described him as "a brave and noble-hearted man."[38]

This was more than could be said of Reeder's successor, Wilson Shannon, who had given up a political career in his home state of Ohio after his support for the Kansas-Nebraska Act had alienated his constituents. Once in Kansas he made his stand in favor of "law and order," as represented by the new Shawnee Mission legislature. By this time the free-soilers were setting up a rival show. They started off by holding their own convention at Big Springs, some fifteen miles west of Lawrence on the Kansas River on September 5. The choice of location was prudent: it was some distance from the extremists in Lawrence and even further from Missouri. At the convention the informal free-soil resistance was transformed into the Free State Party, which was united by its opposition to nonresident voting. Having accepted resolutions proposed by Reeder to create its own legislature—disregarding the formally recognized territorial legislature—the convention then nominated Reeder by acclamation as Kansas' first territorial delegate. The delegates then called for another convention to be held at Topeka, even further up the Kansas River,[39] on September 19. There, after condemning the March 30 elections, the delegates having concluded that the people of Kansas "were left without any legal government" went on to resolve that they were "compelled to resort to the only remedy left—that of forming a government for themselves."[40]

To achieve this result the convention voted to reconvene on October 9, the second Tuesday in the month, knowing that the territorial legislature had called for the election of the territorial delegate to be held on the first Monday, October 1. What is more, the Topeka delegates were intent to go even further and agree on a constitution that could be submitted to the US Congress as the basis for the grant of statehood. They well knew that this was a dangerously radical step, but once it was taken they were able to claim that "the people of Kansas . . . have done, what half the Western States did while territories—called their constitutional conventions."[41]

Predictably J.W. Whitfield, having been first elected in March, was officially reelected on October 1. Nonetheless he was still listed as a candidate in the October 9 election, with Reeder standing against him. The result, needless to say, was the opposite of October 1. With Governor Shannon's certificate of election already in the possession of Whitfield, Reeder had no chance whatever of going to Washington.

Following the October 9 election the free-state constitutional convention met in Topeka, with thirty-seven delegates, from October 23 to November 11, and although, in the face of varied attitudes held by Democrats and Whigs on race, a compromise had to be found to govern the prospective rights of free blacks, a draft constitution that prohibited slavery was finally agreed upon. In the ratification vote, which was held on December 15, there were 1,731 votes for and only 46 against the Topeka constitution. With 1,287 for and 453 against, the vote for the exclusion of free blacks from citizenship was closer. On December 27, James H. Lane, who had emerged as the leader of the dominant Democratic faction, proclaimed that the Topeka constitution, having been ratified by the voters, was in force, and called for elections of state offices on January 15, 1856.[42]

The course of events in the second half of 1855 was extremely significant. Lane—presiding, in June, over a meeting held to organize the Democratic Party in Kansas—endorsed both the Democratic platform of 1852 and the Kansas-Nebraska Act.[43] By October he had given up trying to rally support for the territorial government, and by the end of the year he was leading the opposition to it—a transformation that demonstrated how the free-soil movement was becoming the dominant political force in Kansas. Numbers were beginning to count: although—as noted above—some 3,000 votes were cast in the official election of November 1854, more than half of these were cast fraudulently by Missourians who had crossed into Kansas just for voting day. This was nothing compared to the March elections in 1855, when 6,000 mainly pro-slavery votes were cast, when the number of officially registered voters was less than 3,000. The fact that at the end of the year the independently organized free-state elections—in which border ruffians and like-minded Missourians cast no votes—produced some 1,731 votes in favor of the Topeka constitution left little doubt that on any fair count free-soilers would have a majority. Time was on their side. For one thing, as new townships were established at steadily increasing distances from the Missouri state line, the cost, to Missourians, of intervening actively in Kansas politics also increased substantially; casting a fraudulent vote was beginning to involve more than a steamboat trip up river. All this was happening at a time when the pro-slavers, whether true residents of the territory or Missourians, could not afford to lose ground. In practice, as the situation in Kansas became more problematic (and also more dangerous) there was little to tempt Missourians into the territory unless they were looking for a fight—as indeed some of them were. On the other hand, few free-soilers came from Missouri—although most had to cross the state to reach Kansas—and as the prospect of land in a free state became ever more promising, the more their numbers were likely to increase. True, they also faced a fight, but it was for many one in a good cause—the ultimate abolition of slavery—and with good prospects of victory and prosperity.

Surprisingly, perhaps, pro-slavers did little to interfere with the Topeka elections. They could after all be content with the fact that these were invalid. From an early stage free-staters were ready to resort to arms, and in February 1855 a number of them combined to form the Kansas Legion, "first, to secure to Kansas the blessing and prosperity of being a free State; and secondly to protect the ballot-box from the LEPROUS TOUCH OF UNSCRUPULOUS

MEN." If the Legion failed to achieve either objective in the March and October official elections, its members never gave up their arms. This meant, as Amos Lawrence wrote in July, "that a revolution must take place in Kansas is certain . . . When farmers turn soldiers they must have arms."[44] From May 1855 outside supporters from northern states, from Massachusetts to Iowa, sent Sharps rifles and other munitions for the Kansas Legion and other free-state militias, and by the fall of 1856 sympathizers had raised over $43,000 to buy arms for free-state Kansans.[45] Even before the end of 1855 it was clear that the free-staters, having earlier condemned the pro-slavers for resorting to the threat of violence, were doing just the same.[46]

The year ended with the Wakarusa War, so-called because the line of battle, such as it was, was drawn along the Wakarusa River—a tributary of the Kansas river with Lawrence just to the north, and a much smaller settlement, Hickory Point, just to the south. The war started as a result of land claims disputed between a free-stater, Jacob Branson, and a pro-slaver, Franklin Coleman. Both sides had their local supporters, and on the morning of November 25—following a confrontation between them just outside the blacksmith's shop at Hickory Point—one on Branson's side, Charles Dow, was shot dead by Coleman, who, although he claimed to have acted in self-defense, fled to Missouri, fearing the sort of justice that awaited him in that part of Kansas.

The same afternoon armed men burned down two houses belonging to pro-slavers, while at Branson's house a committee of vigilantes was formed to punish Dow's murderers. After some of its members burned down Coleman's empty house, Douglas County Sheriff Samuel Jones—a prominent pro-slaver—came with his posse, some hours later, to arrest Branson. Leading their prisoner away from Hickory Point, the posse encountered a party of some fifteen armed free-staters, and after an hour's tense confrontation Jones prudently released Branson, whose rescuers brought him safely across the Wakarusa River to Lawrence, where, at 4:00 a.m. he found refuge in the house of the free-state leader, Charles Robinson.

There—given the trouble he was likely to bring with him—Branson was not a very welcome guest. Jones, having lost his prisoner, appealed to Governor Shannon for support. Shannon in turn reported to Washington, "The time has come when this armed band of men, who are seeking to subvert and render powerless the existing government, have to be met and the laws enforced against them, or submit to their lawless domination."[47] Closer to home, Shannon called on the people of the territory to support Sheriff Jones in overcoming this "armed band" of lawless men. Predictably it was Missourians who responded to this appeal, and as many as 1,000 massed along the Wakarusa River. Free-staters, in turn, swarmed into Lawrence to defend the town, where they built circles of earthworks to defend it. While Branson and his party discreetly left Lawrence, James Lane, who was organizing its defense, opened negotiations with Shannon and petitioned the president.[48] Meanwhile, with Missourians routinely intercepting free-staters moving into and out of Lawrence, one of their officers, Major George Clarke, fired his gun at a local man, Thomas Barber, who with his brother, Robert, and brother-in-law, Thomas Pierson, had questioned the major's authority to prevent them returning home to their cabin outside the town. Leaving Thomas Barber to die on the ground after he had fallen, grievously wounded, from his horse, the two others fled back to Lawrence.

On the evening of the same day, Governor Shannon, accompanied by Missouri Senator David Atchison and a senior officer, Colonel Albert Boone,[49] went to the Missouri camp along the Wakarusa, where they talked with the Missouri leaders. The next day, December 7, Shannon and Boone went to negotiate with the free-state leaders in Lawrence's Free State Hotel, where they saw the body of Thomas Barber laid out in a room across the hall. Both Shannon and Boone expressed their regrets, and negotiated a truce with the free-staters. After dining at Robinson's house, Shannon went on to the meet the pro-slavery leaders in Franklin—just outside Lawrence—where he also stopped the territorial militia from carrying out a planned attack on the town.

Negotiations continued on December 8, with Boone and Atchison representing the territorial government, and Lane and Robinson the free-staters, and after five hours a written statement was agreed upon between the two sides. Exonerated from complicity in the Branson rescue, the citizens of Lawrence affirmed their readiness to support the law in any action against a criminal. The document—at least as the free-staters construed it—did not mean that they recognized the legal validity of the territorial legislature. With this in hand Shannon disbanded the military forces around Lawrence, ordering their generals to "repress all demonstrations of a disorderly character and turn back any movement on Lawrence."[50]

Shannon remained in Lawrence where he joined the party celebrating the truce. There, slightly inebriated as a result of free-state hospitality, he rashly signed a document, submitted to him by Robinson, authorizing the free-staters to organize a militia. Robinson's pretext, that the Missourians along the Wakarusa River were planning another attack, was unfounded, but all that interested him was that his revolutionary military force had been legitimized by the governor. As one young militiaman told his parents, "The Gov has come round to our side and all is right."[51] The governor, realizing that the two sides as they confronted each other outside Lawrence could hardly be trusted to maintain the peace, confided to President Pierce his "forebodings as to the future," and asked for authority to call on US troops. This request was not granted, and although Pierce's annual address sent to be read in Congress noted events in Kansas "prejudicial to good order," it also stated, reassuringly, that none required his intervention.[52]

With the free-staters' claim to victory resonating through the northern states, southerners regarded the Wakarusa War as the triumph of lawlessness.[53] Nonetheless, with the siege of Lawrence, the Missourians had overplayed their hand, and with the death of Thomas Barber the free-staters had their first martyr.[54] The new year, 1856, brought little peace, whatever President Pierce might have told the US Congress. On January 15 the free-staters' election for state officers under the Topeka constitution was, at least by Kansas standards, comparatively quiet, although an encounter with a Missouri mob led to the murder of Reese Brown, a free-state leader. President Pierce remained unequivocally on the side of the pro-slavers, and in a special message on January 24 reaffirmed the legitimacy of the territorial government, while condemning the Topeka constitution as "revolutionary" and its supporters as potentially "treasonable."[55] He went on to threaten military intervention, asking Congress for the necessary appropriations.

In February federal troops at Fort Leavenworth were put at Governor Shannon's disposal, but the free-staters still went ahead with assembling their first government at Topeka, where Charles Robinson, the man they had elected as governor, made his inaugural address. Sheriff Jones, who was present—following Shannon's orders—to record the names of the Topeka officers as they took their oaths could be in no doubt as to the threat to law and order implicit in the speeches made not only by Robinson, but also by his attorney general, H. Miles Moore. Although the latter recorded in his journal on March 4, "To day has a new era dawned upon us today . . . the new State of Kansas has been ushered into existence,"[56] both houses of the Topeka legislature voted to wait for Congress' acceptance of statehood before proceeding to enact any laws. Otherwise the legislators were liable to be arrested and charged with treason, as President Pierce had threatened.

However dubious the legitimacy of the first Topeka assembly, the mere fact that it took place was seen as a radical assault on slavery. As David Atchison wrote to Amos Lawrence, "you and your people are the aggressors upon our rights. You come to drive us and our 'peculiar' institution from Kansas. We do not intend, cost what it may, to be driven or deprived of any of our rights."[57] That these words were addressed to Lawrence shows how Atchison—one of the pro-slavers' leading spokesmen—regarded northern emigration to Kansas as the real threat. In Missouri—which Atchison had represented in the US Senate until 1855—life was made increasingly difficult for northerners as they traveled across the state to Kansas. They were harassed on the Missouri River steamboats, and their cargo intercepted. Even so the northern immigrants kept on coming, and what is more they had arms—as often as not smuggled into

Kansas. Kansas City merchants, with an eye to the money to be made from immigrants, helped by protecting goods passing through the city—so that for many it proved to be better than Leavenworth as the point for entering Kansas. In spite of the support given by their home states and the help that they would receive while crossing Missouri, southern immigrants were far fewer. That those who did come found little joy in their new life can be seen from the words of one family letter: "Missouri will do to live in on a pinch, but Kansas territory is worse than nowhere and has been greatly overrated."[58] The reality about southern immigration was well summed up by a Missouri man who wrote, "But I fear this is all too late. The Free-soilers and Abolitionists of the North are ready to pour into the Territory the moment the ice breaks up in the rivers."[59]

As seen from higher up the situation could still be rescued. After the Topeka legislature had adjourned Governor Shannon did not expect any further invasions from Missouri, although, with arms still being smuggled in, he had to admit to "misgivings" about the future—which were indeed well founded. In Washington the Senate Committee on Territories—chaired by Stephen Douglas—with its eye on admitting Kansas to the Union, proposed a constitutional convention in the territory, supported by additional appropriations for law enforcement. The Republican minority called for admission under the Topeka free-state constitution, claiming that Democrats accepted that "the subjugation of white freemen may be necessary, that African slavery may succeed."[60] The issue came to a head on March 17 when Douglas introduced his bill for the admission of Kansas, followed three days later by New York Senator William H. Seward stating his intention to introduce his own bill providing for admission under the Topeka constitution.

Seward's stated intent was followed by petitions from northern states supporting his bill. On April 7, Michigan Senator Lewis Cass presented a memorial from the Topeka legislature asking for admission as a free state, but withdrew it when fellow Democrats pointed out irregularities which cast doubt upon its authenticity. A much more fundamental objection, as Stephen Douglas wrote, was that to accept the memorial meant recognition of the revolutionary process that had created it. The House of Representatives, nonetheless, voted by a majority of two to admit Kansas under the Topeka constitution—a small margin considering that Democrats held barely a third of the seats. In the Senate, with a safe Democratic majority, the vote predictably went the other way, in spite of Seward's plea that Kansas, with "a substantial civil community and a Republican Government" satisfied the requirements for statehood.[61]

A better indication of the climate in the Senate is given by Massachusetts Senator Charles Sumner's two-day speech on May 19 and 20. Having condemned "the Crime against Kansas," "the depraved longing for a new slave State" and "the rape of a Virgin Territory," he compared Douglas to a "noisome, squat, and nameless animal," going on to accuse the elderly and much respected South Carolina Senator A. P. Butler of having taken "a mistress . . . who . . . though polluted in the sight of the world is chaste in his sight—I mean the harlot, slavery."[62] Seward, on April 9, had compared President Pierce with King George III, but Sumner went too far, leading Douglas to ask, "Is it his object to provoke some of us to kick him as we would a dog in the street, that he may get sympathy for just chastisement?" This is more or less what happened. Three days later South Carolina Representative Preston Brooks, a nephew of Butler, attacked Sumner—who was working as his desk in the Senate—with his cane, wounding him so severely that he was unable to return to the Senate for two and a half years. While the north was shocked, the south condemned Sumner for his cowardice while commending Brooks for his "coolness and courage."

While violence between dissenters and supporters of slavery had reached the floor of the Senate, it had continued unabated in Kansas. On the evening of April 22, Sheriff Jones, having camped outside Lawrence after arresting—but only with the support of Federal troops—six free-staters, was shot in the back. Even though he survived, not seriously wounded, the free-state leaders in Lawrence rightly feared general warfare; this was averted only after a public meeting in Lawrence had condemned the attack as an "isolated act" of an "individual."[63] Charles Robinson even suggested that a pro-slavery group—anxious to commit an outrage to frustrate the work of a congressional investigating committee which had arrived on April 18—could have been responsible. At all events, the committee, whose task it was to investigate the alleged voting frauds at the time of the legislative elections in March 1855, found that witnesses would only appear in locales favorable to their political views.[64] After working long hours it found Missourians "deeply implicated" by the testimony of election fraud—so much so that "some of the most important facts have been proven by leaders of the invasion & even by the candidates elected."[65]

On May 5 a grand jury was charged to indict all free-state officials and to abate Lawrence's free-state newspapers and hotel as nuisances. Even before the indictments were made public they came to the notice of free-state officials, who decided that Reeder would be the test case, while Robinson would travel east to raise help. That same evening a marshal came to arrest Reeder, but left after Reeder, having alleged that the indictment was irregular, asked the congressional committee to protect him. Two days later Reeder decided to escape, and by traveling at night in disguise and staying in a succession of safe houses, he eventually reached Kansas City. There, after adopting a new disguise as an Irish laborer, he boarded a steamer downstream to Jefferson City[66] to continue northward overland to the ferry across the Mississippi River to Alton, Illinois, where, in his own words, "For the first time since leaving Lawrence I feel easy and safe."[67] Within days he was making speeches to enthusiastic crowds, with his tour extending through Chicago to Detroit.

Robinson was less fortunate. Traveling with his wife, Sara, downstream on a Missouri River steamboat, he was arrested at Lexington, Missouri, for fleeing the grand jury's indictment. Sara, who was allowed to continue her journey, had hidden in her clothing a copy of the testimony given to the congressional committee, together with "full particulars of our situation & progress"[68] and all this she delivered safely to Washington Republicans on May 13. Meanwhile her husband was taken first to Leavenworth and then on to Lecompton, where in "Uncle Sam's Bastile [sic] on the Kansas prairies"[69] he enjoyed considerable comfort and freedom, even though he was under arrest for usurping office and high treason.[70]

Arresting Robinson was only the partial fulfillment of the first part of the charge to the grand jury; it was time to abate the hotel and newspapers in Lawrence as nuisances—an operation that was almost certain to cause trouble. As early as May 11 Governor Shannon had received a request for federal troops to help protect Lawrence against a force of 500 to 700 Missourians who had surrounded the town. With only a federal marshal and posse, helped by Sheriff Jones, nearby, the governor was powerless to intervene.

After several days of guns firing, and shooting in all directions, Sheriff Jones, heading a new posse, arrived in Lawrence in mid-afternoon on May 21. His purpose was to carry out the grand jury's order. Having allowed the proprietor of the Free State Hotel time to move the furniture out of the building, he had the posse bombard it for an hour, after which he tried blowing it up with gunpowder. With its structure still intact the posse was dismissed, leaving Missourians to set fire to it and go on to loot and burn down other nearby houses, including that of the Robinsons. The newspaper presses were dumped into the river while books and papers were burned in the streets. Such was the Sack of Lawrence: no one was killed but the town was left in ruins, even though its citizens had offered no resistance. Far outside Kansas there was little doubt about who had won the moral victory.

Only three days later, on May 24, John Brown Jr., a free-state settler at Osawatomie, some distance south of Lawrence—determined to avenge the sack of Lawrence—took the law into his own hands in a way that would set him on the path to immortality. His father, also John Brown, had been present at a meeting at Osawatomie in April where it was resolved to condemn the territorial legislature and repudiate compliance with its laws. This little township was situated at the confluence of two rivers, the Pottawatomie and the Marais des Cygnes, along whose banks were a number of small settlements, mainly of pro-slavers. Until the evening of May 24 there had been no great animosity between them and free-state settlers such as John Brown and his family. That night would change everything: hearing the news of the sack of Lawrence, John Brown Jr, as a militia officer in a rifle company, left for the town, leaving behind in Osawatomie a small group of men including his father, his brother, Owen, and his brother-in-law, Henry Thompson, to go on the rampage among the isolated pro-slavery households along the Pottawatomie River, where they hacked four men to death with swords. The first two victims, a father and son, James and William Doyle, were followed by Allen Wilkinson and William Sherman: three separate households were left devastated.

All the victims were connected to the pro-slavery movement, but only Allen Wllkinson, a delegate to the territorial legislature, could be counted as being really significant. Although a number of free-staters defended the killings as a preemptive strike, John Brown himself took another line when asked if he had committed murder: "I did not; but I do not pretend to say that they were not killed by my order, and in doing so I believe I was doing God's service"[71]—a claim calculated to resonate in the religious climate of the American frontier. Even so, judged objectively, these were targeted political assassinations.

However incompatible with free-state policy, what happened on the night of May 24 was the spark that ignited the fire that finally brought a hot war to Kansas. Settlers fled the countryside on both sides to form military companies, and as federal troops disbanded them, they lost little time in reforming. In particular the Pottawatomie massacres justified deploying the US Army against free-state guerrillas, but its main task—which it was quite unable to fulfill—was simply to keep the peace. The forces of law and order had an early setback, when H. C. Pate, a deputy US marshal—who helped capture three of the Brown brothers, together with a brother-in-law—surrendered after another brother, Frederick, had used a ruse to convince him that his force was outnumbered by two companies of free-staters, one commanded by John Brown Sr. This was just one incident in a conflict that led Governor Shannon—quite unable to control events—to withdraw to Kansas City, where Sara Robinson noted on his face "a look of utter weariness, of inability to do anything, or incapacity to know what to do."[72]

If anyone was in control at all, it was the commander of the federal troops, Col. Edwin Sumner—a cousin of the Massachusetts senator. He secured Pate's freedom, advising him to return, together with his men, to Missouri, and disbanded a large force of Missourians led by Col. Whitfield the territorial delegate. He then proceeded to deal with the Topeka legislature, which had been summoned to meet on July 4, while at the same time the town was filled with men arriving for a mass convention. In the legislature, Sumner, interrupting the proceedings of the lower house, told its members to disperse in compliance with proclamations from the president and the acting governor. This immediately provoked a spectator to ask whether "the legislature is dispersed at the point of a bayonet"[73] to which Sumner replied, "I shall use the whole force under my command to carry out my orders." The legislature did not resist its dispersal, and in doing so compromised the federal government into playing into the free-staters' hands—"this being the position the Legislature desired to occupy to be dispersed at the point of a bayonet."[74] Faced with popular condemnation for what had happened in Topeka, President Pierce chose to make Sumner a scapegoat and replaced him with an old friend from the Mexican War, Persifor Smith. Congress then reacted by failing to vote the extra appropriations needed for the military support of the territorial government in Kansas, making it necessary for Pierce to call it into special session three days after it had adjourned for the summer. The army had learned the lesson that it was unwise to stage a showdown with free-staters in Kansas.

An alternative that was still open was to blockade the Missouri River so as to frustrate new emigration to Kansas, but this inevitably provoked protests from the north, including those of the governors of Iowa and Wisconsin—two states from which many emigrants came. Overland routes via Iowa and the Nebraska Territory, beyond the reach of both federal troops and Missourians, were open to new emigrants, whose number included a large force of some 250 to 500 men, led by Jim Lane, and equipped with a cannon as well as rifles. This was in action before the end of August, leaving a larger force of pro-slavers in retreat. At the same time other free-state forces had their successes, inevitably inviting retaliation, sometimes successful, from pro-slavers. The result was general lawlessness with both sides suffering from "drought, robbery, burning, plundering and driving," with the acting territorial governor increasingly at odds with the army. While the former was beholden to Missourians, the latter took its orders from the administration in Washington, which—in the face of mounting congressional opposition and adverse publicity—was becoming increasingly uncomfortable about holding Robinson and his associates in custody at Lecompton on charges of treason. President Pierce, in exchange for Republican cooperation in voting army appropriations, entered a nolle prosequi[75] and ordered General Smith to release the prisoners and provide them with an escort back to Lawrence. There, after being greeted by cheering crowds, they enjoyed an evening of speeches, made by Robinson himself, James Lane, and John Brown, together with many local figures.

The problem of providing a legitimate government for Kansas was still unsolved. The events of the summer demonstrated both the impotence of the territorial legislature and the reluctance of the army to be involved in governing the territory. Because they also showed that the free-staters were gaining the upper hand, pro-slavery supporters in Congress—who in the Senate were in the majority—knew that time was against them. In the summer of 1856 Democratic Senator Robert Toombs of Georgia introduced a bill that would lead to statehood for Kansas via a constitutional convention independent both of the territorial legislature and the Topeka government. There would first be a census enumerating only actual residents of the territory as the basis for listing qualified voters; these would then elect delegates to the convention on the same day as the presidential election due to be held in November.

Although this bill was assured of a majority in the Senate, it failed in the house because of Republican opposition. This was a new factor in American politics, since the Republican Party had only emerged in 1854, as a loose coalition of Anti-Nebraska Democrats, former Whigs whose party was disintegrating, and members of "one-issue" parties, such as the Free-Soilers, dedicated to the eradication of slavery. The new party, united in its opposition to the expansion of slavery into the territories,[76] introduced into the House of Representatives its own bill for Kansas statehood under the Topeka constitution. This was passed by the House, but predictably rejected by the Senate, which once again voted in favor of the Toombs bill. Even President Pierce's support was insufficient to win over the House, so by the end of the session on August 18, no bill for the admission of Kansas had passed Congress.[77]

The congressional debates in the summer of 1856 were overshadowed by the need for all parties to find candidates to fight the presidential elections due in November. Since 1850 two presidents had showed little sense of the need for a robust policy on the most critical issue of the day, the future of slavery in the United States. The first, Millard Fillmore—once described as "a pattern of that outwardly dignified, yet nerveless and heartless respectability, that was more dangerous to America . . . than political recklessness or want of scruple"[78]— might well have saved his country much of the agony of the 1850s if he had used his powers of veto to block the California Compromise, as President Zachary Taylor, to whom he had been vice president, almost certainly would have done had he survived until the end of his term. Franklin Pierce, who succeeded Fillmore in 1853, "might perhaps claim the palm among the presidents of those days, for sheer, deleterious insignificance."[79] Almost everything related so far in this chapter shows how ill-equipped he was to deal with crisis. Democrats, in the summer of 1856, knowing that they must find a stronger man, decided that the diplomatic gifts shown by James Buchanan, a Pennsylvania Democrat, both as Polk's secretary of state and Pierce's ambassador in London, made him the best candidate.

The presidential election of 1856 was remarkable for the first appearance of a Republican candidate, John C. Frémont, a man chosen for his reputation—contested by many—as a hero in the conquest and settlement of California, which he had briefly represented (as related in chapter 9) as one of its first two US senators. There was also a third candidate contesting the election, Millard Fillmore, whose American Party had also emerged out of the ruins of the Whig

Party, which he had already served as president from 1850 to 1853. Between them the two parties opposing Buchanan won a substantial majority of the popular votes, but even so Buchanan, with 174 votes in the electoral college, won over Fremont with 114 votes and Fillmore with only the eight votes of Maryland. These results were full of foreboding for the Democrats, even though the 1856 elections gave them a majority in both houses of the US Congress. In the fifteen slave states the Republicans only won 600 votes—all from Maryland and Delaware—while without the split vote in Pennsylvania, Indiana, and Illinois they would have won the election. A radical division between north and south, "free" and "slave," was taking shape, and this would certainly be critical in the 1860 elections.

The newly elected president was unconcerned, for as he said in his inaugural address on March 4, 1857, the territorial question was "happily, a matter of but little practical importance" since the Supreme Court was about to settle it "speedily and finally." Two days later, the judgment of the Supreme Court, given by the eighty-three-year-old Chief Justice Taney, supported by five associate justices, in the appeal case of *Dred Scott vs. John Sandford*, delivered a bombshell to the politics of slavery. In the time warp of the case so many different states and territories were involved that when it came to deciding whether the appellant, Dred Scott, was slave or free, the federal courts constituted the only possible tribunal. As for what lay behind the case, an army surgeon, Dr. Emerson, had bought Scott as a slave in Missouri in the early 1830s, but had then moved first to Illinois—always a free state—and then on to the Wisconsin Territory, where slavery was excluded by the Northwest Ordinance of 1787.

In 1842 Dr. Emerson, bringing Scott with him, returned to Missouri, where he died, leaving his wife to claim ownership by inheritance of Scott, who in turn, having sought to purchase his freedom and been turned down, sued for it in the federal district court in St. Louis by right of his residence in the Wisconsin territory. At the trial in 1846 the jury found against Scott, but at a retrial in 1850 another jury found in his favor and declared him free by reason of his previous residence on the Wisconsin territory. It was this second verdict that caused the train of appeals that at the end of 1856 ended up in the US Supreme Court, with John Sandford, who had bought Scott from his sister, the original defendant, as respondent. Taney found that under the US Constitution, Scott, as a negro, could not be a citizen, which meant that he was excluded from the entire legal process that had brought him to the Supreme Court.[80] He then added—as an obiter dictum without legal force—that the Missouri Compromise (which had been observed for more than thirty years before its repeal in 1854) was from the very beginning void and unconstitutional. This dictum, if correct, meant that there was never any need for the California Compromise of 1850 and the Kansas-Nebraska Act of 1854: the rights they conferred were inherent in the US

Constitution. Stephen Douglas need never have fought for popular sovereignty in the territories. If the dictum also meant that the whole Republican platform was unconstitutional, so as to leave the Party despondent, a new issue soon gave Republicans a cause to fight for.

THE LECOMPTON CONSTITUTION

The scene now switches back from Washington to Kansas, where the territorial legislature passed a bill to hold a constitutional convention in Lecompton in September 1857. Governor John Geary, who had been appointed to succeed the hapless Wilson Shannon a year earlier, vetoed the bill for its failure to provide for submission of the constitution to the voters.[81] The legislature then overrode his veto, claiming that concessions to the free-staters were no longer necessary with Buchanan safely elected as president. The complaints of the Kansas legislature were too much for Geary, who found the administration in Washington an unreliable ally.[82] After six months in Kansas he wrote to his brother, "I have learned more of the depravity of my fellow men that I ever before knew." With such experience behind him he left Kansas just as James Buchanan was being installed as president.

To succeed Geary, the president appointed an undoubted political heavyweight, Robert J. Walker, who as a "Northerner by birth, a Southerner by adoption, and a Union man by conviction"[83] should have been acceptable to all parties. By the time Walker arrived at the end of May 1857, Frederick P. Stanton, the territorial secretary of state, had already organized the election of delegates to the Lecompton convention on the basis of the census—"bogus" in the opinion of free-staters[84]—authorized by the territorial legislature, which was heavily biased in favor of the pro-slavery counties. Although Walker was welcomed by enthusiastic crowds as his steamboat proceeded up the Missouri River, once in Kansas he gave an inaugural address that antagonized both sides. Then, to pacify the free-staters, who had called a meeting of the Topeka government on June 9, he himself visited this "hamlet of fifteen or twenty houses scattered over a green prairie"[85] on June 6, to promise that any constitution produced by Lecompton—a township hardly more impressive than Topeka—would be submitted to the voters for ratification.

The election of the Lecompton delegates passed quietly. Few crossed over from Missouri to vote, and not many more actual settlers did so. Seven thousand free-staters boycotted the election, and another 10,000 qualified voters had not been registered. The 10 percent or so of the electorate that did vote came mainly from the pro-slavery districts along the Missouri River. The result, predictably, was a pro-slavery constitution. To its supporters it became a considerable hostage to fortune when President Buchanan affirmed his support for Governor Walker's stated commitment to submit it to ratification. This, to southern politicians, was anathema; the risk of rejection was simply too great.

The free-staters then made a significant change of course: at a meeting at Grasshopper Falls in late August they resolved to participate in the elections to the territorial legislature due in October, insisting at the same time that this did not mean abandoning the Topeka movement. Walker reacted by bringing, once again, criminal charges against Charles Robinson, for usurping office. Although the judge instructed the jury in terms that supported these charges, Robinson was nonetheless acquitted. The verdict, however, was overshadowed by the Lecompton convention, where the sixty delegates were—inevitably given the way the election was held—pro-slavery Democrats,[86] seven of whom had actually owned slaves. The delegates' bias became clear when they elected as their presiding officer John Calhoun,[87] who was opposed to submission; needless to say, the more certain it became that free-staters would vote in the October election, the less likely it was that the Lecompton convention would accept submission.

On October 5, Lawrence—which, after the devastation in the summer of 1856, had been rebuilt to becoming a thriving town—witnessed so massive a turnout of voters that the polling stations had to remain open to the end of the following day. The majority, needless to say, were free-staters. On the other side of the line, Oxford, a pro-slavery hamlet close to the Missouri line, and sparsely populated McGee County, each recorded more than 1,000 votes—results so incredible that they were repudiated by Governor Walker. The result was that the territory for the first time had a legislature with a free-state majority.

The Lecompton convention reacted by deciding to send its proposed state constitution for Kansas directly to the US Congress; this was too much for Calhoun and the more moderate delegates, who in the end persuaded the convention to submit for ratification that part of the constitution relating to slavery. The voters would then have to choose between a constitution "with" or "with no" slavery,[88] but with this latter choice only the future importation of slaves would be prohibited. The "peculiar institution" would itself survive in Kansas. Governor Walker, who had always made clear that he would not accept partial submission, decided to go to Washington to present the case against the Lecompton constitution; by doing so he established himself as an ally of the free-staters.

While Walker was away, the free-staters successfully pressured the acting governor, Frederick P. Stanton, to call the territorial legislature into session on December 7, and on that day and at his suggestion, it agreed to reconvene on January 4, 1858, for a second ratification vote on the constitution. Washington, informed two days later of what Stanton had done, dismissed him. This accorded with a decision made by President Buchanan in late November to support the Lecompton constitution, overruling Walker's opposition to it. In particular, the limited scope of a "no slavery" vote was in his view required by the Supreme Court's decision in the Dred Scott case.[89] Walker, considering himself betrayed by the man who had appointed him to be governor, saw his remit as a "forlorn hope" from the start.

If President Buchanan could dismiss Walker and Stanton, he was powerless when Stephen Douglas, a senator from his own party, told him that he was irrevocably opposed to Lecompton, because it "was not the act and deed of the people of Kansas, and did not embody their will."[90] Douglas proposed a new constitutional convention, rejecting both Lecompton and Topeka, but first decided to wait to see how Kansas would react to the partial submission of the Lecompton constitution on December 21. With the free-staters boycotting the election, the constitution "with slavery" won with a ten-to-one majority, 6,000 votes to 600: it followed that the constitution President Buchanan was committed to submit to Congress, if accepted, would admit Kansas as a slave state.

The crucial test came on January 4, 1858, the day appointed by the Lecompton constitution for the election of state officers and by the state legislature for the referendum on that constitution. With some misgivings the free-soilers decided to submit candidates for the state offices. It was the right choice: although initial voting returns gave victory to the pro-slavers, these were fraudulent, and when the true returns were found, buried in a candle box under a Lecompton woodpile, to be opened—in the presence of James W. Denver,[91] Stanton's appointed successor as acting governor—at 2:00 a.m. on the night of January 27, the free-state candidates were the winners. The result was that even if Kansas became a state under the Lecompton constitution "with slavery," both its elected officers and its elected legislature would be committed to its abolition.

One result of the free-staters' double victory was that they no longer needed the Topeka government, which prudently adjourned, to meet again.[92] This was little consolation to President Buchanan, who in face of mounting protests from northern Democrats—including many from his home state of Pennsylvania—still adhered to Lecompton. His problem was that these protests also resonated with northern Democrats in the US Congress, and among those who heard them was Illinois Senator Stephen Douglas, due to stand for reelection at the end of the year, when he would face a formidable Republican opponent—Abraham Lincoln.

With the election of the Thirty-fifth Congress to convene during the first two years of Buchanan's administration (1857–1859) the position of the parties in the House of Representatives was reversed. Where in the previous Congress the Democrats, with only 84 seats, were in a minority, in the new Congress, with 132 seats (out of 237) they had—at least on paper—a comfortable majority. This, in any case, was sufficient, in March 1858, for the House Committee considering the Lecompton constitution to recommend it as the basis for admitting Kansas as the thirty-fourth state of the Union.[93] The issue was hotly contested, with southern representatives threatening secession if Lecompton was rejected.[94] Both sides made Lecompton an issue upon which the future of the Union depended, but the case in favor of it was critically flawed because of the way it had been adopted in Kansas. As one northern Democrat, Michigan Senator Charles Stuart, made clear, the objection to Lecompton was not because of slavery, but because it "overthrew" the people's right to govern themselves:[95] it denied, at the most fundamental level, Stephen Douglas' essential principle of popular sovereignty. For this reason Douglas supported a new bill which called for another ratifying election, but the Senate, in rejecting it, by 33 votes to 25, effectively voted to admit Kansas under the Lecompton constitution.[96]

The Senate vote meant that the battleground would be the House of Representatives. There, although there were forty-eight more Democratic members than there had been in the Thirty-fourth Congress, the majority of these were from northern states where Lecompton was anathema—and there would be another election for all their seats at the end of the year. In the early months of 1858 the number of anti-Lecompton Democrats ready to vote with the Republican minority was sufficient to prevent the Lecompton constitution being passed by the House. In April there was something of a diversion: disregarding everything that was happening in Washington, the Kansas territorial legislature—with the free-state majority gained in October, 1857—passed a bill adopting a new free-state constitution, which had been produced by a convention that it had orchestrated in Leavenworth early in the new year. Although Governor Denver had refused to sign the bill, a member of the convention still brought the Leavenworth constitution to Washington. There Republican Senator William Seward from New York attempted to have it submitted for consideration by Congress instead of Lecompton.

Predictably Seward's attempt failed. Instead a joint Senate-House conference committee—set up in mid-April only after a tie of 108 to 108 in the House was broken by the Speaker's casting vote—met to fashion a compromise.[97] Although the leading role was played by Indiana Democratic Representative William English, by whose name the compromise is known to history, it was Alexander Stephens of Georgia who crafted it. Under Lecompton, as accepted by Kansans in the vote of December 21, 1857, the federal land grant—customarily made to new states on admission to the Union—would be $23 million. The English compromise reduced it to $4 million, so that effectively Kansans would pay a high price for rejecting the amended constitution. James Wilson, an Indiana Republican, spoke for many when he called the compromise "a conglomeration of bribes, of penalties, and of meditated fraud,"[98] while the president, with considerable congressional support said that "it would bring peace to the Union and the Democratic Party."[99] Submitted to Kansas voters on August 2, 1858, the compromise was rejected by 11,300 to 1,788 votes; even though floods and heavy rains kept many voters at home this was a substantial turnout.

Although after this vote there could be little doubt about how the majority of Kansans felt about slavery, pro-slavers still insisted on their rights to own slaves, relying on the Dred Scott decision to support their case. The English compromise was disastrous for the Democratic Party, which in the north was split between Douglas and Buchanan, with neither of them trusted in the south. In the mid-term elections at the end of 1858 every anti-Lecompton Democrat who ran for reelection won, whereas many who were pro-Lecompton lost to Republicans. Douglas himself was only reelected as senator for Illinois because of the way seats were distributed in the state legislature; the Republicans won 4,000 more popular votes. For Abraham Lincoln the way was wide open to campaign for the Republican nomination for the presidency in 1860. He rightly saw Kansas as "the concrete embodiment of the choices facing the nation's future," while the president, in a letter to his niece, wrote, "Poor bleeding Kansas is quiet & is behaving herself in a [sic] orderly manner."[100]

KANSAS AND ABOLITIONISM

James Buchanan, as so often happened in his four years (1857–1861) in the White House, got things wrong. His concentration on such matters as political patronage, which he used unashamedly to gain support in Congress, left him blind to the situation in Kansas as it was after the decisive rejection of the Lecompton constitution. The result of this happening, which had long been feared by the pro-slavery minority in the territory, was that the neighboring state of Missouri had become a slave enclave with free-staters threatening it from almost every side. What counted in the political geography of Missouri was that—except in the far south—it had Illinois to the east, on the other side of the Mississippi River, and Kansas to the west, accessible simply by traveling across country. Arkansas, immediately to the south, may have been even more committed to slavery, but it was a poor state in no position to help buttress the institution in Missouri. The Kansas Territory, after 1858, offered to slaves in both states a refuge to which they could escape, where they would find men dedicated to helping them. It was not for nothing that the fugitive slave legislation of the US Congress, passed under southern pressure, became ever more stringent, but in the climate of the 1850s this did not deter abolitionists, mainly from northern states, from working hard to free as many slaves as possible. Where better to do so than the Kansas Territory, where abolition could count on strong local support?

The cause had produced two extremist free-state leaders, John Brown and James Montgomery, who were only too ready to stir up trouble in southern Kansas where pro-slavers were at their strongest. The first major confrontation occurred at Fort Scott, in February 1859, when a large party of free-staters, led by Montgomery, sought redress for the robbery of a free-state man.[101] Although Judge J. Williams, a federal official, managed to calm them down, Governor Denver still sent troops to Fort Scott to help maintain order. Montgomery retired from Fort Scott, but only to commit atrocities against pro-slavers in the countryside to the north—hoping to drive them into a "stampede" out of Kansas. His men were not discouraged by occasional clashes with the federal troops sent by the governor, but in the end, after stealing hundreds of horses, Montgomery's "murderers, & robbers"[102] provoked retaliation. This was the work of Charles Hamilton, originally from Georgia, who had a record, equal to that of Montgomery, for atrocities against free-staters along the Osage River. At a rally on May 19 Hamilton declared a war of extermination against free-staters, and twenty-five chose to join him. Together they went on the rampage, robbing free-staters and taking prisoners. Eleven captives were marched to a narrow ravine, where Hamilton ordered his men to shoot them. Such was the Marais des Cygnes massacre, and although only five men actually died, Montgomery took it as a declaration of war; this carried over into Missouri after Hamilton and his men retreated across the state line, followed by Montgomery with 150 men and two cannons. This was sufficient to deter Hamilton's force from returning to Kansas, where, in June, Governor Denver made an inspection tour of the devastated southern counties, which included a visit to the site of the Marais des Cygnes massacre. By posting troops along the Missouri state line and suspending a number of writs against free-staters, Denver hoped to persuade Montgomery and other guerrilla leaders to disband their forces. Although this proved to be a vain hope, Kansas, outside the troubled southern countries along the Missouri state line, remained peaceful, with Charles Robinson, the free staters' leader, repudiating Montgomery and supporting the governor.[103] After all, his party was by this time well in control of the legislature.

Denver resigned as governor in September 1858, leaving his successor, Samuel Medary from Ohio, to keep the peace. This, in the southern counties, was still threatened by James Montgomery, who had been joined by John Brown—not a good omen. Montgomery—after making a raid on Fort Scott on December 16, which left one man dead, several houses torched and some $5,000 worth of property looted—offered to cease fighting in exchange for an amnesty from the new governor. His terms were refused, while Medary, with cooperation from the majority of free-staters, was granted authority by President Buchanan to use troops together with $30,000 from Congress toward the costs of enforcing the law along the Missouri state line. After Montgomery won the support of only one free-state legislator, he turned himself, and six other men, in for trial for robbing the mails. The legislature rewarded him by passing an amnesty bill for southern Kansas, which provided that "no criminal offense arising out of a political dispute would be prosecuted, and that such prosecutions [already] in progress would be dismissed."[104] This pleased the citizens of Kansas more than it did those of Missouri, the state in which the mail robbery had actually taken place. The days when Missourians could make a show of force in Kansas were past, and in the years since 1854, when it all started, they had gained nothing. As one Kansas City editor wrote, "We are tired of the eternal wrangle over the territories and the niggers . . . It was the question of Kansas; and although that Territory bled profusely, and Missouri bled much more, practically, yet we are today where we were when the Kansas-Nebraska Bill was passed."[105] If, for all the devastation in "Bleeding Kansas," and the disruption of its economy, the final aggregate death toll for both sides attributable to the slavery issue was only fifty-six,[106] this still counted in an area where the total population numbered less than 30,000.[107]

In March 1859, Kansas voters decided by 5,306 to 1,425 in favor of yet another constitutional convention. This was a poor turnout, reflecting either the difficulties of reaching the polls after a snowstorm or just plain apathy, for as H. Miles Moore noted, "we have been Constitutioned to death."[108] In any case, as seen by most of its members, the work of the free-state party was done, and at a meeting at Osawatomie in May former members organized a Kansas Republican Party which specifically denied that the US Constitution could bring slavery into the territory—so much for Dred Scott and Chief Justice Taney. Finally, in July, the constitutional convention met at Wyandotte to produce a constitution that prohibited slavery, gave women some limited voting rights, and did nothing to prevent black immigration. The most contentious issue was the location of the state capital, with Topeka being the final choice.[109] Democrats opposed Wyandotte's wide conception of liberty, with most of the opposition coming from the old pro-slavery parts of Kansas. On October 4, 1859, 10,421 votes were cast in favor of the constitution and 5,530 against it. By this time men on both sides of the Kansas-Missouri line were ready to forget the past, and cultivate friendly relations across it.

If the territory had moved a long way in five years, it still provided a home for men such as John Brown and James Montgomery, dedicated to abolishing slavery everywhere. The public was largely on their side. When runaway slaves came to Kansas, people looked the other way, with an increasing number actively assisting them—which is just what white men in Missouri had always feared.[110] In December 1858, John Brown had led a force of fifteen men into Missouri where they freed eleven slaves, who then hid for a month along Pottawatomie Creek. Leaving their hiding place on January 20, 1859, the party reached Grinnell, Iowa, a town, whose founder, Josiah B. Grinnell, was a leading abolitionist. With his help the former slaves reached Detroit in mid-March, and crossed by ferry into Canada. Brown himself, in the words of one who met him, was "an earnest fanatic who thinks himself, and declares himself called of God to make war on slavery and to kill whoever comes in the way of his mission."[111]

Brown's sights, however, were set not on Kansas but on the mountains of Virginia, where he believed a small guerrilla force could fatally undermine slavery. Brown, and his eminent backers in the east—known as "the Secret Six"—believed that slavery could only be ended by violence. His first need was for arms and to that end he planned to attack and take over the federal arsenal at Harpers Ferry, at the point where the Shenandoah River joins the Potomac. The assault came on the night of October 16, 1859, and although the arsenal was captured, by the end of the following day Brown and his men were trapped there after it was surrounded by the local militia and angry residents of Harpers Ferry. No slaves came to help them, and the insurrection failed completely.[112] On October 18 Brown and his men surrendered to a force of marines commanded by Col. Robert E. Lee. The press, with banner headlines announcing "THE NEGRO INSURRECTION,"[113] and reports of hundreds of men under Brown's command, was guilty of gross exaggeration. Brown's total force numbered only nineteen men. There was no northern conspiracy, only "the crazy freak of Ossawatomie Brown," a child of the violent frontier of distant Kansas. Brown was tried for treason, and John A. Andrew, the lawyer who defended him, told a group of southern senators investigating what had happened at Harpers Ferry that Brown's invasion of Virginia was in retaliation for Missouri's invasion of Kansas—or, in Andrews own words, "I think that his foray into Kansas was a fruit of a Kansas tree."[114]

The trial of John Brown was not long delayed, and the sentence of death was carried out on December 2, 1859, less than seven weeks after his raid on Harpers Ferry. Whatever his Kansas reputation as a "crazy freak," he saw more clearly than almost anyone that slavery in the United States could not be ended without violence. He was the archetype of "bleeding Kansas," and once war finally came in 1861 he was seen not as insane, but as a prophet.[115] In the words of the best-known song of the civil war, "His soul goes marching on."[116]

Republicans and Rebels

THE LINCOLN-DOUGLAS DEBATES

Eighteen fifty-eight—the year of the famous Lincoln-Douglas debates recounted in chapter 5—is the best starting point for a synoptic view of American political geography of the Civil War. Illinois was then, according to the *New York Times*, "the most interesting political battle-ground in the Union."[1] The battle was between Abraham Lincoln, a Republican, and Stephen Douglas, a Democrat, who, in the course of seven debates, fought their case in every part of Illinois. Both, realizing how much the balance of opinion varied across the state, adapted their arguments to the character, as they judged it, of local audiences, but the important question was how much there was a consistent line on both sides. As the debates moved on from one locality to another, Douglas, in particular, accused Lincoln of inconsistency, so that in the last debate but one, in Quincy—a town which, located on the Mississippi some 130 miles north of St. Louis, was not particularly favorable to Douglas—Lincoln was accused of holding "one set of principles in the Abolition counties, and a different and contrary set of principles in the other counties."[2]

Douglas' core strategy was to establish that Lincoln's party, in Illinois, had emerged in 1854 as a reaction to the Kansas-Nebraska Act as "an Abolition Party, under the name and disguise of a Republican party."[3] This may have been true of the first attempt—centered on Chicago—to organize a party called "Republican" in 1854, but Lincoln, contrary to Douglas's allegations, then played no part.

Nonetheless, by the end of 1855, Lincoln, together with many others, had concluded that Illinois required "a fusion of all the opponents to the existence of slavery in a new political party."[4] This began to take shape at a meeting of sympathetic newspaper editors at Decatur on February 22. Lincoln was present, as the only non-editor, and under his guidance a declaration was drafted calling for the restoration of the Missouri Compromise, upholding the constitutionality of the Fugitive Slave Act, and pledging noninterference with slavery in the states where it already existed.[5] It went on, however, to affirm the basic free-soil doctrine, that "the United States was founded on the principle that freedom was national and slavery exceptional."[6]" It also included proposals focused on special categories of voters such as recent, and mainly Catholic immigrants, and Know Nothings. It mattered little that their concerns shared little common ground.

Although the February meeting adjourned without giving a name to the proposed new party, its declaration was adopted as the platform to be considered by 270 delegates, including Lincoln, who had convened at Bloomington on May 29 to organize the Illinois Republican Party. On the key question of slavery the platform, as finally adopted, went no further than to declare "that Congress had the power and the duty to exclude slavery from the national territories."[7]

Lincoln's vulnerability in debate with Douglas was, however, increased by his speech at Springfield made at the close of the Republican State Convention after he had been adopted as the party's candidate for the US Senate in the elections due in November. This was the famous "house divided" speech, in which Lincoln established a position that allowed for little compromise:

> I believe this government cannot endure, permanently half *slave* and half *free*. I do not expect the Union to be dissolved—I do not expect the house to *fall*—but I *do* expect it will cease to be divided. It will become *all* one thing or *all* the other. Either the *opponents* of slavery, will arrest the further spread of it, and place it where the public mind shall rest in the belief that it is in course of ultimate extinction, or its *advocates* will push it forward, till it shall become alike lawful in *all* the States, *old* as well as *new*—*North* as well as *South*.[8]

Both Lincoln and Douglas had to take into account the final rejection, on August 2, of the Lecompton constitution by Kansas voters. This event confirmed Lincoln's belief in the ultimate extinction of slavery, while Douglas, the champion of "popular sovereignty," had to respect the way the people of Kansas had voted. In the words of both Lincoln and Douglas the devil was in the details—not surprising given that both were very accomplished lawyers. Both sides had a different time warp: for Lincoln the days of slavery were numbered (although he was careful not to suggest that he would play any significant part in bringing about its demise), while for Douglas the institution was permanent. In the third of the debates with Lincoln—in Jonesboro, in the south of the state, where Douglas could count on a sympathetic audience—he asked, rhetorically, "why cannot this Union exist forever divided into free and slave States, as our fathers made it?" The immediate question related, however, not to time but space. The question at the back of everyone's mind must have been whether the territorial limits of slavery, following the Kansas decision to reject it on August 2, 1858, could ever expand.

Lincoln—in his acceptance speech to the Republican state convention—foresaw the possibility of a further decision of the US Supreme Court, that "the Constitution of the United States does not permit a State to exclude slavery from within its limits."[9] Significantly, an opposition amendment of the Kansas-Nebraska Act, designed to recognize this right, was defeated.[10] What is more, the way the Court decided the Dred Scott case in 1857 made the decision that Lincoln feared much more likely. In his own words:

> such a decision is all that slavery now lacks in being alike in all the States. Welcome or unwelcome, such a decision is probably coming, and will soon be upon us, unless the power of the present political dynasty shall be met and overthrown. We shall *lie down* pleasantly dreaming that the people of *Missouri* are on the verge of making their State *free*, and we shall awake to the *reality*, instead, that the *Supreme* Court has made *Illinois* a *slave* State.[11]

All this, in Lincoln's view, was the result, in the first place, of the repeal of the Missouri Compromise by the Kansas-Nebraska Act of 1854, and in the second, of Dred Scott in 1857. Was he then simply arguing for putting the clock back, of more radically, to question the whole legitimacy of the way the Congress had dealt with the Nebraska territory? As chapter 11 shows, it had failed to achieve the expansion of slavery. In 1858 there was no prospect of another slave state joining the Union: Kansas was the last chance of the pro-slavery forces. With Kansas and California both free, what chance would slavery have in any new states carved out of the territory that separated them? It is not surprising, then, that the hard-core slave states in the south worked so hard for authorization of a southern railroad link across the New Mexico territory, but this, then, threatened all the much more realistic and advanced plans for a northern link involving Illinois, which Douglas, seeking reelection as senator, could not conceivably abandon.

At the heart of Douglas' opposition to Lincoln was his conviction that the Republican Party was sectional, in the sense that its platform could only appeal to one part of the nation. This was not how things were in the days when the Whigs were the main opposition to Douglas' own Democratic Party. As he pointed out at the very beginning of the first debate with Lincoln, "prior to 1854 this country was divided into two great political parties, known as the Whig and Democratic parties. Both were national and patriotic, advocating principles that were universal in their application." With the emergence of the Republican Party, the position changed completely. Of the hundred Republicans elected to the Thirty-fifth Congress in 1856 not a single one would represent a slave state. Although this was far from sufficient to give the Republicans a majority in either House, the position could well have changed with the elections due at the end of 1858; this was why the question of sectionalism was so important as to attract nationwide interest in the debates between the two rival candidates for the Senate in Illinois. The 1858 elections brought precisely the result that Douglas warned against, that is, the Republicans, with 116 seats in the House of Representatives—as opposed to eighty-three held by the Democrats—were in effect the majority party.[12] What is more, of the eightythree Democrats, seventy came from slave states: of the remaining thirteen, five came from Illinois. With nine seats altogether in the House of Representatives, this meant that Illinois, in the Thirty-sixth Congress, was—except for California and Oregon on the west coast—the only northern state in which the Republicans were not in a majority in the state representation in Congress.

Judged by this record, Lincoln's performance in the debate was sufficient neither to win for his party a majority representation in Congress, nor to gain sufficient seats in the state legislature to secure his own election to the US Senate. These facts, however, do not give a true picture of the relative strengths of the two parties. Although on a popular vote Lincoln might well have won over Douglas, the parties were evenly balanced, with their relative strengths little changed from the two preceding elections of 1854 and 1856. This was not true, however, of the nation at large, which the election results of 1858 polarized between north and south. This was precisely what Douglas had warned against, and it was little consolation to him that Illinois survived, somewhat dubiously, as a Democratic bastion in the north.

Douglas' accusation, essentially, was that the abolition of slavery was the issue that lay behind this unprecedented situation, and that this was a cause that Lincoln, according to the record, supported. If, as a result of the free-state vote in Kansas—less than three weeks before the first of the Lincoln-Douglas debates on August 21, 1858—there was no real possibility of the further territorial expansion of slavery in the United States (in spite of Dred Scott), then the abolitionist platform must go further than mere preservation of the status quo: in other words, its target was the "peculiar institution" as it existed in the fifteen slave states, where, in the Thirty-sixth Congress, the Democratic Party found its main strength and support.

Confronted by Douglas' challenge, Lincoln refuted the charge of sectionalism by claiming—notably at the fifth debate, at Galesburg on October 7—that:

> the evidence brought forward to prove the Republican party guilty in this respect was that in the Southern portion of the Union the people did not let the Republicans proclaim their doctrines amongst them, [and] that they had no supporters, or substantially none, in the slave States.

Lincoln went to ask for Douglas'

> attention to the fact that he felicitates himself to-day that all the Democrats of the free States are agreeing with him, while he omits to tell us that the Democrats of any slave

State agree with him. If he has not thought of this, I commend to his consideration the evidence in his own declaration, on this day, of his becoming sectional too.

This question was only too apt, given Douglas' refusal to cast his Senate vote in favor of Kansas' Lecompton constitution—as related in chapter 11. It was also prophetic, since (as related later in this chapter) when it came to the Democratic presidential convention adopting Douglas as its candidate in 1860, this was too much for the representatives of a number of slave states in the deep south—who simply walked out. This was what Lincoln had foreseen when he went on to say, "I see the day rapidly approaching when [Douglas'] pill of sectionalism, which he has been thrusting down the throats of Republicans for years past, will be crowded down his own throat".

As to the charge that he was an "abolitionist," Lincoln's response was based on resolutions which Douglas claimed to have been adopted by an anti-Nebraska state convention held at Springfield in 1854 which Lincoln—contrary to what Douglas alleged—had neither attended nor later endorsed. What is more this convention did not even pass the resolutions attributed to it: Douglas had been deliberately misled by a newspaper editor. None of this really mattered when it came to the way Lincoln's views were perceived in the slave states: there was more than enough in what he said in the fifth and sixth debates (at Galesburg and Quincy on October 7 and 13) to justify the view that he was at heart an abolitionist. Indeed this was a part of his appeal to many northern voters, not so much in Illinois in 1858, as in the free states generally when he stood for president in 1860. Even so, Lincoln's opening speech in the fourth debate—at Charleston on September 18—made clear that he was "not in favor of bringing about in any way the social and political equality of the white and black races".

THE RACE FOR THE PRESIDENCY

Where Lincoln then stood on key issues can best be judged by studying the famous speech made at the Cooper Union in New York on February 27, 1860. Much of what he said merely reaffirmed positions—such as that relating to sectionalism—which he had taken during the 1858 debates in Illinois. At the same time, having denied the charge that Republicans had made "the slavery question more prominent than it formerly was," he went on to say, "We admit that it is more prominent but we deny that we made it so. It was not we, but you who discarded the old policies of our fathers"—a theme central to the whole speech, and argued in considerable detail. At this point, however, Lincoln found it necessary to disown John Brown, pointing out Douglas' failure "to implicate a single Republican in his Harper's Ferry enterprise."[13] Lincoln's words were essentially conciliatory:

> It is exceedingly desirable that all parts of this great Confederacy shall be at peace, and in harmony one with another. Let us Republicans do our part of have it so. Even though provoked, let us do nothing through passion and ill temper. Even though the Southern people will not so much as listen to us, let us calmly consider their demands, and yield to them, if in our deliberate view of our duty, we possible can.

The will to conciliate was confirmed near the end of the speech:

> Wrong as we think slavery is, we can afford to let it alone where it is, because that much is due to the necessity arising from its actual presence in the nation; but can we, while our votes can prevent it, allow it to spread into the national territories, and to overrun us here in these Free States?[14]

The Cooper Union speech was a triumph for Lincoln. Horace Greeley of the *New York Tribune*, who in 1847 had been the first editor to mention his name in a national newspaper,[15] declared that "Mr Lincoln is one of nature's orators, using his rare powers solely and effectively to elucidate and convince, though their inevitable effect is to delight and electrify as well."[16] The day after the speech four New York newspapers printed it in full, while outside the city it was issued as a Republican tract by newspapers in Albany, Detroit, and Chicago. It was also a bold move on Lincoln's part to appear on stage in the home state of William Seward, a US senator and a leading contender for nomination as the Republican candidate in the presidential election coming at the end of the year

By this time Lincoln himself was clearly an "unannounced presidential aspirant."[17] There were already two others besides Seward, Salmon P. Chase of Ohio and Edward Bates of Missouri. Two matters were essential for Lincoln's success: first, the Republican convention must be held in Chicago, and second the Illinois delegation must then be unanimous in supporting him. As to the site of the convention, although most of the Republican Party's strength was in eastern states such as Ohio and New York, it was recognized that its success depended on winning key western states, notably Illinois and Missouri. This meant a convention either in Chicago (which would favor Lincoln) or St. Louis, the hometown of Edward Bates. Lincoln got his way on both these matters, having prepared the ground by speaking throughout Illinois of the suitability of the other three candidates. His message was that where Seward and Chase could win in the north of the state they would lose in the south, whereas with Bates it would be the other way round.[18] The implication was that Lincoln, coming from the center of the state would be acceptable in both north and south.

This still left open the question as to how Lincoln would fare among Republican delegates from outside Illinois. His strongest card was that with all his experience of confronting Stephen Douglas in debate he would be the most effective opponent if Douglas, as expected, was chosen by the Democratic convention as the party's candidate for president. At the convention, which met at Charleston, South Carolina, on April 23, Douglas and his supporters did their best to avoid discussion of slavery, knowing well that the stand he had taken in Illinois on key issues, such as the limited consequences of Dred Scott,[19] was not acceptable to southern delegates.

This strategy failed when an Alabama delegate, William Yancey, proposed that the Democratic platform should include a federal slave code. This proposal, if accepted, would be disastrous for the party's chances in the northern states, but even so it was only narrowly defeated. Yancey denounced the convention and walked out, followed first by the other Alabama delegates and then by those from Mississippi, Louisiana, Florida, Texas, North and South Carolina, and even Delaware. Their stand was made clear by the words of a South Carolina delegate, William Preston: "slavery is our King; slavery is our Truth; slavery is our Divine Right."[20]

In terms of national politics the Democratic Party was well rid of such members, but then without southern votes its presidential candidate had little chance of being elected. This is exactly what happened. Although Lincoln's appeal to Republicans was weakened as a result of the disarray of the Democrats at Charleston, on May 18 the Chicago convention still elected him on the third ballot, after Seward had led in the first two. He had the advantage of being perceived as the candidate most likely to win three key states, Pennsylvania, Indiana, and Illinois, which had not voted for Frémont in 1856.[21] At the same time his prospects in the presidential election improved substantially when in June, the southerners who had walked out at Charleston, held a new convention at Richmond, Virginia, where John C. Breckinridge of Kentucky—James Buchanan's vice president—was adopted as their own presidential candidate. The northern Democrats, left to pick up the pieces as best they could, confirmed the nomination of Stephen Douglas as the Democratic candidate. This meant that both Breckinridge and Douglas would oppose Lincoln in November, creating a situation in which the Democratic votes would be divided. There was also a new Constitutional Union Party, with John Bell of Tennessee as its presidential candidate. The position, therefore, was the reverse of that in the 1856 presidential election when the anti-Democratic vote was split as a result of Millard Fillmore—the last Whig president (1850–1853)—contesting the election as candidate for that party, while John C. Frémont was the much stronger Republican candidate.

With the presidential election in November, Lincoln won all nineteen free states, in some, such as Vermont, with an overwhelming majority, and in others, such as California, only by a narrow margin. All this was sufficient for 180 out of

303 electoral votes. As to the fifteen slave states, Lincoln was in ten of them not even a candidate, and only in Missouri did he obtain more than 10,000 votes. Although, over all, Douglas came second in the number of votes, Missouri was the only state to give him all its nine electoral votes—with another three (out of seven) coming from New Jersey. With twelve electoral votes in all he was thus far behind Breckinridge with seventy-two from eleven southern states, and even Bell, with thirty-nine from Kentucky, Tennessee, and Virginia.

The success of Lincoln was also reflected in the congressional elections, according to which the Democrats would have been in a minority in both houses. Combining this result with that of the presidential election produced exactly the result that Stephen Douglas had repeatedly warned against during the debates with Abraham Lincoln in 1858: the Republicans would govern as a sectional party, owing political loyalty only to the northern states. This ruled out any legislative policy favorable to southern interests, whatever the constitutional safeguards might be. After all that Lincoln had said about the consequences of Dred Scott, what would this case be worth under his presidency? And as the voting showed in November 1860, the south was divided, and the north solid. To the south, in its own perception, the Union had nothing to offer, at least to judge from what had happened to the Democratic Party at Charleston in June. A reaction was to be expected and it was not long in coming.

THE CONFEDERATE STATES OF AMERICA

Four days after the election, on November 10, 1860, the legislature of South Carolina unanimously authorized a state convention on December 6 to consider future relations with the Union. On December 20 delegates from every part of the state met in the largest hall in Charleston to sign the Ordinance of Secession[22]—to considerable public acclamation. By the end of February 1861, South Carolina had been followed by Alabama, Florida, Georgia, Louisiana, Mississippi, and Texas. The Ordinance of Secession declared that "the Constitution of the United States of America is no longer binding on any of the citizens of this State," which in some cases was then described as "sovereign and Independent."[23]

While all this was going on there was a colossal power vacuum in Washington. James Buchanan would be president until March 4, by which time such support as he had once had in Congress had been drastically reduced as a result of eight southern states seceding from the Union. That this process meant a corresponding increase in the power of the Republicans in what was the lamest of all possible lame-duck Congresses made it next to impossible for Buchanan to take any effective action. There was little chance of the congressional

Republicans producing any constructive policy, although it is worth noting that with so many southern Democrats absent a favorable vote for Kansas enabled it to be admitted as the thirty-fourth state of the Union on January 31, 1861. This was no help to Buchanan, who "was torn between his belief that secession was unconstitutional and his conviction that nothing could be done to prevent it."[24] Lincoln, at the same time, had no legal standing until the ballots of the electoral college were officially counted on February 13—less than three weeks before the day appointed for the inauguration of the president whose name would then be proclaimed. Appeals to modify positions he had taken during his election campaign—such as are clearly delineated in the Cooper Union speech—went unheard. They were just "the trick by which the south breaks down every Northern man," which, if Lincoln fell for it, would make him "as powerless as a block of buckeye wood."[25] His response to all who appealed to him was biblical: "they seek a sign, and no sign shall be given them."[26]

Lincoln, whatever his formal status before February 13, was kept busy at home in Springfield preparing for the time, beginning on March 4, when he would be in the White House. As early as November 21, 1860, when Lincoln began a three-day conference in Chicago with his prospective vice president, Hannibal Hamlin—whom he had never previously met—he began to choose the advisers who would help him form his administration.

Lincoln would inevitably be breaking new ground because the Republicans had never been in office before. Given that the antecedents of party members were divided between anti-slavery Whigs and free-soil Democrats, Lincoln had to balance his choice of advisers with this in mind. At the same time he wished to include all his three rivals for the nomination, that is William Seward and Edward Bates, both former Whigs and Salmon P. Chase, a former free-soil Democrat. They would then also represent their home states of New York, Missouri, and Ohio. This fitted in with the geographical distribution of cabinet posts which Lincoln had in mind, with one member coming from New England, two from New York and New Jersey in the northeast, two from Ohio, Indiana, and Illinois in the northwest, and two from the critical border states of Missouri, Kentucky, Maryland, and Delaware. The list was finally completed with the names of Gideon Welles of Connecticut (on the recommendation of Hamlin), William Dayton of New Jersey (the only former Whig), Caleb Smith of Indiana, and Montgomery Blair of Maryland.

This was by no means as simple as it now looks on paper. With these choices, others with a claim to office were left out. What is more, a mere list did not determine how the offices would be allocated. Lincoln needed all the diplomacy he could master to persuade Bates that he should accept Seward as secretary of state, and this was far from being the only case of dispute about the allocation of different cabinet offices—although no one protested against Welles becoming secretary for the navy. Much more serious, in political terms, was the absence of anyone from Pennsylvania, always a key state—and destined to be the more so in a Congress with only northern members. In Pennsylvania, with resources in coal and steel placing it at the heart of the American industrial revolution, an acceptable politician had to support the traditional Whig high-tariff policy. Lincoln had hoped that with New Jersey sharing the same interests, his nomination of Dayton would satisfy any claim from Pennsylvania. The reason was that the Republican Party in Pennsylvania was divided into factions at loggerheads with each other. What is more, the strongest candidate, Senator Simon Cameron—a self-made man who started off as a newspaper editor and went on to make a fortune in iron and railroads—had any number of enemies. Finally, while traveling by train on his way to inauguration in Washington, Lincoln hinted that he might actually retain one or two members of Buchanan's cabinet. This was too much for Pennsylvania's coal and iron magnates, who closed ranks and agreed to support Cameron.

Choosing a cabinet was only one part of Lincoln's activities in Springfield as he waited to leave for Washington. His offices in the state capitol were thronged with people seeking patronage and favors, offering both advice and criticism or just asking to meet him. All the time this was happening the nation, of which Lincoln was soon to be the chief magistrate, was disintegrating. Attempts were made to compromise with the south, so as to entice the states that had seceded back into the Union. They were bound to fail. Lincoln was immovable when it came to allowing slavery to be extended into the national territories, and no compromise would be acceptable to the south without some concession on this matter.

With no such prospect, six southern states, South Carolina, Florida, Mississippi, Alabama, Georgia, and Louisiana—later to be joined by Texas—sent representatives to Montgomery, Alabama, where in February 1861 they drew up a constitution for the new Confederate States of America.[27] At the same time these states were seizing federal military installations within their borders, so that even before Lincoln assumed office, Fort Pickens at Pensacola, Florida, and Fort Sumter at Charleston, South Carolina, were the only two major southern forts left in federal hands.

The seeds of crisis were sown. On Lincoln's first day in the White House Major Robert Anderson reported from Fort Sumter that he would have to surrender in about six weeks unless the garrison received new provisions. Making the fort secure would require some 20,000 well-disciplined men. The problem confronting Lincoln was appalling. Only the day before, in his first inaugural address, he had promised to avoid "bloodshed or violence . . . unless it be forced upon the national authority. The power confided to me will be used to hold, occupy and possess the property, and places belonging to the government."[28]

This commitment, according to the advice of General Winfield Scott, was impossible to honor at a time when the entire US Army numbered only 16,000 men—and most of these were scattered among forts along the Indian frontier far beyond the Mississippi River. Others, however, more optimistic, considered that Fort Sumter could be resupplied from the sea. The alternative—evacuating the military garrison—would be utterly ruinous politically.[29]

Lincoln was able to send two men who knew the state well to South Carolina, with one to report on the Union defenses at Fort Sumter, and other on the state of public opinion. The first report was positive: Fort Sumter could be resupplied by sea at night. The second report was extremely bleak: "separate nationality is a fact; there is no attachment to the Union . . . positively nothing to appeal to." On the contrary, any attempt to reinforce Sumter would be seen as an act of war. Even more discouraging advice was to come from Winfield Scott. To retain the loyalty of the upper south, including Virginia, Scott's home state, not only must Sumter be evacuated but also Fort Pickens—where there was no problem about bringing in new supplies.

On March 29 Lincoln summoned a cabinet meeting to consider the right course of action. Seward was all for following Winfield Scott's advice and abandoning both Sumter and Pickens, but he was alone. Where Bates and Smith insisted that Pickens must be held "at all hazards,"[30] Chase, Wells, and Blair insisted on also holding Sumter. With considerable interoffice and interservice rivalry, separate expeditions were organized for both forts. On April 6 Lincoln sent a special messenger to Governor Francis Pickens of South Carolina, to inform him that an attempt would be made to resupply Fort Sumter, but with provisions only, and no arms. While this may have been a breach of security, it made little difference to the outcome; on April 12, while the Union ships lay helpless offshore, the Confederates bombarded Fort Sumter. After thirty-four hours the garrison surrendered.

The Civil War had begun, but Lincoln preferred to see it as a rebellion, or an insurrection of individuals who had joined in "combinations too powerful to be suppressed by the ordinary course of judicial proceedings."[31] Although he consistently refused to recognize the Confederate States of America, his actions as president and commander in chief were often only consistent with accepting that the Union, confronted by something more than a problem of law enforcement, was actually engaged in a war between two belligerent powers. Confederate soldiers, when captured, would not be tried as criminals, nor sailors as pirates. Naval actions directed against the seceding states took the form of a blockade, in international law consistent only with acknowledging the existence of a separate state. Leading politicians, such as the Pennsylvania Republican leader, Thaddeus Stevens—well versed in the law—took issue with Lincoln regarding this decision, but his response was that not of a jurist, but a politician: "I am a good enough lawyer in a Western law court, I suppose, but we don't practice the law of nations up there, and I supposed Seward knew all about it and I left it to him."[32]

In practice this meant that so long as hostilities continued, Lincoln would act as commander in chief, rather than as chief magistrate. In the former role there were battles to be won, with minimal interference from Congress and the judiciary and, where militarily necessary, little regard for human rights. In the latter role, Lincoln's writ could hardly run in those parts of the nation that his forces did not control. The question which faced him in the early summer of 1861, after the fall of Fort Sumter, was where the line would be drawn between the two sides.

On April 12 there were still eight slave states which had not seceded. Of these, four, Virginia, Tennessee, Arkansas, and North Carolina, lost little time in doing so. They all joined the Confederacy, which provocatively moved its capital to Richmond, Virginia. Although the secession of Virginia was a serious loss to the Union, the state had been steadily declining during all the years in which Lincoln had been active in politics. Going back even further to 1809, the year of his birth—and the first year of the Eleventh Congress (1809–1811)—Virginia then had twenty-two seats in the US House of Representatives, while Ohio, only admitted to the Union in 1805, had but one. Virginia's representation was also greater than that of any other state, which accorded also with the fact that the first three nineteenth-century presidents, Jefferson, Madison, and Monroe, were also Virginians. In the Twenty-third Congress (1833–1835), Ohio's representation had increased to nineteen. Although Virginia, with twenty-one representatives, remained very strong, both New York, with thirty-three, and Pennsylvania, with twenty-five, were some way ahead. With the Thirty-seventh Congress (1861–1863), these numbers were the same, but Virginia's representation had fallen to thirteen, of whom only five Unionists actually took their seats. Significantly these all represented districts in the mountainous part of the state bounded, on the northwest, by the Ohio River. Virginia, therefore, by joining the Confederacy—and with its state capital becoming that of the new nation—was in a position to recover the status it had lost over the previous generation. Much more serious for Lincoln's prospects was the fact that Virginia was just across the Potomac River from Washington.

This made it critical that Maryland, on the same side of the Potomac, should remain loyal to the Union. Although its representation in the Thirty-seventh Congress (1861–1863) had declined from eight to six in the course of thirty years, the loss, far less serious than in Virginia, was largely attributable to the remarkable population growth in more western states during this period. Maryland remained important, both politically and economically. Although when Fort Sumter fell all six representatives, together with the state governor,

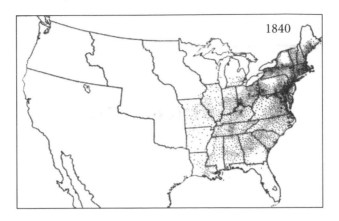

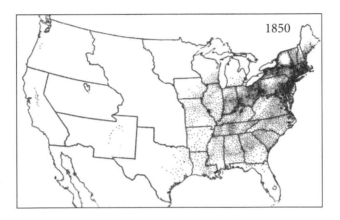

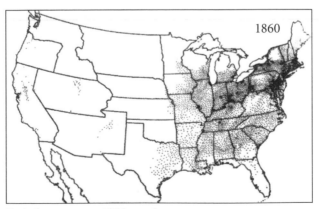

Each dot represents 5000 people

Population change, 1840–60.

were Unionists, they showed little backbone when it came to supporting Lincoln. Baltimore, important both as a seaport and as a northern railroad hub, had a large population sympathetic to the southern cause—so much so that the Sixth Massachusetts Regiment, on its way to defend Washington, was attacked by a secessionist mob, leading both the mayor and the state governor to request Lincoln to send no more troops through, or close to the city. During a week when Washington was virtually under siege, Baltimore secessionists destroyed the railroad bridges linking the city with the north and cut the telegraph lines. Lincoln, desperate for reinforcements, was finally rescued by General Benjamin F. Butler and the Seventh New York Regiment, which had reached Washington by taking ferries down Chesapeake Bay to Annapolis to continue on by train to the capital—an operation that first required repairing the damage done to the line by local secessionists.[33] This opened the way for thousands of troops to follow on. They were just in time. The Maryland legislature, meeting in Frederick on April 26, decided against secession. Even so, General Butler—just to be on the safe side—occupied Federal Hill, overlooking Baltimore Harbor, on May 13. Lincoln, having suspended the writ of habeas corpus along the route between Washington and Philadelphia, soon found this act questioned by Chief Justice Taney—himself a citizen of Maryland—but Lincoln ignored him.

With Maryland secured more or less for the Union, Delaware was bound to remain loyal. This still left the loyalty of Kentucky and Missouri extremely problematic. As must be clear from earlier chapters, Lincoln had close political ties to both states, and Kentucky, at least, had elected Unionists to represent it in Washington. As in Maryland this was not enough to guarantee loyalty. Nonetheless, during a period of uneasy neutrality, Lincoln had promised that "if Kentucky made no demonstration of force against the United States, he would not molest her."[34] This was prudent, for as Lincoln correctly observed, support for the Union was growing faster than for the Confederacy. Indeed he was able to create a new Military Department of Kentucky, to include all the state within a hundred miles of the Ohio River. The Union hold became firm in September 1861, when Confederate forces crossed over from Tennessee and headed for Bowling Green in the southwest of Kentucky, intending to capture the town and use it as a base for attacking Louisville. The Kentucky legislature, furious at this breach of the state's neutrality, ordered the Union flag to be raised over the state capitol in Frankfort, declaring its allegiance with the Union. It also passed the "Non-Partisan Act," which provided that "any person or any person's family that joins or aids the so-called Confederate Army was no longer a citizen of the Commonwealth."

Missouri, with six out of its seven congressmen Democrats, was much more uncertain, as can be seen by the way it had supported the cause of slavery in Kansas during the 1850s. Although two-thirds of all residents had come from southern states, in St. Louis, critically, the greater part of the population supported the Union. Here the substantial number of European immigrants, of which some 65,000 Germans constituted the majority, were a major factor. In St. Louis Lincoln also had the support of both the powerful Blair family (which had raised seven regiments for the Union cause), and the military commander, Nathaniel Lyon—who had succeeded in forcing the surrender of the garrison at Camp Jackson just outside the city, where the troops supported the Confederacy. Outside St. Louis, however, Governor Claiborne Jackson mobilized support for the Confederacy, leading to battles being fought in many different parts of the state. Although Union forces, by winning at Boonville on June 17, 1861, secured central Missouri, Confederate forces won a number of victories in the south, along the Mississippi, and in the west in the counties next to Kansas. Lyon's Union forces, in turn, had captured Jefferson City, the state capital, and appointed Hamilton Gamble—who as chief justice of Missouri had dissented in the Dred Scott case—as provisional governor.

In the late fall of 1861, Claiborne Jackson, encouraged by success in battle, convened a special session of the Missouri legislature to meet at Neosho in the far southwest corner of the state. With complete disregard for Gamble's appointment as provisional governor, an Ordinance of Secession passed with a safe majority, and on November 28 the Confederate Congress voted to admit Missouri as the twelfth state. This counted for little, for Jackson had no prospect of mobilizing the whole state for the Confederacy from so remote a base. On the contrary, after a series of more or less indecisive battles during the winter of 1861–1862 on both sides of the frontier between Missouri and Arkansas, Union forces, by winning a strategic victory at Pea Ridge, just inside Arkansas, on March 8, 1862, effectively secured the whole of Missouri for the Union. By this time the Union, after yielding to the force majeure of Confederate land forces on both sides of the Mississippi river at Columbus, Kentucky in November 1861—in a conflict in which the Missourian, General Ulysses S. Grant, first saw action—was busy organizing a fleet of ironclad gunboats to operate on the river. When this sailed downstream in the early summer of 1862 the Confederate forces had nothing to meet it beyond a number of converted paddle-steamers armored with cotton bales. These "cottonclads," after first losing to the Union fleet at Island Number Ten—now no more as a result of the changing course of the Mississippi—finally made a stand at Memphis, Tennessee. There, on June 6, in a battle lasting an hour and a half and watched by the citizens from the Chickasaw Bluffs, the Union fleet sank or captured almost every opposing ship, losing only one man to the 160-odd lost to the Confederates. The Union commanders then landed their forces and took control of a city which had become the leading entrepôt, inland, of the southern plantation economy. Already, on April 28, Captain David Farragut, USN, having led an oceangoing fleet along the Gulf Coast and up the lower reaches of the Mississippi, had captured New Orleans—the leading harbor and much the largest city of the Confederacy—after five days of action. With the exception of Vicksburg, approximately halfway between Memphis and New Orleans, the Mississippi River was lost by the Confederacy, leaving the two states on the other side, Arkansas and Texas, completely isolated. Governor Jackson's initiative in establishing the confederate state of Missouri had proved completely futile, while acting governor Hamilton Gamble, confirmed in office, became a staunch ally of Lincoln.[35]

THE BALANCE OF POWER IN THE CIVIL WAR

The balance of power between the Union and the Confederacy, as it developed in the political geography of the Civil War in the course of 1862, provides the key to the further history of both sides. On almost any analysis the Union was much more powerful. On the basis of the 1860 US census the population of the states which would support the Union in 1861 was some twenty-two million, with just over nine million people in those which would joint the Confederacy.[36] The ratio of these population figures to each other did not, however, reflect relative strengths when it came down to such matters as railroads,[37] industrial development, population growth, migration to California and the west, ocean shipping—in all of which the position of the north was disproportionately stronger.[38] Mobility, particularly of troops and armaments, from one part of the country to another, was far less of a problem for the north than for the south. All these factors meant that the war aims of the south were much more restricted. Particularly as the war went on, survival on the terms put forward toward the end of the Thirty-sixth Congress (which confirmed the Dred Scott decision) were all that the south was asking for—so much so that one is left to wonder why the war was ever perceived as unavoidable. The south was never going to conquer the north, whose great cities would never be captured. The north, on the other, was never going to be satisfied with anything but total victory. Given the balance of power, as described above, no one could have foreseen how long this would be in coming. The reasons are almost entirely military, that is, in the long-term fighting capacity of both sides. In the end this was not so much a question of the will to fight of the soldiers in the field or even of the merits of the generals who commanded them and the battles that they chose to fight, but of the logistical support that they could count on. Here the Union, for the reasons—largely economic—stated at the beginning of this paragraph, consistently had the upper hand.

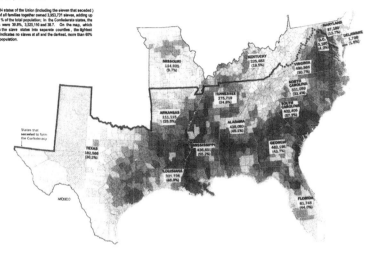

Slavery in 1861.

The geography of the eastern United States determined from the start that the war must be fought on two fronts, separated by the densely wooded hills of the Appalachians, which, stretching across the western parts of New York, Pennsylvania, and Virginia, the border areas of Virginia and Kentucky, North Carolina, and Tennessee, finally ended in the north of Georgia and Alabama. West of the Appalachians this meant that the war would be fought mainly in Kentucky and Tennessee, while on the eastern side it would be mainly in Virginia. In both theaters the Union was far ahead of the Confederacy when it came to shipping, whether in the west on the Mississippi and its tributaries, or in the east and south along the Atlantic and Gulf coastline. There, in the first year of war, the recapture of Norfolk left the Union in complete control of Chesapeake Bay, while further south, key confederate ports, from Wilmington, North Carolina, on the Atlantic to Mobile, Alabama, on the Gulf of Mexico, were effectively blockaded by the US Navy.[39] In men of war, merchantmen, and troop transporters, the Confederacy was far behind the Union, although in the first year of fighting it was able to take over a number of US Navy ships in southern harbors. One of these, the *USS Merrimac*—scuttled by the Union when the navy yard in Norfolk, Virginia, fell to Confederate forces in April 1861—was salvaged and converted to become a novel and successful ironclad warship, the *CSS*[40] *Virginia*. After demolishing two wooden frigates of the

Union navy, it finally met its match in the hastily constructed *USS Monitor*, built according to the same principles. The actual sea battle was a draw, from which both ships withdrew, never to engage again, but the design principles—notably the use of iron armor-plating and screw propellers—became standard in naval architecture.[41] All in all, the most important strategic consequence of the imbalance of naval power was that the Union could supply and transport its troops by water—and here it was critical that it dominated the Mississippi and its tributaries in the west and Chesapeake Bay, together with its important tidal rivers, in the east. To give one instance of what this meant, in the key early battle of Shiloh—fought in April 1862—the day was saved for the Union forces by the arrival of reinforcements brought down the Tennessee River.[42] Without this capacity Confederate generals preferred to fight their battles inland, as at Antietam in September 1862 or Gettysburg in July 1863—although occasionally, as with the Rappahannock, at Fredericksburg, Virginia, in December 1862, a river was a useful first line of defense.

In the Civil War there was never any question of a single continuous fortified line, stretching from Kansas to Virginia to separate the areas controlled, respectively, by Union or Confederate forces. Instead there were only the established frontiers between the states, which for the most part consisted—in the words of President Lincoln[43]—of nothing more than "surveyor's lines, over which people may walk back and forth without any consciousness of their presence." This was one reason why limited commerce, both of men and goods, was always possible between the two sides, so that—particularly in the early days of the war—men supporting the cause of the other side from wherever they happened to be, could cross over to volunteer to fight for that cause. (This process critically lost the Confederacy many of its specialist railroad men.) Many such men chose to stay at home, with the result that Union supporters were strong in the hills of western Virginia and the mountainous frontier area shared by Tennessee and North Carolina, while Confederate supporters were numerous in western Missouri, where, particularly in 1864, they organized militias to fight local Union forces.

Such local support for the other side never much influenced the course of war. Both Union and Confederate generals allowed important strategic considerations to determine the course of their campaigns, and it is this factor which decided where the key battles were fought. In February 1862, General Ulysses Grant's spectacular capture of two Confederate strongholds in northwest Tennessee, Fort Donelson, and Fort Henry, was the first move in a campaign planned to capture the key railroad junction at Corinth in northern Mississippi—an operation which, if successful, would break the Confederates' main east-west supply route along the Memphis and Charleston Railroad. Grant's success led the Confederate generals to withdraw their troops from

almost the entire state of Tennessee so that they could be used to establish a
defensive line to the west of the Tennessee River, less than a day's march north
of Corinth. This determined the site of the critical battle of Shiloh, which, after
appalling casualties suffered by both sides, ended—following the last-minute
arrival of reinforcements—in a Union victory.

In the early fall of 1862, General Braxton Bragg, commander of the
Confederate Army of the Mississippi, planned a campaign to turn the tables and
capture Louisville, Kentucky, the most important river port on the Ohio. This
time the Union generals had to withdraw their troops from Tennessee to block
the Confederate advance across Kentucky—which in late September nearly
succeeded in reaching its objective. The Confederate troops, however, halted
their advance at Bardstown, some forty-odd miles south of Louisville, and on
October 1, a new Union commander, General Don Carlos Buell, left the city,
with a large force to confront Bragg. This led to the decisive battle of Perryville
on October 8, which, if hardly a defeat for the Confederate forces, still led
Bragg to withdraw them, heavily outnumbered, back to Tennessee. Louisville
was saved after an ignominious defense; its loss to the Union would have been
catastrophic, so the Confederate strategy was well conceived. Critically, as so
often happened throughout the war, it was the numbers that won the battle.

Neither this book, nor this chapter of it, is intended to be a narrative history
of the Civil War; there are more than enough already. At every stage the politics
of Lincoln's Washington reacted to the course of the war. At much the same
time as Bragg failed to capture Louisville, General Robert E. Lee, commander
of the Confederate Army of Northern Virginia, followed, with no greater
success, a comparable strategy east of the Appalachians. Following a number
of significant victories in central Virginia, Lee's plan was to proceed up the rich
Shenandoah Valley—where the harvest could help feed his troops—and then
cross the Potomac River into northern Maryland in a movement designed to
encircle Washington. By chance his plan of campaign fell into Union hands,
enabling the Union generals to shadow the advancing Confederate forces. Lee
decided to confront the Union army just east of the small town of Sharpsburg,
and just short of Antietam Creek where his troops would have the advantage
of the high ground. With casualty lists as appalling as they had been at Shiloh
in April, Lee finally had to give up the battle, and withdraw to Virginia. Once
again, numbers were on the side of the Union generals.

EMANCIPATION

On July 12, 1862, Lincoln pleaded with both the senators and representatives
of the four slave states loyal to the Union—Delaware, Kentucky, Maryland, and

Missouri—to endorse a plan for the emancipation of slaves, pointing out that in their states slavery would soon yield to the "mere friction and aberration of war" while at the same time northern anti-slavery sentiment "is still upon me and is increasing."[44] With the congressmen quite unpersuaded, Lincoln had to bide his time. Nonetheless, only a day later, on July 13, he told two members of his cabinet, William Seward and Gideon Welles, that he "had about come to the conclusion that we must free the slaves or be ourselves subdued."[45] He had plainly not given up on the question of emancipation.

On the other side of the battle lines Lee had always counted on a victory in northern Maryland as the way to ending the war on terms favorable to the Confederacy. It was not to be. His defeat at Antietam opened the way for Lincoln, in Washington, to announce a decisive change in the Union's political objectives. Within a week of the battle, President Lincoln, on September 22, 1862, proposed a constitutional amendment providing for the long-term emancipation of slaves.[46] In a process that could continue until January 1, 1900, compensation would then be paid to the slave owners, who, after that date, would forfeit their entitlement to it. At the same time it would be open to the Congress "to provide for colonizing free colored persons, with their own consent, at any place or places without the United States." The appeal of this first emancipation proposal, which was made in a spirit of compromise, was that it would shorten the war on financial terms that would only have to be met over a long period of time, rather than committing the Union to meeting the steadily mounting costs of continuing to fight on until unconditional surrender by the Confederate forces. Little was said about the saving of human lives, because the "subject [was] presented exclusively in its economical aspect."[47] The social problem inherent in this early proposal was that of absorbing a vast colored population of freed slaves into the population at large. In Lincoln's view the Union could meet this challenge; already in Delaware, Maryland, and the District of Columbia, the ratio of free Negroes to the general population was higher than it would be, in the nation at large, if all the existing approximately four million slaves were emancipated.[48]

Lincoln's address of December 1, 1862, is above all remembered for its final words:

> We shall nobly save, or meanly lose, the last best hope of earth. Other means could succeed; this could not fail. The way is plain, peaceful, generous, just—a way which, if followed, the world will forever applaud and God forever bless.[49]

Lincoln's eloquence did not win the day. The elections held in November 1862 had already cost him his majority in both houses of Congress. Then, in mid-December, Union forces, engaged in an attempt to capture Richmond, the Confederate capital, were decisively defeated at Fredericksburg, only sixty miles south of Washington. Northern governors had already told the president that unless he moved against slavery they would be unable to meet their quotas for new troops. European powers were also reported to be close to recognizing the Confederacy unless he did so.[50] Emancipation would also have the advantage of encouraging slaves in the Confederate states to desert their masters, even to the point of fighting for the Union cause.

On January 1, 1863, Lincoln, after much hard thinking, finally ordered—in his capacity of commander in chief in a time of war—that "all persons held as slaves within [certain] designated States, and parts of states, are and henceforward shall be free."[51] The states designated were ten out of the eleven which had joined the confederacy, except for such designated parishes in Louisiana and counties in Virginia as were either in Union hands or had declared their loyalty to the Union. (The latter would be admitted later in the year as the new state of West Virginia.) Tennessee, already substantially in Union hands, was not designated. Lincoln went on to declare that "such persons of suitable condition will be received into the armed service of the United States to garrison forts, positions, stations and other places, and to man vessels of all sorts in said services."[52] The abolition of slavery, a cause long supported in the northern states, was now government policy, giving the hard-pressed Union forces a cause worth fighting for. Barely three years after his death John Brown had won the day.

Victory for the abolitionist cause was at this stage qualified by expediency. Because the emancipation proclamation only applied to territory not in Union hands, it had no immediate impact on either side of the line of battle. When victory came, however, it would be immediately enforced within the prescribed geographical limits, leaving little future for slavery in the four slave states not subject to it—the more so given the considerable numbers of free negroes in their population. As a declaration of policy, therefore, its reach extended across all the states, both north and south. At the end of the day not a county would be exempt from it. This still left Lincoln with the formidable task of winning the war.

THE ROAD TO APPOMATTOX

Following the Emancipation Proclamation, Lincoln, under pressure from within his own cabinet—coming particularly from Charles Sumner—was by the spring of 1863 urging the massive recruitment of negro troops in those parts of the Confederacy in Union hands. He told Andrew Johnson of Tennessee, whom he had appointed military governor of the state, that "the colored population is the great *available* and yet *unavailed* of, force for restoring the Union."[53] In the Mississippi Valley this led to the recruitment of some twenty regiments of Negro soldiers, who went on to acquit themselves well in battle. At the same time Governor John Andrew of Massachusetts was authorized to raise two regiments of black troops. With few negroes in the state, he allowed his recruiting officer, Major George Stearns to cast his net more widely. Stearns then approached Frederick Douglass, the renowned free negro leader, who answering his call, traveled throughout the north, urging negroes to enlist. Although the initial response was encouraging—allowing the famous Fifty-fourth Massachusetts Regiment to be formed[54]—resistance arose as a result of the fact that negro soldiers would both be paid less, and denied the enlistment bounty, while at the same time they faced an ordinance of the Confederate Congress "dooming to death or slavery every negro taken in arms, and every white officer who commands negro troops."[55] While this was dealt with by an appropriate Order of Retaliation, the administration's failure to take immediate action on pay led Douglass to confront the president directly. This was made possible by an invitation to the White House, where Douglass was captivated by Lincoln's "transparent countenance."[56] Lincoln immediately acknowledged the justice of Douglass' cause, and promised that "in the end [negro troops] shall have the same pay as white soldiers," a promise echoed later the same day by Secretary of War Edwin Stanton.[57] Douglass, however, declined the secretary's invitation to become assistant adjutant general charged with recruiting black soldiers along the Mississippi.

All this was taking place during a very hot July in Washington. The month had started with two great victories, one, on July 3, at Vicksburg in the west, and the other, on July 4, at Gettysburg. The fall of Vicksburg to General Grant—after a siege of forty-six days had brought the Confederate garrison close to starvation—meant that the whole length of the Mississippi was in Union hands, leaving Confederate troops in Texas, Louisiana, and Arkansas completely cut off. The victory at Gettysburg turned back Robert E. Lee's second attempt to invade Pennsylvania by sending his Army of Northern Virginia across western Maryland. His defeat at Antietam in 1862 had not discouraged him. As in 1862, the Union forces failed to follow up their victory, allowing the surviving remnant of Lee's army to retreat safely to Virginia, where they would continue to fight until the end of the war in 1865.

In the summer of 1863 Lincoln also had to combat copperhead subversion in the northwest. In May, in his home state of Ohio, a former congressman, Clement Vallandigham, after inciting "a large crowd to a frenzy with his passionate denunciations of a failed war,"[58] was arrested by General Burnside, the local Union commander. Within hours Vallandigham was tried for treason and sentenced to imprisonment for the rest of the war. Following Lincoln's suspension of habeas corpus Vallandigham was denied the writ, an action leading to considerable local unrest. Lincoln, determined to be loyal to his subordinate, General Burnside, supported his action, but commuted the sentence to banishment within the Confederate lines, observing that there "Vallandigham's copperhead body could go where his heart already was."[59] Lincoln restored his position with the American public by writing a letter to a New York "war" Democrat, Erastus Corning, in which he explained that Vallandigham was arrested "because he was laboring with some effect to prevent the raising of troops, to encourage desertion from the army, and to leave the rebellion without an adequate military force to suppress it."[60] The letter—as always planned—was released to Horace Greeley's *New York Tribune*, and this first publication then led on to its reaching an astonishing ten million homes.[61] Later in the summer Lincoln wrote another letter intended for publication, this time to his Springfield friend and leading Illinois Republican, James Conkling. His intention was to repudiate copperhead rumors that he had secretly rejected several viable peace proposals. Once again publication was a triumph in public relations, with the *New York Times* going on to commend to its readers a long list of Lincoln's previous writings, which, taken together, made him "the most popular man in the Republic. All the denunciations and all the arts of demagogues are perfectly powerless to wean the people from their faith in him."[62]

In the late summer months of 1863 the Confederate forces withdrew across the whole strategically important area of eastern Tennessee to the point that on September 7 their commander, General Braxton Bragg, ordered the evacuation of the key railroad junction of Chattanooga, just north of the Georgia state line. This was the beginning of the way of the Union's planned invasion of Georgia, with as its first goal the key city of Atlanta.[63] Knowing this full well, General Bragg saw the opportunity of enticing the General Rosecrans' Union army into a trap, which took the form of fighting a battle at Chickamauga Creek, just inside Georgia, on terrain deliberately chosen for the tactical advantages it gave to the Confederate army. Three days (September 18–20) of fighting gave Bragg the victory he had sought, but at such an appalling cost in casualties to both sides that he was unable to follow it up by recapturing Chattanooga.

Rosecrans, defeated at Chickamauga, was relieved of his command on October 20. General Ulysses Grant, appointed to succeed him, insisted that he could do nothing without reinforcements—and Bragg, on the other side was in a similar situation. Whereas in November a substantial Union force commanded by General William T. Sherman arrived to reinforce the Union Army, no such help could be sent to the Confederate forces opposing it. By the end of the month the much-strengthened Union army resumed its advance into Georgia, and this time Bragg was powerless to stop it. Chickamauga proved to have been a Pyrrhic victory, and the Union army continued its advance in a campaign known to history as "Sherman's march to the sea"—which only ended with his capture of Savannah in December 1864. When, however, Atlanta fell to Sherman on September 4, the war in the deep south was effectively won—the more so after Mobile, Alabama, the last Confederate seaport, fell to Admiral David Farragut at almost the same time. Effectively this meant that the war would finally be fought out in Virginia, where, in its last year, all the major battles were fought. Although what happened at the Wilderness, Spotsylvania and New Market in May, or at Cold Harbor in June 1864, brought little glory to the Union forces, the great number of casualties on both sides was fatal to the Confederate army. There were no longer sufficient men or material to reinforce it. Although this army still defended Petersburg—the most important railroad town north of Atlanta—throughout the winter, the supply routes by river and railroad were under Union control. With the fall of Petersburg on April 3, 1865, Richmond was also lost, with the Confederate president Jefferson Davis and his government—on Lee's advice—abandoning the city only at the last moment. On the next day Abraham Lincoln, with his wife and younger son, Tad, were passengers on the *USS Malvern*, Farragut's flagship, as it sailed up the James River, and after transferring to a shallow-draft barge they arrived in Richmond. After lunch in the Confederate White House they made an extensive tour of the city. Not only throngs of negroes, some shouting "Bless the Lord, Father Abraham's come,"[64] came out to greet him, but also countless working-class white men. In the more fashionable residential districts, however, "blinds or shades were drawn and no faces were to be seen."[65]

Lee tried to escape westward with the remnants of his army—in all some 28,000 men—hoping to find essential new supplies. When he arrived outside the small town of Appomattox, the railroad station was already occupied by Union cavalry, and the last chance of feeding his soldiers was gone. At the invitation of General Grant, Lee came to a private house in Appomattox,[66] where in the afternoon of April 9, 1865, Lee agreed to Grant's terms of surrender for his army. At his request Grant then authorized that rations from Union stores be provided for Lee's starving soldiers, who were then left with the prospect of returning to homes devastated by a war which, at one time or another, had been fought in almost every state from which they came. Except for Lee's incursion into southern Pennsylvania in 1863—which ended at Gettysburg—this was not the fate of any free state. Although the Union, as much as the Confederacy, had paid a terrible price in human lives,[67] the war gave a considerable impulse to its economy, which, when peace came, was on the threshold of vast further expansion—much of it planned during the war years. The southern plantation economy, deprived for four years of its overseas markets, and—by the end of the war—of any prospect of reverting to slave labor, faced a bleak future.

THE POLITICAL LEGACY OF ABRAHAM LINCOLN

After the secession of the Confederate states in 1861, both the area and the population of the territory that was part of the Union as defined by the states still represented in the US Congress, was inevitably considerably smaller than it had been at the time of the November elections, both for the president and the Congress, in 1860. Nonetheless it was this reduced territory that defined the political base of Abraham Lincoln during his entire period in office from his inauguration on March 14, 1861, to his untimely death, at the hand of an assassin, on April 15, 1865—barely a week after the terms of surrender had been agreed between General Ulysses S. Grant and General Robert E. Lee at Appomattox. In this period there was, however, one significant change that would never have been possible in normal times: this was the admission of West Virginia, a state carved out of Virginia, as the thirty-fifth state of the Union on June 23, 1863.

The political geography of the United States, such as it was at the end of 1864, became critical when it came to both houses of Congress voting—with the two-thirds majority required by the Constitution—for the thirteenth amendment which would establish, in perpetuity and for the whole of the United States, the emancipation of slaves as proclaimed by Lincoln on January 1, 1863, with respect to the territory then under Confederate control. The problem was that the Thirty-eighth Congress, which at the end of 1864 had entered its final lame-duck session, had been elected in November 1862 at a time when the reverses suffered by Union forces in the Civil War had lost the Republican Party essential popular support. The fact that as a result of this election the Democrats held seventy-two out of the 184 seats in the House of Representatives meant that the amendment could not pass the House without some Democratic and Unionist support. The amendment, which had already failed in the House in 1864, was reintroduced on January 6, 1865, and after long hours of debate was passed by 119 votes for and fifty-six against on January 31—a result only achieved after five Democrats had been persuaded to change their votes.[68] Although twenty state legislatures (out of thirty-six) ratified the amendment almost immediately, the seven further votes necessary were not passed until the end of the year. Lincoln never saw the final consummation of the cause which history, more than any other, associates with his name.

No plans for the future of the United States are to be found in Abraham Lincoln's second inaugural address, given on March 4, 1865, after the electoral college—in accordance with the results of the election in November 1864—had voted for him to be president with an overwhelming majority.[69] The address is remembered, rightly, for its eloquence rather than its substance. It was only on April 11, 1865, two days after Lee's surrender at Appomattox, that Lincoln, in an address made to a crowd of several hundred assembled on the lawn, stated that the problem then confronting the nation could be summed up in one word, "reconstruction." The principle, implicit in Lincoln's words, was that the initiative must come from within each seceding state. Here the free parishes of Louisiana, mentioned in the emancipation proclamation, had already taken the first steps, which Lincoln commended:

> some twelve-thousand voters in the heretofore slave-state of Louisiana have sworn allegiance to the Union, assumed to be the rightful political power of the State, held elections, organized a State government, adopted a free-state constitution, given the benefit of public schools equally to black and white, and empowering the Legislature to confer the elective franchise upon the colored man. Their Legislature has already voted to ratify the constitutional amendment recently passed by Congress, abolishing slavery throughout the nation.[70]

Lincoln's support for the new legislature of Louisiana was made clear by a rhetorical question at the end of his address: "Can Louisiana be brought into proper practical relation with the Union *sooner* by *sustaining* or by *discarding* her new State Government?"[71] He plainly saw the measures taken by Louisiana as a general blueprint for other seceding states to rejoin the Union. Dying only four days later, he never had time to elaborate further on how this could be achieved in practice.

Endnotes

Notes to Chapter 1: The American Scene in 1809

1   A. G. Bogue, *From Prairie to Corn Belt: Farming on the Illinois and Iowa Prairies in the Nineteenth Century* (Chicago: University of Chicago Press, 1963), 149.
2   K. J. Winkle, *The Young Eagle* (Lanham, MD: Taylor Trade Publishing, 2001), 7.
3   R. B. Bernstein, *Are We to be a Nation: The Making of the Constitution* (Cambridge: Harvard University Press, 1987), 9.
4   S. Mihm, *A Nation of Counterfeiters: Capitalists, Con Men, and the Making of the United States* (Cambridge: Harvard University Press, 2007), 41; the Constitution granted the US Congress the exclusive right to mint coins, which it delegated to the US Treasury, after this was established on September 2, 1789.
5   *Young Eagle*, 5.
6   R. C. Walter and D. J. Merritts, "Natural Streams and the Legacy of Water-powered Mills." *Science* 319 (2007), 299–304.
7   A. W. Eckert, *A Sorrow in Our Heart: the Life of Tecumseh* (New York: Bantam Books, 1993), 11.
8   *Young Eagle*, 7.
9   Rhode Island, on May 29, 1790, became the last state to ratify the constitution.
10 A. de Tocqueville, *Democracy in America*, 2 vols. (New York: Bantam Classics, 2000), 419.
11 D. H. Donald, *Lincoln* (New York: Simon and Schuster, 1995), 34–5.
12 Ibid., 394.
13 Ibid., 393.
14 H. S. Klein, *A Population History of the United States* (Cambridge: Cambridge University Press, 2004), 85, records some 678,000 slaves in 1790—the year of the first US census—but there were also a small number of free negroes.
15 Connecticut, Massachusetts, and New Hampshire were the three states where slavery was already banned; New York would follow in 1827, Rhode Island in 1842, New Jersey in 1846, Connecticut in 1848, and Pennsylvania in 1850, but in all these states the slave population was quite insignificant long before slavery was formally banned—so much so that they counted politically as "free" rather than "slave."
16 E. J. McManus, *A History of Negro Slavery in New York* (New York: Syracuse University Press, 1966), 182–83.

17   C. Malone, *Between Freedom and Bondage: Race, Party and Voting Rights in the Antebellum North* (London: Routledge, 2008), 4, Table 1.1. After the Civil War, the Fifteenth Amendment to the US Constitution, finally ratified on February 3, 1870, provided that no government in the United States may prevent a citizen from voting based on that citizen's race, color, or previous condition of servitude.

18   D. B. Davis, "He Changed the New World." *New York Review of Books*, May 31, 2007, 54–8, 55.

19   *Nation of Counterfeiters*, 11.

20   W. A. Dunaway, *Slavery in the American Mountain South* (Cambridge: Cambridge University Press, 2003), 60–2.

21   W. K. Scarborough, *Masters of the Big House: Elite Slaveholders of the Mid-Nineteenth Century South* (Baton Rouge: Louisiana State University Press, 2003), 139.

22   This process, which continued until nearly the end of the nineteenth century, was the result of defeat in battle and the imposition of treaties consistently leading to Indian territory being lost to American settlers; see the map in M. Gilbert, *The Routledge Atlas of American History* (London: Routledge, 2006), 37.

23   Although North Carolina accepted, in principle, the creation of a separate territory out of its lands beyond the Appalachians in 1781, these only became the Southeast Territory, by virtue of an act of Congress, on May 26, 1790; formal acceptance of this act was a condition for North Carolina's admission as the twelfth state of the Union on November 21, 1788.

24   In 1803 the federal Orleans Territory was constituted out of that small part of the whole purchase containing the delta of the Mississippi, including the city of New Orleans, and extending up to latitude 33° north. The state of Louisiana as it then became in 1812 was much smaller than it now is, since it could not include the so-called Spanish parishes, which—as related in earlier in this chapter—were only acquired from Spain in 1820.

25   In the First Congress (1789–1791) all the representatives from four states, Connecticut, New Hampshire, New Jersey, and Pennsylvania, were elected "at large."

26   H. S. Klein, *A Population History of the United States* (Cambridge: Cambridge University Press, 2004), 89.

27   The exact number counted was 7,239,881, which included 1,377,808 negroes, of whom nearly 90 percent were slaves in the southern states.

28   The three mid-Atlantic states scored highest, with 28 percent of the national population, in 1810, 1820, and 1830.

29   According to the 1861 census, the British population in that year was 29,070,930.

30   In the most recent census, that of the year 2000, it was located in Phelps County, Missouri: *Population History of the United States*, 92.

31   A simple formula allows one to find the years of the N-th Congress in the nineteenth century: the first year is then $2N - 13$, so that of the Tenth Congress, for instance, was 1807 ($1800 + 2 \times 10 - 13$). To know the Congress in session in a given year, say $1800 + n$, add 13, and divide by 2, so that, 1807, gives $7 + 13 = 20$, which divided by 2, equals 10. This is sufficient for a book about Abraham Lincoln.

32   Two from Massachusetts, and one each from Delaware and New York.

33   S. Wilentz, *The Rise of American Democracy: Jefferson to Lincoln* (New York: W.W. Norton and Company, 2005), 190.

34   A. M. Schlesinger, *The Age of Jackson* (London: Eyre and Spottiswood, 1946) is the standard text.

35   *Democracy in America*, 413.

36   Described in detail in C. Malone, *Between Freedom and Bondage: Race, Party and Voting Rights in the Antebellum North* (London: Routledge, 2008).

37   *Democracy in America*, 426, footnote.

38   M. Gilbert, *The Routledge Atlas of American History* (London: Routledge, 2006), 52.

39   *Slavery in the American Mountain South*, 109.

40   From Spanish colonial times slaves had been employed in sugar plantations in Louisiana, a practice that continued in the state of Louisiana.

41   Cotton, since early plantation days, has consistently been much the largest cash crop in US agriculture; over the course of time the plantations have moved steadily westward, so that northwest Texas is now the most intensively cultivated area.

42   Until slave trading in the District of Columbia was abolished by Congress in 1850, Washington's Georgia Pen was notorious for the inhuman way the trade was carried on. For an eyewitness description of what the traffic in slaves meant to the city of Baltimore, see F. Douglass, *On Slavery and the Civil War: Selections from his Writings* (Mineola: Dover Publications, 2003), 31.

43   This article provided for extradition between the separate states, but without mentioning crimes relating to slavery.

44   P. Finkelman, *Slavery in the Courtroom: An Annotated Bibliography of American Cases* (Washington: Library of Congress, 1985), is the standard sourcebook.

45   *Rise of American Democracy*, 331.

46   Ibid., 332.

47   Ibid., 335–6.

Notes to Chapter 2: The American Riverboat

1   M. Twain, *Life on the Mississippi* (New York: Signet Classics, 1961), 37.

2   Quoted in Steamboating on the Mississippi: St. Louis' Riverboat Heritage (http://www.usgennet.org/usa/mo/county/stlouis/steamboat.htm), accessed July 24, 2008.

3   K. J. Winkle, *The Young Eagle* (Lanham, MD: Taylor Trade Publishing, 2001), 21.

4   L. C. Hunter, *Steamboats on the Western Rivers: An Economic and Technological History* (Cambridge: Harvard University Press, 1949), 15.

5   J. E. Davis, *Frontier Illinois* (Bloomington: Indiana University Press, 1998), 222.

6   Oliver Evans, a western pioneer, had seen the advantages of high-pressure engines for steamboats as early as 1785 (according to his own account) but the steamboat he launched in 1803 was a failure; he had more success introducing high-pressure engines for industrial use in the west. *Steamboats on the Western Rivers*, 7.

7   *Steamboats on the Western Rivers*, 17.

8   F. Donovan, *River Boats of America* (New York: Thomas E. Crowell Company, 1966), 52.

9   *Steamboats on the Western Rivers*, 64.

10   Ibid., 62.

11   See Chapter 1.

12   Longitude 112° west is accepted as the eastern boundary of a climate zone with exceptionally low precipitation. As can be seen by any traveler across the continent this line divides the Dakotas, Nebraska, Kansas, Oklahoma, and Texas, each into a dry, sparsely populated western zone, and a more densely settled, wet eastern zone.

13   *River Boats of America*, 7.

14   Ibid., 92.

15   Texas was until 1836 part of Mexico, while the Oklahoma territory (which was part of the Louisiana Purchase) was a reservation for Indians from the states east of the Mississippi; see also chapter 5.

16   See Chapter 1.

17   Quoted in Steamboating on the Mississippi. (http://www.usgennet.org/usa/mo/county/stlouis/steamboat.htm), accessed July 24, 2008.

18   Ibid., 95.

19   Ibid., 111.

20   N. Etcheson, *Bleeding Kansas: Contested Liberty in the Civil War Era* (Lawrence: University Press of Kansas, 2004), 94.

21   Oklahoma retained its status as Indian territory until it became the forty-sixth state of the Union in 1907. Kansas was admitted at the thirty-fourth state in 1861 and Nebraska as the thirty-seventh in 1867.

22   These figures come from the chapter "Recollections of a Steamboat Captain," in W. B. Stevens, *St. Louis The Fourth City 1764–1909* (Chicago: S.J. Clarke Publishing, 1909).

Notes to Chapter 3: The British Connection

1   C. L. Rossiter, "Nationalism and American Identity in the Early Republic," in S. Wilentz (ed.) *Major Problems in the Early Republic 1787–1848* (Lexington: D.C. Heath & Co., 1992), 14–23.

2   The eighth president, Martin Van Buren, born in December 1782, lived less than a year as a British subject.

3   See R. W. Carwardine, *Lincoln* (London: Pearson Education, 2003), 56 and 60.

4   See H. R. Helper, *The Impending Crisis of the South* (New York: Burdick, 1860), a book regarded by the south as highly subversive when it first appeared, for the argument that demographic changes in the United States would ensure victory for the north in any contest with the south.

5   D. H. Donald, *Lincoln* (New York: Simon and Schuster, 1995), 54.

6   From Monticello, August 12, 1810, reproduced in J. P. Kaminsky (ed.), *Citizen Jefferson: The Wit and Wisdom of a American Sage* (Madison, WI: Madison House, 1994), 29.

7   The Polly decision of 1800, noted by D. R. Hickey, *The War of 1812: A Forgotten Conflict* (Champaign: University of Illinois Press, 1990), 10, concerned an American-owned ship seized while on a voyage from Marblehead, Massachusetts to Bilboa. The British captor claimed that since the cargo consisted of Havana sugar and Caracas cocoa being shipped to Spain it was a lawful prize. The owners argued that the cargo, bought in Havana, had been entered at the customs house at Marblehead and duties paid. They pointed out that the cargo had been off-loaded, the ship put on stocks for repairs, new insurance taken and new clearances obtained; therefore the voyage was not direct. The court found for the owners. For the details of this decision, and its consequences, see, T. Holmberg, *The Acts, Orders in Council, &c. of Great Britain [on Trade], 1793–1812* (Cambridge: Kentrolman Ltd., 2003).

8   *War of 1812*, 9.

9   W. R. Borneman, *1812: The War that Forged a Nation* (New York: Harper Perennial, 2004), 19–20.

10   *War of 1812*, 11.

11   *1812*, 30–1.

12   The boundaries of this territory were defined by the Northwest Ordinance of 1787; see Chapter 1.

13   *1812*, 37.

14   Ibid., 49.

15   Ibid., 51.

16   Ibid., 159.

17   *War of 1812*, 139.

18   *1812*, 185–89.

19   Ibid., 226–29.

20   Ibid., 231–32.

21   Ibid., 242–44.

22   Ibid., 246.

23   Ibid., 203–15.

24   *War of 1812*, 289.

25   Ibid., 290.

26   Ibid., 296.

27   The land battle of Waterloo was still to come in 1815.

28   *1812*, 273–91.

29   *War of 1812*, 299.

30   Ibid.

31   C. K. Harley, "Trade: Discovery, Mercantilism and Technology," in R. Floud and P. Johnson (eds.), *The Cambridge Economic History of Modern Britain, Vol. 1, Industrialisation, 1700–1860* (Cambridge: Cambridge University Press, 2004), 175–203, 185.

32   E. Hobsbawm, *Industry and Empire* (London: Penguin Books, 1959), 51.

33   "Trade: Discovery, Mercantilism and Technology," 189.

34   E. Wolf, *Europe and the People without History* (California: University of California Press, 1982), 280.

35 Succeeded William H. Harrison, who died after only one month in office.
36 G. G. van Deusen, *The Jacksonian Era 1828–1848* (London: Hamish Hamilton, 1959), 173.
37 Ibid., 188.
38 See A. Nevins (ed.), *Polk: The Diary of a President 1845–1849, Covering the Mexican War, the Acquisition of Oregon, and the Conquest of California and the Southwest* (London: Longmans, Green and Co., 1952), xvii.
39 *Jacksonian Era*, 213.
40 D. Hurd, *Robert Peel: A Biography* (London: Weidenfeld and Nicolson, 2007), 274–77, 356–57.
41 A. M. Schlesinger, *The Age of Jackson* (London: Eyre and Spottiswood, 1946), 398 and 443.
42 *Lincoln*, 140.
43 Described, ibid., 321, as "an entirely proper step."
44 The reaction of the British government is described in Chambers, J., *Palmerston: The People's Darling.* (London: John Murray, 2004), pp. 486–87.
45 Lincoln, 321.
46 Ibid., 323.
47 Salmon P. Chase.
48 *Lincoln*, 323.
49 R. J. Carwardine, *Lincoln* (London: Pearson Education, 2003), 307.
50 D. H Donald, *Lincoln* (New York: Simon and Schuster, 1995), 379.
51 Ibid., 415.
52 Ibid., 547.

Notes to Chapter 4: Spanish America: Independence and the Monroe Doctrine

1 A. Pagden, "Heeding Heraclides: Empire and its Discontents, 1619–1812," in R. L. Kagan and G. Parker (eds.), *Spain, Europe and the Atlantic World: Essays in Honour of John H. Elliott* (Cambridge: Cambridge University Press, 1995), 327.
2 Ibid., 328.
3 Ibid., 333.
4 This became fourteen when Panama (previously part of Colombia) became an independent state in 1903.
5 N. A. Graebner, *Empire on the Pacific: A Study in American Continental Expansion* (New York: Ronald Press, 1955), 387.
6 J. K. Mahon, *The War of 1812* (Gainesville: University of Florida Press, 1972), 148.
7 See D. H. Donald, *Lincoln* (New York: Simon and Schuster, 1995), 323, 499.
8 M. Gilbert, *The Routledge Atlas of American History* (London: Routledge, 2006), 41.
9 S. V. Connor, *Texas: A History* (Northbrook: AHM Publishing Corporation, 1971), 67.
10 The precise definition of this frontier is the line running due north from the point where latitude 32° north crosses the Sabine River.
11 *Texas*, 56.

12 Ibid., 56–7.

13 Ibid., 87.

14 Ibid., 89.

15 Ibid., 95.

16 Ibid., 96 relates Sam Houston's background.

17 Ibid., 103.

18 Ibid.

19 Ibid., 172.

20 "Slavery Up Close," *Time*, July 4, 2005, 61.

21 G. G. van Deusen, *The Jacksonian Era 1828–1848* (London: Hamish Hamilton, 1959), 83.

22 Quoting from Lincoln's second inaugural address: "Both parties deprecated war; but one of them would *make* war rather than let the nation survive; the other would *accept* war rather than let it perish."

23 *Lincoln*, 123.

24 Ibid., 125.

25 The natural frontiers of Texas are the Rio Grande, the Gulf Coast, the Sabine, and the Red Rivers. Apart from the short, straight-line frontier linking the two rivers (see note 10 above), the remaining frontiers as established in 1850 are the line running due north from the point where the Red River crosses longitude 100° west up to latitude 36°30" north, then this parallel of latitude west to longitude 103° west, then due south to the point where the meridian crosses latitude 32° north, and from this point due west to the Rio Grande; *Texas*, 163.

Chapter 5: Illinois: Land of Lincoln

1 J. E. Davis, *Frontier Illinois* (Bloomington: Indiana University Press, 1998), 161–2; the losers were the settlers in the Wisconsin Territory, which only became a state in 1848.

2 P. W. Gates, *The Illinois Central Railroad and Its Colonization Work* (Cambridge: Harvard University Press, 1934), 17.

3 Ibid., 16.

4 Invented 1831; later International Harvester, one of Chicago's largest businesses.

5 K. J. Winkle, *The Young Eagle* (Taylor Trade Publishing, 2001), 20, from Indiana.

6 For land sales in Illinois, see *Frontier Illinois*, Table 1, 205.

7 By the end of the 1850s only Ohio had more railroad mileage than Illinois.

8 T. L. Carlson, *The Illinois Military Tract: A Study of Land Occupation, Utilization and Tenure* (Champaign: University of Illinois Press, 1971) is the standard text.

9 *Illinois Central Railroad*, 99.

10 House Executive Documents, Twenty-sixth Congress, first session, 1840, vol. 7, doc. 262.

11 *Illinois Central Railroad*, 100.

12 Ibid., 101.

13 *Frontier Illinois*, 279.

14 Ibid., 304–6.

15 The most dramatic and far-reaching conflict involved the Mormons, who, led by Joseph Smith, had established, in 1839, the central gathering place for their Church of Jesus Christ of Latter-day Saints at Nauvoo, Illinois. Mormons collected there from all over the United States and from Great Britain, eventually to reach a population of about 15,000. The state charter obtained from the Illinois legislature in 1840 permitted the city to form a militia and to organize municipal courts, which Smith hoped would protect the Mormons from the persecution they had experienced elsewhere.

Smith's controversial innovations, such as plural marriage, in which men married multiple wives, turned some highly placed Mormons against him. They organized a reformist movement and published a newspaper exposing the self-styled prophet. When Smith as mayor closed down the paper and destroyed its press, non-Mormon citizens in the surrounding towns demanded his arrest. Opposition had already been building against the Mormons because of their growing influence in county politics. On June 27, 1844, while Smith was awaiting trial, a lynching party invaded the jail in nearby Hamilton where he was held, and shot and killed him.

Brigham Young, who succeeded Smith as president of the church, remained in Nauvoo but local opposition did not subside. On February 6, 1846, the first party of Mormons left Nauvoo for the west, and the remainder followed within a year. Although Nauvoo was for a short period the largest city in Illinois, nothing of the drama that took place there seemed to have made any impact upon Abraham Lincoln.

16 *Frontier Illinois*, 371.

17 For a full description of the case, see J. J. Duff, *A. Lincoln, Prairie Lawyer* (Austin, TX: Rinehart and Company, 1960), chapter 20.

18 Of these, two, Harrison and Taylor, were elected (in 1840 and 1848)—only to die in office—with the remaining two, Tyler and Fillmore, then succeeding to the White House (in 1841 and 1850).

19 See B. Vandervort, *Indian Wars of Mexico, Canada and the United States 1812–1900* (London: Routledge, 2006), 122–26.

20 T. C. Pease, *The Story of Illinois* (Chicago: University of Chicago Press, 1949), 108.

21 A. M. Schlesinger, *The Age of Jackson* (London: Eyre and Spottiswood, 1946), 76.

22 Ibid., 80.

23 Ibid., 109.

24 Ibid., 112.

25 G. G. van Deusen, *The Jacksonian Era 1828–1848* (London: Hamish Hamilton, 1959), 97.

26 The significant breakthrough only came with the Federal-Aid Highway Act of 1956, enacted on the initiative of President Dwight D. Eisenhower. Initial federal planning for a nationwide highway system dates back to 1921 when the Bureau of Public Roads asked the US Army to provide a list of roads it considered necessary for national defense; the result was the Pershing Map, named after the commander of the US forces in the First World War.

27 D. H. Donald, *Lincoln* (New York: Simon and Schuster, 1995), 36.

28   S. Mihm, *A Nation of Counterfeiters: Capitalists, Con Men, and the Making of the United States* (Cambridge: Harvard University Press, 2007), 315.

29   A. W. Eckert, *A Sorrow in Our Heart: the Life of Tecumseh* (New York: Bantam Books,1993), 672.

30   *Age of Jackson*, 451.

31   Both quotations come from ibid., 451–52.

32   *Lincoln*, 111.

33   Ibid., 178.

34   Ibid., 180.

35   Ibid., 181.

36   Ibid., 183.

37   Ibid., 192.

38   Ibid., 194.

39   A. Lincoln, *Great Speeches* (Mineola: Dover Publications, 1991), 25; see also Lord Charnwood, *Abraham Lincoln* (New York: Pocket Books Inc., 1954), 158; *Lincoln*, 206.

40   Matthew 12:25; Mark 3:25.

41   *Lincoln*, 208.

42   See Chapter 11.

43   *Lincoln*, 214.

44   Ibid., 224.

45   Ibid., 226.

Chapter 6: King Cotton

1   See Chapter 1.

2   See Chapter 4.

3   S. W. Mintz, *Sweetness and Power: The Place of Sugar in Modern History* (London: Viking, 1985), 53.

4   See the map and table in L. C. Gray, *History of Agriculture in the Southern United States to 1860*, vol. 2 (Cranbury, NJ: Augustus M. Kelley, 1973), 759, and also W. K. Scarborough, *Masters of the Big House: Elite Slaveholders of the Mid-Nineteenth Century South* (Baton Rouge: Louisiana State University Press, 2003), appendices C and D.

5   From a very early stage in the nineteenth century, cotton was used mainly for men's wear, with denim jeans now accounting for 65 per cent of this market; see chapter 1, footnote 18.

6   In the third of the Lincoln-Douglas debates: see also Chapter 12.

7   See also Chapter 11, (for attack on Sumner).

8   See C. W. Ramsdell, "The Natural Limits of Slavery Expansion," *Mississippi Valley Historical Review* 16:2 (September 1929), 151–71.

9   See Chapter 1.

10   *History of Agriculture*, 687.

11   See Chapter 1.

12   This now comprised the "Florida parishes" of Louisiana.

13   See B. Vandervort, *Indian Wars of Mexico, Canada and the United States 1812–1900* (London: Routledge, 2006), 115–19.

14   The United States rate of natural increase substantially exceeded that of any other plantation economy. H. S. Klein, *A Population History of the United States* (Cambridge: Cambridge University Press, 2004), 84.

15   There are various estimates for the number of slaves illegally imported into the United States before 1860, but the number generally accepted is approximately 250,000; see *History of Agriculture*, 649 and M. Gilbert, *The Routledge Atlas of American History* (London: Routledge, 2006), 52.

16   *Population History*, 83.

17   *Masters of the Big House* is the best modern study.

18   As the nineteenth century went on, both France and the German states became important markets for American cotton, with the seaports of Le Havre and Hamburg expanding to accommodate this trade. Significantly, the ships returning to America often carried immigrants, German more often than French, who after landing at New Orleans would proceed up the Mississippi, generally to settle in free states bordering the upper river. The German community in St. Louis later played a critical role (as described in chapter 12) in ensuring that Missouri, in 1861, remained loyal to the Union.

19   *Population History*, 97, graph 3.8.

20   See W. A. Dunaway, *Slavery in the American Mountain South* (Cambridge: Cambridge University Press, 2003) for a recent modern study.

21   In Alabama, at the heart of the cotton belt, all the twenty-five largest plantations in 1860, as listed by Scarborough, *Masters of the Big House*, 456–58, cultivated only cotton.

22   In 1860 55.2 percent of the population of Mississippi and 57.2 percent of that of South Carolina were slaves; *Time*, July 4, 2005, 61.

23   Even today, it is still ahead in dollar terms of all other products of US agriculture.

24   See *Masters of the Big House*, chapter 4, "Agrarian Empires."

25   *History of Agriculture*, 689.

26   *History of Agriculture*, 147.

27   Ibid., 144; Louisiana sugar plantations, with two crops every year, suffered even greater losses.

28   Ibid., 146.

29   Ibid., 147–48.

30   One Mississippi owner lost more than a hundred slaves; ibid.

31   Ibid., 149.

32   Ibid., 155.

33   See F. Douglass, *On Slavery and the Civil War: Selections from his Writings* (Mineola: Dover Publications, 2003), 31, where the author describes how as a child he saw handbills distributed throughout his native Maryland offering "CASH FOR NEGROES."

34   *History of Agriculture*, 903.

35   *Masters of the Big House*, 161.

36   Ibid., 162.

37   Ibid., 164.

38   Ibid., 239.
39   Ibid., 240.
40   Ibid., 264.
41   *History of Agriculture*, 811 and 831.
42   See map in Dunaway, *Slavery in the American Mountain South*, 49.
43   For a short description of railroads in the southern states, see *Masters of the Big House*, 226–30.
44   *Slavery in the American Mountain South*, 99.
45   Ibid., chapters 3 and 4.
46   Ibid., 139.
47   Ibid., 143.
48   Ibid., 141.

Chapter 7: The Missouri Compromise

1   Under the Northwest Ordinance of 1787; see Chapter 1.
2   G. Moore, *The Missouri Controversy 1819–1821* (Lexington: University of Kentucky Press, 1953), 3.
3   S. Wilentz, *The Rise of American Democracy: Jefferson to Lincoln* (New York: W. W. Norton and Company, 2005), 182.
4   Quoted *Missouri Controversy*, 9.
5   Quoted ibid., 11.
6   Ibid.
7   Ibid., 66.
8   Ibid., 33.
9   Ibid., 35.
10   Ibid., 50.
11   Ibid., 51.
12   Ibid., 18.
13   Ibid., 19.
14   Ibid., 20.
15   Ibid., 62.
16   Quoted ibid., 259.
17   Quoted ibid., 262.
18   Ibid., 87.
19   Except for the southeast "boot-heel," between the St. Francis and the Mississippi Rivers, which extends south to 36° north.
20   *Missouri Controversy*, 88.
21   Ibid., 90.
22   Ibid., 92.
23   Ibid., 93.
24   Ibid., 100.
25   Ibid., 100.

26   Ibid., 101.
27   Ibid., 103.
28   Ibid., 104.
29   Quoted ibid., 140.
30   Ibid., 145.
31   e.g. by his role in the nullification crisis of 1830 by which South Carolina claimed that a state had the right to nullify a federal statute within its boundaries.
32   Note how Clay sat at different times in both houses of Congress, and was also absent for certain terms.
33   D. H. Donald, *Lincoln* (New York: Simon and Schuster, 1995), 165.
34   *Missouri Controversy*, 173.
35   Ibid., 174.
36   Ibid., 178.
37   Ibid.
38   Quoted from Clement Eaton, the eminent contemporary historian of the antebellum south, ibid., 251.
39   Ibid., 351.

Chapter 8: Railroads

1   This was only two years after the opening of the world's first passenger railroad, Britain's Liverpool and Manchester Railway, in 1830.
2   The New York Central, the Erie Railroad (quite separate from the canal but built with much the same economic rationale), the Pennsylvania Railroad and the B&ORR.
3   The Atlantic and St. Lawrence Railroad between Portland, Maine (in the United States) and Montreal.
4   T. Crump, *A Brief History of the Age of Steam* (London: Constable and Robinson, 2007), 138.
5   J. E. Davis, *Frontier Illinois* (Bloomington: Indiana University Press, 1998), 355.
6   Ibid., 375.
7   Note also that the Canadian Pacific Railroad reached Vancouver in 1885.
8   New Mexico was the name given to that part of the territory ceded to the United States after the Mexican War and now comprised in the states of New Mexico and Arizona (see also chapter 9).
9   L. L. Richards, *The California Gold Rush and the Coming of the Civil War* (New York: Alfred A. Knopf, 2007), 145.
10   Ibid., 146.
11   Ibid., 153.
12   Ibid., 154.
13   T. G. Otte and K. Nielson (eds.), *Railroads and International Politics: Paths of Empire, 1848–1945* (London: Routledge, 2006), 10.
14   Ibid., and see also B.W. Bacon, *Sinews of War: How Technology, Industry and Transportation Won the Civil War* (Presidio, 1997), 127–38.

15 Ibid., 11.

16 The story of the Andrews raid, as related in this chapter, is based on R.S. Bonds, *Stealing the General: The Great Locomotive Chase and the First Medal of Honor* (Yardley: Westholme Publishing, 2007).

17 "In the end it was the greater skills of the Union forces in making strategic use of railways that led to the Confederate surrender at Appomattox in April 1865": *Railroads and International Politics*, 11.

18 Missouri still did not count as a free state.

Chapter 9: California Stikes Gold

1 See chapter 3.

2 By the Treaty of Nootka of 1790, Spain had surrendered to Britain its rights to this territory; W. Bean, *California: an Interpretive History* (McGraw-Hill Book Company, 1973), 52.

3 This comprised the whole of the present states of California, Nevada, and Utah, and a part of Arizona, Colorado, New Mexico and Wyoming; *New York Public Library American History Desk Reference*, 2nd ed. (New York: Hyperion, 2003), 88.

4 See the map in *California*, 45.

5 For the full story see *California*, section 7.

6 Speaking in Congress in opposition to the bill providing for the annexation of the Mexican territories; http://en.wikipedia.org/wiki/William_W._Wick.

7 L. L. Richards, *The California Gold Rush and the Coming of the Civil War* (New York: Alfred A. Knopf, 2007), 45.

8 *New York Public Library*, 79.

9 *California Gold Rush*, 13.

10 Ibid., 19.

11 Ibid., 20.

12 M. H. Shutes, *Lincoln and California* (Stanford: Stanford University Press, 1943), 2.

13 This followed from the admission of Wisconsin as the thirtieth state of the Union in 1848.

14 This was the opinion of no less than President James Polk, who—presiding over the Mexican War—wrote in his diary that the agitation about slavery's expansion was "not only mischievous but wicked" because "there is no probability that any territory will ever be acquired from Mexico in which slavery could ever exist," as quoted in J. M. McPherson, "The Fight for Slavery in California," *New York Review of Books*, October 11, 2007.

15 *California Gold Rush*, 62.

16 Ibid., 65.

17 Ibid., 58.

18 Ibid., 68.

19 Ibid., 73.

20 *Lincoln and California*, 9.

21 As noted in chapter 10 this meant closing the notorious Georgia Pen.
22 *California Gold Rush*, 183.
23 *California*, 173.
24 The January date for opening a new Congress came in only after the Civil War.
25 *California Gold Rush*, 186.
26 Ibid., 193.
27 See chapter 11.
28 *California Gold Rush*, 107.
29 Ibid., 223.
30 Ibid., 225–6.
31 The news was transmitted from San Francisco by the electric telegraph in time of it to be reported in the *New York Times* of October 11.
32 *Lincoln and California*, 57.
33 Ibid., 86.
34 *California Gold Rush*, 230.

Chapter 10: Washington: 1847–1849

1 Quoted J. H. Silbey, *The American Political Nation, 1838–1893* (Stanford: Stanford University Press, 1991), 181.
2 D. H. Donald, *Lincoln* (New York: Simon and Schuster, 1995), 120.
3 Ibid., 120.
4 Ibid., 121.
5 S. Wilentz, *The Rise of American Democracy: Jefferson to Lincoln* (New York: W. W. Norton and Company, 2005), 402.
6 Ibid., 123.
7 Ibid., 124.
8 Ibid., 125.
9 O. V. Burton, *The Age of Lincoln* (New York: Hill and Wang, 2007), 27.
10 Ibid.
11 *Rise of American Democracy*, 557.
12 *Lincoln*, 128.
13 Ibid., 126.
14 Ibid., 127.
15 Ibid., 129.
16 Ibid., 130.
17 Vice president, who became president after the death of Taylor in 1850.
18 *Lincoln*, 131.
19 Ibid., 132.
20 Quoted ibid., 134.
21 Ibid., 134.
22 J. F. Pacheco, *The Pearl: A Failed Slave Escape on the Potomac* (Chapel Hill, NC: University of North Carolina Press, 2005), 13.

23 Even so, the largest producers of wheat and corn in Maryland and Virginia still kept substantial numbers of slaves; W. K. Scarborough, *Masters of the Big House: Elite Slaveholders of the Mid-Nineteenth Century South* (Baton Rouge: Louisiana State University Press, 2003), 138.

24 *Lincoln*, 136.

25 Ibid., 137.

26 P. Irons, *A People's History of the Supreme Court* (London: Penguin, 1999), 142.

27 Quoted, ibid., 143.

28 41 US (16 Pet) 539 (1842); for summary see P. Finkelman, *Slavery in the Courtroom: An Annotated Bibliography of American Cases* (Washington: Library of Congress, 1985), 60–3.

29 *The Pearl*, 1.

30 *American Political Nation*, 181.

31 Until 1845, a letter sent more than 400 miles cost 25 cents; thereafter the rate for a letter weighing not more then ½ ounce was 10 cents for more than 300 miles, which in 1851 went down 3 cents for distances up to 3,000 miles: J. E. Davis, *Frontier Illinois* (Bloomington: Indiana University Press, 1998), 373.

32 D. M. Henkin, *The Postal Age: The Emergence of Modern Communications in Nineteenth-Century America* (Chicago: University of Chicago Press, 2006), 22.

33 Ibid., 8.

34 *Lincoln*, 137.

Chapter 11: Bleeding Kansas

1 L. L. Richards, *The California Gold Rush and the Coming of the Civil War* (New York: Alfred A. Knopf, 2007), 119.

2 Ibid., 132.

3 Ibid., 142.

4 Since 1863 Wheeling has been in West Virginia.

5 O. V. Burton, *The Age of Lincoln* (New York: Hill and Wang, 2007), 69.

6 Ibid., 70.

7 D. H. Donald, *Lincoln* (New York: Simon and Schuster, 1995), 168.

8 This vast area also includes the present states of North and South Dakota, admitted to the Union only in 1889.

9 S. Wilentz, *The Rise of American Democracy: Jefferson to Lincoln* (New York: W. W. Norton and Company, 2005), 672.

10 Ibid.

11 Ibid.

12 N. Etcheson, *Bleeding Kansas: Contested Liberty in the Civil War Era* (Lawrence: University Press of Kansas, 2004), 43.

13 See chapter 6.

14 The words quoted are a paraphrase from D. Zarefsky, *Lincoln, Douglas and Slavery: In the Crucible of Public Debate* (Chicago: University of Chicago Press, 1990), 220.

15 *Bleeding Kansas*, 29.

16 Ibid., 30.

17 Ibid., 31.

18 Ibid., 32.

19 Ibid., 33.

20 Ibid., 36–7.

21 Ibid., 39.

22 The Creek War of 1836 (also known as the Second Creek War or the Creek Alabama Uprising) was a conflict fought between the United States and factions of the Creek Nation in 1836 and 1837. The war took place in the border region between Alabama and Georgia along the Chattahoochee River. It resulted in a defeat for the Creek forces and the removal of the Creek people from their native lands to the Indian Territory in present-day Oklahoma; see http://en.wikipedia.org/wiki/Creek_War_of_1836.

23 *Bleeding Kansas*, 47.

24 Ibid., 47.

25 Ibid., 48.

26 Ibid., 46.

27 Fort Leavenworth is now a major US Army base.

28 *Bleeding Kansas*, 53.

29 Ibid.

30 Ibid.

31 Ibid., 54.

32 This was just before the end of Atchison's final six-year term in the US Senate.

33 *Bleeding Kansas*, 55.

34 Ibid., 59.

35 Ibid., 60.

36 Ibid., Sebastopol did not actually fall until September 1855.

37 Ibid., 68.

38 Ibid., 69.

39 Topeka became the capital of Kansas following the grant of statehood in 1861.

40 *Bleeding Kansas*, 72.

41 Ibid., 73.

42 Ibid., 76.

43 Ibid., 71.

44 Ibid., 76.

45 Ibid., 77.

46 Ibid., 78.

47 Ibid., 82.

48 Ibid., 83.

49 Grandson of the famous pioneer, Daniel Boone; see Chapter 1.

50 *Bleeding Kansas*, 86.

51 Ibid.

52 Ibid., 87.

53 Ibid.

54 Ibid., 88.
55 Ibid., 91.
56 Ibid., 93.
57 Ibid., 94.
58 Ibid., 95.
59 Ibid., 96.
60 Ibid., 97.
61 Ibid., 98.
62 Ibid., 98–9.
63 Ibid., 102.
64 Ibid., 102.
65 Ibid.
66 The capital of Missouri state.
67 *Bleeding Kansas*, 106.
68 Ibid., 103.
69 Ibid., 125.
70 Ibid., 113.
71 Ibid., 111.
72 Ibid., 115.
73 Ibid., 116.
74 Ibid., 117.
75 A legally binding undertaking not to proceed with any action.
76 *Bleeding Kansas*, 23.
77 Ibid., 128.
78 Lord Charnwood, *Abraham Lincoln* (New York: Pocket Books, 1954), 108.
79 Ibid., 110.
80 *Dred Scott v. Sandford*, 60 U.S. (19 How.) 393 (1857).
81 *Bleeding Kansas*, 141.
82 Ibid., 142.
83 Ibid., 143.
84 Ibid., 145.
85 Ibid., 147.
86 Ibid., 151.
87 Calhoun, as well as being a friend of Stephen Douglas, had previously given Abraham Lincoln lessons in surveying. *Bleeding Kansas*, 152.
88 Ibid., 156.
89 Ibid., 159.
90 For these words see inter alia the third Lincoln-Douglas debate.
91 Denver previously represented California in the US Congress; the capital city of Colorado is named after him.
92 *Bleeding Kansas*, 166.
93 Ibid., 170.
94 Ibid., 171.
95 Ibid., 172.

96   Ibid., 174.
97   Ibid., 179.
98   Ibid., 180.
99   Ibid., 182.
100 Ibid., 189.
101 Ibid., 191.
102 Ibid., 192.
103 Ibid., 197.
104 Ibid., 199.
105 Ibid., 200.
106 *Age of Lincoln*, 76.
107 This was the figure given by Douglas in the fourth of the debates with Abraham Lincoln in the summer of 1858; see Chapter 12. The fact is that the English amendment required a minimum of 93,420 resident voters for Kansas to be admitted as a state makes clear that this number had not been reached in 1857.
108 *Bleeding Kansas*, 201.
109 Ibid., 206.
110 Ibid., 204.
111 Ibid., 203.
112 A number of contributions to T. P. McCarthy and J. Stauffer (eds.), *Prophets of Protest: Reconsidering the History of American Abolitionism* (New York: New Press, 2006) claim that there was some slave support.
113 *Bleeding Kansas*, 209.
114 Ibid., 212.
115 Ibid., 217.
116 The song originated with soldiers of the Massachusetts Twelfth Regiment and soon spread to become the most popular anthem of Union soldiers during the Civil War. Many versions exist. Its tune inspired Julia Ward Howe, after she heard troops sing the song while parading near Washington, to write her lyrics for the same melody, "The Battle Hymn of the Republic."

Chapter 12: Republicans and Rebels

1   D. H. Donald, *Lincoln* (New York: Simon and Schuster, 1995), 214.
2   Ibid., 223.
3   Ibid., 216, Ottawa, August 21.
4   Ibid., 189.
5   Ibid., 189–90.
6   Ibid., 190.
7   Ibid., 191.
8   A. Lincoln, *Great Speeches* (Mineola: Dover Publications, 1991), 25.
9   Ibid., 30.
10   Ibid., 26.

11   Ibid., 30–1.

12   This included four small parties, with thirty-nine seats in all, likely to support the Republicans.

13   *Great Speeches*, 45.

14   Ibid., 51.

15   *Lincoln*, 115.

16   Ibid., 239–40.

17   Ibid., 240.

18   Ibid., 242.

19   This was the "Freeport" doctrine, named for the location of the second Lincoln-Douglas debate.

20   O. V. Burton, *The Age of Lincoln* (New York: Hill and Wang, 2007), 102.

21   *Lincoln*, 247.

22   Ibid., 118.

23   Ibid., 119.

24   *Lincoln*, 257.

25   Ibid., 260.

26   Ibid., 261.

27   Ibid., 267.

28   *Great Speeches*, 56.

29   *Lincoln*, 287.

30   Ibid., 289.

31   Ibid., 302.

32   Ibid., 303.

33   B. W. Bacon, *Sinews of War: How Technology, Industry and Transportation Won the Civil War* (New York: Presidio, 1997), Chapter 1.

34   *Lincoln*, 300.

35   For Gamble's contribution to the Union cause, see D. K. Boman, *Lincoln's Resolute Unionist: Hamilton Gamble, Dred Scott Dissenter and Missouri's Civil War Governor* (Baton Rouge, LA: Louisiana State University Press, Southern Biography Series, 2007).

36   Derived from "Slavery Up Close," *Time*, July 4, 2005, 60–1.

37   *Sinews of War*, 127.

38   While the total populations of north and south were in the ratio of 71 to 29 percent, the ratios, respectively, for manufacturing output were 92 to 8, with firearms 97 to 3, textiles 93 to 7, coal 97 to 3 and pig iron 94 to 6. Cotton production was, however, 96 to 4 in favor of the south, where it was the mainstay of the market economy; J. Spiller, T. Clancy, S. Young and S. Mosley, *The United States 1763–2001* (London: Routledge, 2005), 91.

39   Ibid., 38.

40   Abbreviation for *Confederate States Ship*.

41   T. Crump, *A Brief History of the Age of Steam* (London: Constable and Robinson, 2007), 299–301.

42   See J. Shaara, *Civil War Battlefields: Discovering America's Hallowed Ground* (Ballantine Books, 2006), 17; this book can be recommended for its commentary on the ten major battles of the Civil War.

43 *Great Speeches*, 88.

44 *Lincoln*, 362.

45 Ibid., 362.

46 *Great Speeches*, 89–91.

47 Ibid., 96.

48 Ibid., 95.

49 Ibid., 97.

50 *Lincoln*, 374.

51 Ibid., 99.

52 Ibid., 100.

53 *Lincoln*, 431.

54 D. K. Goodwin, *Teams of Rivals: The Political Genius of Abraham Lincoln* (New York: Simon and Schuster, 2005), 549.

55 Ibid., 550.

56 Ibid., 551.

57 Ibid., 552.

58 Ibid.

59 Ibid., 523.

60 Ibid., 524.

61 Ibid., 525.

62 Ibid., 556.

63 See Chapter 8.

64 *Lincoln*, 576.

65 Ibid., 577.

66 The restored Maclean House is now open to the public as part of the Appomattox Court House National Historical Park.

67 The total mobilization of both sides has been estimated at 2.6 million, with the number of dead, 618,000 and of wounded, 472,000; H. S. Klein, *A Population History of the United States* (Cambridge: Cambridge University Press, 2004), 108.

68 For a detailed account, see *Teams of Rivals*, 686–90.

69 The popular vote was 2,218,388 to 1,812,807 for Lincoln; this was sufficient for 213 out of 233 votes in the Electoral College; http://en.wikipedia.org/wiki/United_States_presidential_election,_1864.

70 *Great Speeches*, 112.

71 Ibid., 113.

Dunaway, W. A., *Slavery in the American Mountain South*. Cambridge University Press, 2003.

Eckert, A. W. *A Sorrow in Our Heart: The life of Tecumseh*. New York: Bantam Books,1993.

Etcheson, N. *Bleeding Kansas: Contested Liberty in the Civil War Era*. Lawrence, KS: University Press of Kansas, 2004.

Ferguson, A. *Land of Lincoln: Adventures in Abe's America*. New York: Atlantic Monthly Press, 2007

Finkelman, P. *Slavery in the Courtroom: An Annotated Bibliography of American Cases*. Washington: Library of Congress, 1985.

Gates, P. W. *The Illinois Central Railroad and Its Colonization Work*. Harvard University Press, 1934.

Gilbert, M. *The Routledge Atlas of American History*. London: Routledge, 2006.

Goodwin, D. K. *Teams of Rivals: the Political Genius of Abraham Lincoln*. New York: Simon and Schuster, 2005.

Graebner, N. A. *Empire on the Pacific: A Study in American Continental Expansion*. New York: Ronald Press Company, 1955.

Gray, L. C. *History of Agriculture in the Southern United States to 1860*. Vol II, Cranbury, NJ: Augustus M. Kelley, 1973.

Harley, C. K. "Trade: discovery, mercantilism and technology", in R. Floud and P. Johnson (eds.), *The Cambridge Economic History of Modern Britain, Vol. 1, Industrialisation, 1700–1860*. Cambridge University Press, 2004.

Helper, H. R. *The Impending Crisis of the South*. New York: Burdick, 1860.

Henkin, D. M. *The Postal Age: The Emergence of Modern Communications in Nineteenth-Century America*. University of Chicago Press, 2006.

Hickey, D. R. *The War of 1812: A Forgotten Conflict*. Champaign, IL: University of Illinois Press, 1990.

Hobsbawm, E. *Industry and Empire*. London: Penguin Books, 1959.

Holmberg, T. *The Acts, Orders in Council, &c. of Great Britain [on Trade], 1793–1812*. Cambridge (UK): Kentrotman Ltd, 2003.

House Executive Documents, 26th Congress, 1st session, 1840, vol VII.

Hunter, L. C. *Steamboats on the Western Rivers: An Economic and Technological History*. Harvard University Press, 1949.

Hurd, D. *Robert Peel: A Biography*. London: Weidenfeld & Nicolson, 2007.

Irons, P. *A People's History of the Supreme Court*. London: Penguin, 1999.

Kaminsky, J. P. ed. *Citizen Jefferson: The Wit and Wisdom of a American Sage*. Madison, WI: Madison House 1994

Klein, H. S. *A Population History of the United States*. Cambridge University Press, 2004.

Lincoln, A. *Great Speeches*. New York: Dover Publications, 1991.

Bibliography

Bacon, B. W. *Sinews of War: How Technology, Industry and Transportation Won the Civil War*. New York: Presidio, 1997.

Bean, W. *California: an Interpretive History*. New York: McGraw-Hill, 1973.

Bernstein, R. B. *Are We to be a Nation: The Making of the Constitution*. Harvard University Press, 1987

Bogue, A. G. *From Prairie to Corn Belt: Farming on the Illinois and Iowa Prairies in the Nineteenth Century*. University of Chicago Press, 1963.

Boman, D. K. *Lincoln's Resolute Unionist: Hamilton Gamble, Dred Scott Dissenter and Missouri's Civil War Governor*. Baton Rouge, LA: Louisiana State University Press, 2007.

Bonds, R. S. *Stealing the General: The Great Locomotive Chase and the First Medal of Honor*. Yardley, PA: Westholme Publishing, 2007.

Borneman, W. R. *1812: The War that Forged a Nation*. New York: Harper Perennial, 2004.

Burton, O. V. *The Age of Lincoln*. New York: Hill and Wang, 2007.

Carlson, T. L. *The Illinois Military Tract: A Study of Land Occupation, Utilization and Tenure*. University of Illinois Press, 1971.

Carwardine, R. J., *Lincoln*. Harlow: Pearson Education, 2003.

Chambers, J. *Palmerston: The People's Darling*. John Murray, 2004.

Charnwood, Lord. *Abraham Lincoln*. New York: Pocket Books Inc., 1954.

Connor, S. V. *Texas: A History*. Arlington Heights, IL: AHM Publishing, 1971.

Crump, T. *A Brief History of the Age of Steam*. London: Constable-Robinson, 2007.

Davis, D. B. "He Changed the New World." New York Review of Books, May 31, 2007, pp. 54–8.

Davis, J. E. *Frontier Illinois*. Bloomington, IN: Indiana University Press, 1998.

De Toqueville, A. *Democracy in America*, Vols. I and II. New York: Bantam Classics 2000.

Donald, D. H. *Lincoln*. New York: Simon and Schuster, 1995.

Donovan, F. *River Boats of America*. New York: Thomas E. Crowell, 1966.

Douglass, F. *On Slavery and the Civil War: Selections from his Writings*. New York: Dover Publications, 2003.

Duff, J. J. *A. Lincoln, Prairie Lawyer*. Austin TX: Rinehart & Company, 1960.

McManus, E. J. *A History of Negro Slavery in New York*. Syracuse University Press, 1966.

McPherson, J. M. "The Fight for Slavery in California" (review of Richards 2007). *New York Review of Books*, October 11, 2007.

Mahon, J. K. *The War of 1812*. Gainesville, FL: University of Florida Press, 1972.

Malone, C. *Between Freedom and Bondage: Race, Party and Voting Rights in the Antebellum North*. London: Routledge, 2008.

Mihm, S. *A Nation of Counterfeiters: Capitalists, Con Men, and the Making of the United States*. Harvard University Press, 2007.

Mintz, S. W. *Sweetness and Power: The Place of Sugar in Modern History*. New York: Viking, 1985.

Moore, G. *The Missouri Controversy 1819–1821*. Lexington, KY: University of Kentucky Press, 1953.

Nevins A. ed. *Polk: The Diary of a President 1845–1849 Covering the Mexican War, the Acquisition of Oregon, and the Conquest of California and the Southwest*. Harlow: Longmans, Green & Co., 1952.

New York Public Library American History Desk Reference, 2nd ed. New York: Hyperion, 2003.

Otte, T. G. and K. Nielson, eds. *Railroads and International Politics: Paths of Empire, 1848–1945*. London: Routledge, 2006.

Pagden, A. "Heeding Heraclides: empire and its discontents, 1619–1812", in R. L. Kagan and G. Parker (eds.), *Spain, Europe and the Atlantic World: Essays in Honour of John H. Elliott*. Cambridge University Press, 1995.

Pease, T. C. *The Story of Illinois*. University of Chicago Press, 1949.

Ramsdell, C. W. "The Natural Limits of Slavery Expansion." *Mississippi Valley Historical Review* 16 no. 2 (September 1929), pp. 151–71.

Richards, L. L. *The California Gold Rush and the Coming of the Civil War*. New York: Alfred A. Knopf, 2007.

Rossiter, C. L. "Nationalism and American Identity in the Early Republic." In S. Wilentz, (ed.), *Major Problems in the Early Republic 1787–1848*. Lexington, MA: D. C. Heath, 1992, pp. 14–23.

Scarborough, W. K. *Masters of the Big House: Elite Slaveholders of the Mid-Nineteenth Century South*. Baton Rouge, LA: Louisiana State University Press, 2003.

Schlesinger, A. M. *The Age of Jackson*. London: Eyre and Spottiswood, 1946.

Shaara, J. *Civil War Battlefields: Discovering America's Hallowed Ground*. New York: Ballantine Books, 2006

Shutes, M. H. *Lincoln and California*. Stanford University Press, 1943.

Silbey, J. H. *The American Political Nation, 1838–1893*. Stanford University Press, 1991.

"Slavery Up Close", *Time*, July 4, 2005, pp. 60–1.

Spiller, J, T. Clancy, S. Young, and S. Mosley. *The United States 1763–2001*. London: Routledge, 2005.

Stevens, W. B. *St. Louis: The Fourth City 1764–1909*. Chicago, IL: S. J. Clarke Publishing, 1909.

Twain, M. *Life on the Mississippi*. New York: Signet Classics, 1961.

Vandervort, B. *Indian Wars of Mexico, Canada and the United States 1812–1900*. London: Routledge, 2006.

Van Deusen, G. G. *The Jacksonian Era 1828–1848*. London: Hamish Hamilton, 1959.

Walter, R. C. and D. J. Merritts. "Natural Streams and the Legacy of Water-powered Mills", *Science* 319, pp.299–304.

Wilentz, S. *The Rise of American Democracy: Jefferson to Lincoln*. New York: W.W. Norton, 2005.

Wilentz, S. ed. *Major Problems in the Early Republic 1787–1848*. Lexington, MA: D.C. Heath and Company, 1992.

Winkle, K. J. *The Young Eagle*. Lanham, MD: Taylor Trade Publishing, 2001.

Wolf, E. *Europe and the People without History*. University of California Press, 1982.

Zarefsky, D. *Lincoln, Douglas and Slavery: In the Crucible of Public Debate*. University of Chicago Press, 1990.

Index

The names of US states are followed by the standard abbreviation, e.g. Iowa (IA), and this is also used to indicate the state of any given place, e.g. Davenport (IA), and occasionally of rivers